AMERICAN GOVERNMENT

The Author

Wallace S. Sayre is Eaton Professor of Public Administration at Columbia University. He received his B.A. from Marshall College in West Virginia and his M.A. and Ph.D. from New York University. He has been a member of the faculties of The City College of New York and Cornell University and has been active in governmental service as Civil Service Commissioner for New York City, Director of Personnel for the Office of Price Administration, and as consultant to the State Department, the U.S. Atomic Energy Commission, the Tennessee Valley Authority, Brookings Institution, and the Public Administration Clearing House. The author of several monographs and numerous articles, he is a member of the American Society for Public Administration and the American Political Science Association. He was Editor-in-chief of the *Public Administration Review* from 1951 to 1953 and has been Associate Editor of the *American Political Science Review* since 1956. His most recent major study (with Herbert Kaufman) is *Governing New York City: Politics in the Metropolis.*

COLLEGE OUTLINE SERIES

AMERICAN GOVERNMENT

Fifteenth Edition

Wallace S. Sayre
Columbia University

With Self-Scoring Examination by Samuel Smith

BARNES & NOBLE, INC. · NEW YORK

Publishers · Booksellers · Founded 1873

This book is an original work (No. 14) in the original College Outline Series.
It was written by a distinguished educator, carefully edited, and manufactured
in the United States of America in accordance with the highest standards of
publishing.

PREFACE

This, the fifteenth edition of *American Government,* is complete and up-to-date. The material, old and new, has been related to the newest interpretations in the field. *American Government* reflects not only the tremendous changes in the American governmental system in the three decades since the first edition—decades of depression and recovery, war and victory, and more than a decade of cold war—but also a new understanding of our governmental process which thirty years of study by our political scientists has developed.

The generous receptions of the fourteen preceding editions of *American Government* have confirmed my belief that the outline has both abstract and concrete justification. An outline or syllabus is of value because it organizes and defines the student's task, lends perspective to a course of study, and minimizes the routine aspects of learning. Neither a substitute for a textbook nor for the lectures, an outline is an effective supplement.

The *American Government* outline has specific as well as general uses, particularly where it serves as an introduction to political science. First, in summarizing the descriptive material, it is a useful tool for both the instructor and the student. Second, in freeing the instructor and the student from time-consuming exposition of structure, it allows the placement of emphasis on the more important analyses of function and process.

The study of government is most effective when the generalizations of the classroom are related and compared to the current developments in governmental institutions. In this way, an illuminating appraisal of current events is encouraged.

This outline is adaptable for use with all the leading American Government textbooks. A Quick Reference Table to Standard Textbooks and a Tabulated Bibliography are provided to simplify the correlation of the subject matter of the outline and the textbooks. Thus, this outline is particularly useful for review purposes.

W. S. S.

TABLE OF CONTENTS

CHARTS AND MAPS

TABULATED BIBLIOGRAPHY
OF STANDARD TEXTBOOKS
and
QUICK REFERENCE TABLE
TO STANDARD TEXTBOOKS

TABULATED BIBLIOGRAPHY
OF STANDARD TEXTBOOKS

This *College Outline* is keyed to standard textbooks in two ways:

1. If you are studying one of the following textbooks, consult the cross references listed here to find which pages of the *Outline* summarize the appropriate chapter of your text. (Roman numerals refer to textbook chapters, Arabic figures to corresponding *Outline* pages.)

2. If you are using the *Outline* as a basis for study and need a fuller treatment of a topic, consult any of the standard textbooks in the Quick Reference Table on pp. xvi–xix.

Burns, J. M., and Peltason, J. W. *Government by the People.* 5th ed., Englewood Cliffs: Prentice-Hall, 1963.
II (10–17); III (18–22); IV (22–25); V (22–23, 108–112); VI (115–116); VII (120); VIII (114–120); IX (113–114); X–XIII (123–132); XIV (30–32); XV (64–83); XVII–XVIII (28–36); XXIX (52–63); XX (84–94); XXII–XXIII (95–101); XXIV (167–171); XXV–XXVI (172–178); XXVII (189–194); XXIX (133–137); XXX (138–143); XXXI (144–152); XXXII (153–157); XXXIII (158–162); XXXIV (163–166); XXXV (59–63).

Carr, R. K., Bernstein, M. H., and Murphy, Walter F. *American Democracy in Theory and Practice.* 4th ed., New York: Holt, Rinehart and Winston, 1963.
III (10–17); IV–V (18–27); VI (113–114, 120–121); VII (123-132); IX (29–32); XIII (64–69); XIV (69–83); XVI (28–36); XVII (37–39); XVIII (37–51, 59–63); XIX–XX (84–94); XXI–XXIII (113–120); XXV (183–188); XXVI (172–178); XXVII (195–198); XXVIII (199–202); XXIX (203–207); XXX–XXXI (95–101, 211–215); XXXII (167–171).

Eliot, Thomas H. *Governing America: The Politics of a Free People.* 2nd ed., New York: Dodd, Mead, 1964.
I (4–9); II (10–22); III (22–27); IV (24); V (84–94); VI–VIII (114–120); X (123–132); XI (29–32, 132); XII (120–122); XIII–XIV (64–83); XV (28–29, 32–36); XVI (37–51); XVII (84–94); XVIII (172–194, 199–202); XIX (117, 163–165, 203–210); XX (195–198); XXI (95–101, 167–171).

Ewing, C. A. M., and Phillips, J. C. *Essentials of American Government.* New York: American Book Company, 1962.
I (1–9); II (10–27); III (22–23, 102–112, 207); IV (113–120); V (123–132); VI (29–32, 120–122, 125, 131–132); VII (64–77); VIII (78–83); IX (28–29, 32–39); X (41–58); XI (59–61); XII (84–94); XIII (183–194); XIV (172–182); XV (199–202); XVI (195–198); XVII (203–210); XVIII (167–171); XIX (95–101, 211–215); XX (133–137); XXI (138–143); XXII (144–148); XXIII (149–152); XXIV (184); XXV (163–166, 205–206); XXVI–XXVII (153–162).

Ferguson, J. H., and McHenry, D. E. *The American System of Government.* 8th ed., New York: McGraw-Hill, 1965.
II (4–9); III (10–17); IV–V (18–27, 102–107); VI (108–112); VII–VIII (114–120); IX (113–114, 120–122); XI–XII (29–32, 123–132); XIII–XIV (64–77); XV–XVI (28–36); XVII (84–94); XVIII (183–194); XIX–XX (95–101, 211–215); XXI (167–171); XXII (172–182); XXIII (45–51); XXIV (199–209); XXV (195–198); XXVI (133–137); XXVII (138–143); XXVIII (144–148); XXIX (149–152, 163–166); XXX–XXXI (153–162).

Ferguson, J. H., and McHenry, D. E. *Elements of American Government.* 6th ed., New York: McGraw-Hill, 1964.
I (10–22); II (22–27); III (22–23, 102–110); IV (110–112); V (113–114); VI (114–120); VIII (123–132); IX (120–122); X (64–83); XI (28–36); XII (37–51); XIII (59–63); XIV (84–94); XV (95–101, 211–215); XVI (167–171); XVII (183–194); XVIII–XIX (172–180); XX (199–207); XXI (195–198); XXII (133–143); XXIII (144–152); XXIV (158–162); XXV–XVI (153–157).

Irish, M. D., and Protho, J. W. *The Politics of American Democracy.* 3rd ed., New York: Prentice-Hall, 1965.
II (2–9); III (10–22); IV (22–27, 108–112); VI (123–132); VIII (29–32, 120–122); IX (34–36, 64–83); X (28–36); XI (37–63); XII (84–94); XIII (113–122); XIV (167–171, 203–207); XV (95–101).

Johnson, C. O. *American National Government*. 6th ed., New York: Crowell, 1964.

I (4–8); II (14–22); III (22–27); IV (108–112); V (84–94); VI–VII (114–120); VIII (113–114, 120–122); IX–XI (29–32, 123–132); XIII (64–77); XIV (78–83); XV–XVI (28–29, 32–39); XVII (39–63); XVIII (183–188); XIX–XXI (172–177); XXII (195–198); XXIII (199–202); XXIV (203–210); XXV (95–101); XXVI (211–215); XXVII (167–171).

Odegard, Peter H., with Baerwald, Hans H. *The American Republic*. New York: Harper & Row, 1964.

VI (120–122); VII–IX (123–132); XI (10–17); XII–XIII (18–27); XV–XVI (64–83); XVII–XVIII (28–36); XIX (37–63); XX–XXI (84–94, 163–166); XXII–XXIV (114–120); XXV (108–112); XXVII (133–152); XXVIII (153–162); XXIX (172–182, 209–210); XXX (199–209); XXXI–XXXII (95–101, 211–216); XXXIII (183–188).

Phillips, J. C. *State and Local Government in America*. New York: American Book Company, 1954.

I–II (108–112); III (133–137); IV–V (123–132); VII–VIII (138–143); IX–X (144–147); XI (148–152); XII (184); XIII (61–62); XIV–XVII (153–157); XVIII (158–162); XIX (165–166); XX (210); XXIII–XXIV (205–207); XXV (196).

Redford, E. S., Truman, D. B., Hacker, A., Westin, A. F., and Wood, R. C. *Politics and Government in the United States*. New York: Harcourt, Brace & World, 1965.

III (10–25); IV (25–27, 108–112); V (127–131); VI (123–127, 131–132); VIII (120–122); IX (29–32); X (32–36); XI (37–51); XIII (64–83); XIV (52–63); XVI (84–94, 149–152); XVIII (114–120); XIX (113–114, 120–122); XX (172–182); XXI (195–198); XXII (199–210); XXIII (183–188); XXIV–XXV (95–101, 167–171); XXVII (133–152), XXVIII (153–162).

Saye, A. E., Pound, M. B., and Allums, J. F. *Principles of American Government*. 4th ed., Englewood Cliffs: Prentice-Hall, 1962.

I (4–9); II (10–17); III–IV (18–27); V (114–120); VI (113–114); VII (120–132); VIII (28–32); IX (32–36); X (95–101); XI (37–63); XII (64–77); XIII (78–83); XIV (84–94); XV (133–162).

Young, William H. *Ogg and Ray's Essentials of American Government*. 9th
    ed., New York: Appleton-Century-Crofts, 1964.
    II (14–22); III (22–27, 108–112); IV (114–120); V (113–114, 120–122);
    VII (123-132); VIII (29–32); IX (64–77); X (78–83); XI (34–36); XII
    (28–29, 32–34); XIII (37–51, 59–63); XIV (84–94); XV (172–178); XVI
    (199–202); XVII–XVIII (195–198); IX (203–207); XX (95–101); XXI
    (167–171); XXII (183–188); XXIII (133–137); XXIV (138–143); XXV
    (144–148); XXVI (165–166, 178–180, 205–207); XXVII (184–195);
    XXVIII (149–152); XXIX–XXXIII (153–162).

Young, William H. *Ogg and Ray's Introduction to American Government*.
    12th ed., New York: Appleton-Century-Crofts, 1962.
    I (4–13); II (14–27); III (108–112); IV (114–120); V (113–114); VI
    (120–122); VIII (123–132); IX (132); X (29–32); XI–XIII (64–83);
    XIV–XV (28–29, 32–36); XVI (37–44, 52–58); XVII (49–52, 59–63);
    XVIII (84–94); XIX (172–182); XX (199–202); XXI (195–196); XXII
    (197–198); XXIII (203–210); XXIV (95–101); XXV (167–171); XXVI
    (183–188); XXVII (133–137); XXVIII (138–143); XXIX (144–148);
    XXXII (149–152); XXXIII–XXXV (153–157); XXXVI–XXXVII
    (158–162).

QUICK REFERENCE TABLE TO STANDARD TEXTBOOKS

Bold-face type indicates chapters. *Italic* type indicates pages.

Chapter in This Outline	Topic	Burns & Peltason	Carr, Bernstein & Murphy	Eliot	Ewing-Phillips	Ferguson & McHenry (A.S.G.)	Ferguson & McHenry (E.A.G.)	Irish & Protho
I	The Study of Government		*1–2*		**1**	**2**		
II	Theories of State and Government		**3**	*7–16*		**3**	*1–7*	
III	English and Colonial Background	**2**	**3**		*14–16*		**3**	
IV	The First State and National Governments	**2**	**3**	*19–26*	*17–20*	**3**	*7–11*	*85–92*
V	The National Constitution and Its Principles	**3–5**	**4**	*26–45,* **4**	*20–23*	**4, 5**	*11–38*	*92–123*
VI	The Presidency	**17–18**	**16–17**	*301–351,* **15**	*110–129, 177–189*	*221–225,* **15, 16**	*143–154,* **11**	**10**
VII	The National Administration: The President and the Departments		*446–459*	*484–499*	*171–177, 191–197*	*314–317*	*199–201*	*395–402*
VIII	The National Administration: The Agencies and Commissions			*499–516*	*197–202*	*317–318*	*201–205*	*434–444*
IX	Federal Administrative Reorganization	**19**			*202–206*		*197–199*	
X	The Civil Service	*470–472*	*459–467*	*516–523*	**11**	*341–352*	**13**	*444–456*
XI	The Organization of Congress	**15–16**	**13–14**	*390–413*	**7**	**13**	**10**	**9**
XII	The Powers of Congress	**15–16**	**13–14**	*371–389*	**8**	**14**		**9**
XIII	The Federal Judicial System	**20**	**19–20**	**5,** *546–561*	**12**	**17**	*221–230*	**12**
XIV	Foreign Affairs	**22–23**	**30–31**	*674–692, 698–716*	*371–386*	**19**	*239–260*	**15**
XV	Territories and Possessions	*102–105*				*93–98*	*49–53*	
XVI	The States and the Federal Government	*79–103*	**5**	**3**	*34–60*	**5, 6**	*40–49,* **4**	**4**

Chapter	Title	8–9, 11	6, 21, 23	6, 7, 8	4, 103–110	7–9	5, 6 139–142	13 270–278
XVII	Citizenship, Civil Rights, and Suffrage	13						
XVIII	**The Political Party System**	**13**	**7, 10**	**10, 290–301**	**98–101**	**10–12**	**8**	**6**
XIX	The State Constitutions	29			20	26	398–404	
XX	The State Legislature	30			21	27	404–411	
XXI	The Governor and the State Administration	746–754			22	28	414–421	
XXII	The State Judicial Systems	754–760			23	29	421–425	
XXIII	County and Local Government	32			518–522	30	25	
XXIV	Municipal Government and Administration	33			26, 523–531	31	24	
XXV	The Nature of Law and Its Enforcement	806–809		524–546, 610–615	489–491	620–633	230–236	
XXVI	The National Defense	24	32	692–698	18	21	16	605–611
XXVII	Government and Business	608–619, 633–638	26	580–590, 661–673	14	22	18, 19	
XXVIII	Government Finance	27	25		247–259	32, 386–398	287–296	
XXIX	Government and Money and Banking	35		565–580	259–267	398–403	296–298	
XXX	Government and Natural Resources	638–647	27	600–609, 642–661	16	25	21	
XXXI	Government and Labor	620–627	28	590–600	15	536–543	350–351, 353–362	
XXXII	Social Security and Public Health	648–658	742–758	615–616, 619–629	332–349, 484–495	521–527, 531–536	351–353, 362–370	599–605
XXXIII	Education and Housing	658–665	758–764	629–631	338–342, 24	527–531	370–373	
XXXIV	International Organizations	582–587	787–791		386–394	20	260–264	

See pages xii–xv for complete list of titles.

QUICK REFERENCE TABLE TO STANDARD TEXTBOOKS (Cont.)

Bold-face type indicates chapters. *Italic* type indicates pages.

	Title							
XVI	The States and the Federal Government	73–95	25	1–2	113–130	90–101	3	3
XVII	Citizenship, Civil Rights, and Suffrage	6, 7, 8	23	4–6	18, 19	5–6	4, 5	4–6
XVIII	The Political Party System	9, 10, 11	7–9		5, 6	7	7	8
XIX	The State Constitutions		27	3		430–435	23	27
XX	The State Legislature		27	7–8	864–870	435–437	24	28
XXI	The Governor and the State Administration		27	9–10	876–882, 885–886	437–439	25	29
XXII	The State Judicial Systems		27	11	490–492, 882–884	439–441	28	32
XXIII	County and Local Government		28	14–17	28	441–444	29, 30	33–34
XXIV	Municipal Government and Administration		28	18	28	444–446	31, 32	35–37
XXV	The Nature of Law and Its Enforcement	100–103	21	19	17			25
XXVI	The National Defense	27			781–784, 805–814		21	19
XXVII	Government and Business	19, 20, 548–554, 558–565	677–688		20		15	26
XXVIII	Government Finance	18	33	12–13	23		22, 579–594	
XXIX	Government and Money and Banking	554–558					337–340, 511–513	
XXX	Government and Natural Resources	22			21		17, 18	21–22
XXXI	Government and Labor	23	706–709		717–721		16	20
XXXII	Social Security and Public Health	631–640, 643–655	702–706	23	721–731		399–414, 563–568	566–583
XXXIII	Education and Housing	640–643, 655–660	673–677, 697–702	23	715–717, 731–733		414–419	
XXXIV	International Organizations	26	32		785–787	269–275		617–623

See pages xii–xv for complete list of titles.

Chapter 1

THE STUDY OF GOVERNMENT

The study of government and politics has long been a major preoccupation of the western mind. Within the past century the process of identification and understanding of the laws of society and government has become known as *political science*.

RELATED SOCIAL SCIENCES

Political science, only one of the social sciences, draws heavily upon the contributions made by other social sciences just as they draw upon political science.

History. As the story of past politics, history is almost inseparable from the study of government—the historian relating the rise and fall of governments, of constitutions, of parties, and of domestic and foreign policies, and the political scientist furnishing the analysis and appraisal of governmental institutions which guide the narrative of the historian.

Sociology. As the science of society, sociology provides political science with data concerning the origins and nature of social institutions and the interrelationships among individuals and groups within a society.

Psychology. As the science of human behavior, psychology is invaluable to the political scientist in his analysis of political motivation, public and group opinion, and the influence of leadership in political affairs.

Economics. As the study of the production and distribution of wealth, so increasingly the concern of government, economics shares with political science the analysis of the role of the state in economic affairs, the systems of taxation, and governmental regulatory institutions.

Geography.   Involving the study of man's relation to his physical environment, geography provides political science with data concerning the organized political relationships of man in reference to state boundaries, land utilization, commerce, military affairs, and population distribution.

Fields of Political Science

Political scientists, in their research activities, their writings, and their organization of university curricula, usually divide political science into the following major fields:

Political Theory.   This aspect of political science pertains to the study of the ideas of the outstanding political thinkers of the past and present. The ability to interpret and appraise the teachings of both classical writers and contemporary theorists involves a knowledge of what the important writers have said concerning the nature and end of social and political institutions.

Constitutions and Constitutional Law.   Written constitutions have been one of the most significant contributions of the Western world to the practice of government. These constitutions, and the hypotheses developed by courts, legislatures, and executives in applying them to the recurring problems of government, are a major concern of the political scientist. In constitutional law provision is made for the organization of the chief units of government, definition of their respective powers, location of supreme power in the state, and the establishment of the basic rights of the citizens.

International Relations among Governments.   The relations between states in both peace and war constitute a third major field of study for political scientists, who have contributed to the slow development of an international code of state relationships. The conduct of relations between governments through international organizations, including several official agencies, and through diplomacy are subjects which increasingly interest the political scientist.

Comparative Government. The analysis and evaluation of the general structure and processes of modern governments is a further field of study for political scientists. Comparative analyses of governmental processes and descriptions and analyses of national governmental organizations absorb an increasing amount of attention from students of government. This is also true of the comparative studies of state and local governments in America and throughout the world.

Political Processes. The study of public and group opinion, of political parties, of campaigns and elections, of interest groups, of propaganda, of institutional attitudes and behavior in the conduct of government, and of the formation of governmental policy through the lawmaking process, constitute a fifth major field of study for political scientists.

Public Administration. The management of public business is the most recent addition to the specialties of political science, but its overwhelming importance in the twentieth century has led to a rapid development in this field, with political scientists making significant contributions to general theories of administration and to specialized administrative problems, particularly problems of fiscal, personnel, and judicial administration.

Chapter 2

THEORIES OF STATE AND OF GOVERNMENT

The state is the basic institution with which political science deals. It can perhaps be more successfully described than defined.

ORIGINS OF STATE

Essential Elements. The elements necessary to the state are usually considered to be: (1) people, (2) territory, (3) unity, (4) political organization, (5) sovereignty, and (6) permanence.

Whether a state exists does not depend upon the size of the population, the amount of territory to which it claims title, or the form of its political organization. Without the supreme temporal power, sovereignty, a community cannot be treated as a state.

The origins of the state as an institution have challenged the curiosity of man since the days of Plato. From this unceasing conjecture several theories have emerged, which, whatever their accuracy, have profoundly influenced political institutions.

Divine Rights Theory. The notion that the state was of supernatural origin, that the divine spark of orderly association was implanted in every human being, and that kings or emperors were the vicegerents of divinity, had wide acceptance in the Middle Ages and was, for a long time, the main support of monarchy as a form of government.

4

Governmental Contract Theory. An idea developed by French writers in the eighteenth century set forth that the state was the result of a contract between rulers and their subjects. Under the supposed contract the king was obligated to rule justly and the people were obligated to yield obedience to him. Violation of the supposed contract by either party was held to release the other from its terms. This theory is expressed in the American Declaration of Independence.

Under the *social contract theory* the people were held to have contracted with each other to establish a government and to grant it powers. This theory differed from the preceding one in that the officials of the government were not parties to the contract. The device of the constitutional convention is an outgrowth of the social contract theory.

Neither of the contract theories is now regarded as historically accurate but both have had a profound effect upon our political thinking.

Force Theory. It has been believed by many that the state is a product of force and conquest. This theory, like the others, lacks actual proof; and it is now believed that force alone offers an inadequate explanation. "Blood and iron" more likely consolidated existing states than originated the institution.

Anthropological or Evolutionary Theory. Although the family was once regarded by anthropologists as the germinal state, there is now a general belief among them that the factors of kinship and neighborhood led to the formation of communities which became states when custom and taboo were formalized and entrusted to authority for enforcement. This is the most satisfactory theory in the light of present knowledge.

FUNCTIONS OF THE STATE

Men have unceasingly differed as to the functions of the state. Anarchistic, individualistic, totalitarian, and collectivist theories are among those which have been embraced and advocated at various times, by various countries.

Anarchistic Theory. The state is, in the eyes of the philosophic anarchist, an unnecessary and undesirable institution, arbitrarily depriving men of their liberty. For the state, he would substitute a system of "voluntary associations." These associations, however, would not differ materially from the state as an institution.

Individualistic Theory. Of paramount importance in its influence upon political institutions is the theory that the state, being a necessary evil, should be strictly limited to the preservation of order and the protection of the rights of the individual. This concept has had wide circulation during the past two centuries. It has been the philosophic weapon of democracy, and has been enthusiastically adopted by a growing capitalism. The theory has had great value in aiding the development and maintenance of individual freedom and in making possible individual opportunities. However, the individualistic theory may be criticized on several points. It assumes a conflict between liberty and regulation, when the two are more often compatible. It assumes an enlightened self-interest as universal, a dubious assumption. Some feel it is a theory which has never been found practicable in application. An additional observation is that the state inevitably extends its functions beyond the limitations set forth in the theory.

Totalitarian Theory. As it was practiced in Nazi Germany and Fascist Italy and as it is being practiced in Communist Russia and in its satellites, totalitarian theory sees the state demanding and receiving total control, loyalty, and obedience.

In formal theory, communism, fascism, and nazism seem to have little in common. Communism in theory claims to be international, while fascism and nazism were aggressively nationalistic. Communism promises the emancipation of the proletariat and the preparation of the way for an order of greater freedom. Fascist and Nazi theories recognized no ultimate decline of the state. Communism would abolish the private ownership of the means of production; fascism and nazism in theory accepted private property. But all three movements utilize the central principle of dictatorship. The Communists describe their dictatorship as a temporary measure. To the Nazis and Fascists dictatorship was an integral part of their philosophy.

In actual practice there are many significant similarities in the Fascist, National Socialist, and Communist movements. In each case the demands of the state, as interpreted by the dictator and the party in power, are the prime concern. This means that the basic rights of the individual as we know them are almost completely abrogated. Freedom of assembly, press, speech, and religion are strictly curtailed. Secret police, large military establishments, and militant youth indoctrination in the principles of the particular system are methods employed to perpetuate the power of the ruling group. All three movements construct a monolithic society, in which only one political party and only one system of thought are tolerated by the ruling group and in which dissent is suppressed by the imposition of such heavy penalties as imprisonment, exile, or loss of employment.

Collectivist Theory. Of increasing importance in an industrial world, the collectivist theory sees the state as a constantly expanding institution which will eventually absorb all activities "clothed with a public interest." The complexity of industrial civilization, the inequities of the capitalistic system, the breakdown of private enterprise in many fields, all argue, say the collectivists, for a co-operative commonwealth in which state action replaces private initiative. Though in its extreme forms collectivism puts forth several doubtful arguments, it is undoubtedly true that the individualistic theory is being modified in the general direction of collectivism.

GOVERNMENTS DEFINED AND CLASSIFIED

Government is best defined as the organized agency of the state, expressing and exercising its authority. Governments are variously classified in accordance with their most outstanding features, the ones which clearly differentiate them.

Formal Exercise of Power.   Governments are frequently classified as *autocracies, oligarchies,* or *democracies* according to the legal and formal exercise of authority within the state. Thus an autocracy is a government in which all authority is vested in a single person; an oligarchy, one in which a few persons are the rulers; and a democracy, one in which the generality of the people share and exercise authority through elective officers and representative institutions. None of these exists in a pure form. It is very difficult to determine the actual center of authority in any state.

Distribution of Power.   Governments are called unitary or federal according to the distribution of power. A unitary government is definitely centralized in its governmental organization, with local units such as counties, cities, and towns serving mainly as administrative areas. Great Britain has a unitary form of government. Each of the fifty states of the United States has a unitary form of government.

In a federal form of government political authority is divided between self-governing parts and the national government, each operating within its sphere of action as defined in the constitution. The United States has a federal form of government.

Constitutions.   A further classification is based on a distinction between states in which the constitutions consist of important statutes, precedents, and usages which have never been consolidated or arranged in a single comprehensive document (e.g., Great Britain), and states with written constitutions which are the fundamental law and which may be enforced by the courts, as in the United States.

Organization of the Executive.   Governments are also classified as to the manner in which the executive is organized. The two main groups thus distinguished are *cabinet,* or parliamentary governments, in which the executive is chosen by and is responsible to the legislative body, and *presidential* governments, in which the executive is independently elected and is not responsible to the legislature.

Nearly all governments can be listed under one of the

headings in each category. For example, the United States is a democracy, has a federal system, has a written constitution, and has a presidential government; Great Britain is a democracy, has a unitary system, has an unwritten constitution, and has a parliamentary government.

Chapter 3

ENGLISH AND COLONIAL BACKGROUND

The American government is an offshoot of the British government of the seventeenth and eighteenth centuries. The charters of English liberties and the English traditions of local self-government are the beginnings of American political institutions. The Magna Charta, the Petition of Right, and the Bill of Rights are as much the heritage of Americans as of Englishmen. Common law was first developed by English courts and still is the basic law in forty-seven states of the United States. Such American institutions as the bicameral legislature, the independent judiciary, the county, and the municipal corporation have their antecedent roots in English history.

COLONIAL POLITICAL INSTITUTIONS

Colonial political institutions are even more definitely the antecedents of present-day governmental organizations.

Colonial Charter. The first settlements were made either by individual proprietors or by trading companies. The latter had charters granted by royal authority which, in specific terms, gave authority to establish governments for colonies. These colonial charters gave the colonists a familiarity with government limited by a written document. Charters were granted to the inhabitants of Connecticut and Rhode Island in 1663; and the second charter of Massachusetts was granted in 1691. With the exception of these three, all charters had been revoked by *quo warranto* long before the American Revolution.

Charters were always grants from the Crown. In Rhode Island and Connecticut the charters which allowed the inhabitants to choose all officers proved so satisfactory that they were continued, with slight change, as state constitutions until 1842 and 1818 respectively.

By 1760 there were three "proprietary" colonies (Pennsylvania, Delaware, and Maryland) and two "republican" colonies with charters (Connecticut and Rhode Island); the remainder were royal colonies. Massachusetts is usually classified as a royal colony because its governor was appointed and instructed by the Crown. Instructions to the governor were the basic documents for the government of a royal colony. The royal governor was associated with a council composed of inhabitants of the colony appointed by the Crown, and he was obligated to call an assembly.

Colonial Governor. The chief executive of the colony was the colonial governor. He was the supervisor of its internal administration and the commander-in-chief of its forces, and he might veto acts of its legislature. The powers of the colonial executive set the pattern of American executive organization. The state governors of today, as well as the President, derive many of their powers from colonial precedent: the appointing power, the veto, and independence from legislative control.

Colonial Council. The upper house of the colonial legislature was known as the council. The consent of this body was necessary for many administrative acts. Including the governor, it was the highest court of the colony from which there was an appeal only to the Judicial Committee of the Privy Council in Great Britain.

Colonial Assembly. The most significant institution of colonial self-government was the popular assembly, which, though operating under restrictions imposed by royal instructions or charters, a limited suffrage, and a defective basis of representation, nevertheless won the exclusive power to initiate revenue laws and to make specific appropriations. In some royal colonies during the French and Indian War, the assembly appointed commissions to supervise expenditures of colonial funds. By degrees the assembly gained authority to make general laws in spite of frequent use of the governor's veto and the royal disallowance of colonial laws. In all colonies except Maryland, Rhode Island, and Connecticut, laws had to be sent to England for royal approval. A special act of Parliament provided that all laws, by-laws, usages, and customs in the colonies repugnant to laws made in England relative to colonial affairs should be null and void.

Colonial Judiciary. The colonial courts were closely modeled after English forms, commonly including three grades of tribunals: the justices of the peace, the county courts, and the courts of appeal. The justices of the peace and the judges in the county courts were appointed by the governor; the judges in the courts of appeal were composed usually of the governor and his council.

Colonial Local Government. The development of township government in New England, county government in the South, and mixed county and town systems in the Middle Colonies provided models upon which later local governments have been based. A striking difference between the colonial period and our own is that key local officers are no longer appointed by state officials but are elected by the local voters.

British Control of the American Colonies. A considerable degree of uniformity among colonial institutions was obtained by officers of the Crown in Great Britain, notably by the Board of Trade which corresponded with all the colonies and was responsible for preparing, interpreting, and amplifying the instructions to the colonial governors. After 1765 Parliament passed laws affecting the internal affairs of the colonies. Previously its legislation had affected the colonies mainly through regulation of their commerce.

Colonial Attempts at Union. As early as 1643, the communities of Plymouth, Massachusetts Bay, Connecticut, and

New Haven united in a league of friendship and arranged that each should send two delegates to a joint conference every year. This was the New England Confederation. In 1696, William Penn proposed a union under a royal commissioner and a congress composed of two delegates from each colony. Benjamin Franklin's Albany Plan of Union was proposed in 1754 as a confederation for mutual defense. This plan, like its predecessors, failed to pass beyond the proposal stage; but when the colonies finally realized the urgency of united action, these colonial attempts at union and the subsequently organized bodies for united protest against Great Britain (e.g., the Stamp Act Congress, the Committees of Correspondence, and the First Continental Congress) were useful patterns for the Second Continental Congress and its "Articles of Confederation."

Chapter 4

FIRST STATE AND NATIONAL GOVERNMENTS

The American Revolution, unlike the French and Russian revolutions, did not have a simple class basis. In one of its political aspects, the conflict represented the protests of substantial property owners against restrictions on their commercial and economic activities. At the other extreme, it was radical, or "popular," demanding such changes as were necessary to establish the "equality of man" and the "inalienable rights" which were rallying cries of the major part of the population. There were many gradations in society and all participated in the revolution on one side or the other.

Between 1775 and 1781 the Continental Congress exercised the functions of a central government. This institution established a continental army and navy, made a treaty of alliance with France, borrowed money at home and in Europe, issued currency, declared independence, appointed a committee to draft the Articles of Confederation, and recommended to the states that they establish state constitutions. The Congress performed executive work through committees. Its resolutions were enforced by the self-appointed committees of correspondence.

EARLY STATE GOVERNMENTS

Early state governments were revolutionary and *de facto*. The most radical governments were those of North Carolina and Rhode Island; the most radical constitution was that of

Pennsylvania. The earliest state constitutions, except that of New York and possibly that of Massachusetts, reflected the reaction against royal authority, executive control, and undue interference by the British Parliament. These relatively brief documents reflected the ascendancy of radicalism during the actual course of the revolution. This radical trend was demonstrated by the development of the following definite governmental concepts.

Popular Sovereignty. The early state constitutions were specific in their declaration that all ultimate authority resided in the people and that government rested upon the consent of the governed.

Doctrine of Limited Government. The early state constitutions were also specific in declaring that government possessed only such powers as were voluntarily and definitely bestowed upon it by the people.

Private Rights. The state constitutions took great pains to specify and guarantee a body of individual rights and privileges in lengthy "bills of rights."

Separation of Powers. As a general method of restricting possible governmental tyranny the separation of powers was emphasized, especially in the constitution of Massachusetts. It was not, however, so rigidly conceived as in our present-day systems.

Legislative Supremacy. The most significant governmental concept of the early state governments, and most indicative of the radical ascendancy, was the virtual supremacy of the legislative body over other departments of the government. The governor was made subordinate in all states except New York and Massachusetts, and he was actually elected by the legislature in a majority of the states.

ARTICLES OF CONFEDERATION

The Articles of Confederation reflected local jealousies and a fear of centralized authority as well as the controlling influence of the popular movement. Much can be said for the wisdom of this first attempt to set up by written document a continental government. On the positive side, the Articles gave Congress power to declare war, make treaties, coin money and regulate its value, borrow money, punish piracies, and adjudicate captures. It also originated privileges and immunities, established the principle of full faith and credit, and provided for the delivery of fugitives from justice.

In reflecting the as yet undeveloped character of American federalism, the Articles of Confederation was characterized by four main features.

State Sovereignty.   The union under the Articles was but a loose confederation of states, each of which insisted upon retaining its full and unimpaired sovereignty.

Method of Operation.   The government of the Confederation had no direct relationship with the citizens living under it, but dealt instead with the governments of the states.

Inadequate Governmental Machinery.   The government of the Confederation was confined to a legislative assembly. There was no adequate executive organization; there were no courts for the union.

Lack of Power.   The government under the Articles was subject to rigid limitations upon its powers. In many matters the consent of nine states was necessary before any action was possible. Congress could enforce no decisions—it could only advise and request. For its financial support Congress could only borrow money, issue paper money, or make requisitions on the states; it could not levy taxes. To amend the Articles in any way the consent of every state was required.

FAILURE OF CONFEDERATION

The failure of the government of the Confederation to operate successfully is attributed to the following factors in addition to those enumerated in the preceding section.

Financial Difficulties.   Borrowing and issuance of fiat notes were eventually impossible. The states failed to meet in part or whole the financial requisitions made upon them by Congress. Efforts to amend the Articles so as to grant the power to levy import duties were defeated by New York and

Rhode Island. Congress could not meet its obligations. The credit of the Confederation declined and eventually disappeared.

Depreciation of the Currency. The currency systems of both state and central governments declined under the weight of excessive issues of fiat money. The central government was without power to stabilize the system.

Commercial Warfare. Congress lacked power to regulate commerce among the several states. As a result, the states set up tariff barriers against each other, throwing the commercial relations of the union into chaos.

State Non-Co-operation. As the power and prestige of the government of the Confederation gradually declined, there was an increasing tendency on the part of the states to disregard all obligations and to adopt an intransigent attitude toward proposals from Congress.

MOVEMENT FOR REVISION

The movement to revise the Articles by conferring additional power upon the central government began as early as 1780, when Hamilton, Madison, Washington, and Jay advised strengthening the Confederation. In 1782, the New York Assembly advocated a general convention for the purpose of revision. Congress perennially discussed the problem. In 1786, the negotiations between Maryland and Virginia over boundary disputes resulted in a definite proposal for a national convention.

Annapolis Convention. The Annapolis Convention was attended by delegates from five states: New York, New Jersey, Pennsylvania, Delaware, and Virginia. Under the leadership of Hamilton and Madison it adopted a resolution for a general convention of delegates from all the states to meet in Philadelphia in May, 1787. Congress reluctantly endorsed the idea in February of that year, and the activities of Hamilton, Madison, Washington, and others gave it sufficient prestige to attract delegates from every state except Rhode Island.

Chapter 5

THE NATIONAL CONSTITUTION AND ITS PRINCIPLES

The Constitutional Convention which was assembled in Philadelphia in May, 1787, was composed of fifty-five members, representing twelve states.

Leaders of the Convention. Nearly all the important leaders of the young republic were in attendance at the convention. James Madison and George Washington represented Virginia. Other prominent figures included Alexander Hamilton of New York; Benjamin Franklin and Gouverneur Morris of Pennsylvania; Rufus King of Massachusetts; William Paterson of New Jersey; and Samuel Johnson and Roger Sherman of Connecticut. Prominent among the nonsigners of the Constitution were Elbridge Gerry of Massachusetts and Edmund Randolph and George Mason of Virginia. For various reasons the delegates to the convention did not include in their membership such outstanding Americans as John Adams, Samuel Adams, Thomas Jefferson, Thomas Paine, John Hancock, and Patrick Henry.

Political Philosophy of the Convention. The convention was, in contrast to the temper of the Revolution, a conservative body. Thirty-three of its members were lawyers and eight were businessmen. Their training and interests were generally conservative. Many of the leaders were doubtful of the virtues of democracy, and Alexander Hamilton and Gouverneur Morris were very critical of it.

Economic Interests of the Convention. The convention in its membership reflected the predominance of the four important groups of interests which had been most active in the movement for revision: money, public securities, manufacturing, and trade and shipping. Professor Beard [1] has shown that forty of the members held public securities, fourteen were land speculators, eleven were interested in mercantile, manufacturing, and shipping activities, and fifteen were slaveholders. The small farmer and debtor classes were virtually without representation.

Work of the Convention

The convention was called to meet May 14, 1787, but it was not until May 25 that a quorum assembled.

Organization and Procedure. At the first session Washington was unanimously selected as chairman of the convention. It was then decided that voting should be by states, each state having one vote; that the deliberation of the convention should be behind closed doors and kept secret; that a quorum should be seven states; and that a majority vote would be competent to ratify all decisions.

Decision to Form a National Government. Within five days of its organization the convention made a momentous decision when it adopted Randolph's resolution "that a national government ought to be established consisting of a *supreme* legislative, executive, and judiciary." Thus the revision of the Articles, for which the convention had been called, was dropped and the delegates proceeded to work out a new instrument of government on entirely different lines.

Proposals Considered by the Convention. Although the convention was undoubtedly influenced by the forms of government already in existence, particularly the Articles and certain state constitutions (New York's most of all), it gave most of its time to consideration of specific plans laid before it by various delegates.

THE VIRGINIA PLAN. Introduced by Edmund Randolph on May 29, it proposed: (1) A national legislature, to consist

[1] Charles A. Beard, *An Economic Interpretation of the Constitution of the United States*, 1913, Macmillan.

of the two houses, members of the first to be elected by the
people of the states and members of the second to be elected
by the first from lists nominated by state legislatures. Voting
in the legislature was to be proportional to taxes paid by the
states (to the national government) or to the number of free
inhabitants. The powers of the legislature were to be increased and were to include the right to veto state legislation.
(2) A national executive, to be chosen by the national legislature. (3) A national judiciary, the judges of which were to
be chosen by the national legislature and to hold office during
good behavior. This was called the "large state plan."

THE PINCKNEY PLAN. Presented on the same day by Charles
Pinckney of South Carolina, it proposed: (1) A congress of
two houses, the first to be chosen by the people and the
second by the first. (2) A president to be chosen by the congress for a term of seven years. (3) A national court of appeals. (4) Congressional power to approve or veto acts of state
legislatures.

THE NEW JERSEY PLAN. Introduced on June 15, by William
Paterson of New Jersey, it represented the opposition to the
Virginia Plan. It proposed: (1) Revision of the Articles,
rather than adoption of a new government. (2) A congress
consisting of one house as under the Articles but having
power to levy certain imposts and to regulate trade and commerce. (3) A national executive, plural in composition,
elected by the congress and without veto power. (4) A supreme court, the judges to be appointed by the executive and
to serve during good behavior.

Compromises of the Convention.   The convention did not
adopt, as a whole, any of the formal proposals before it, although the Virginia Plan was most influential in determining
the result. Many compromises were made before the convention reached agreement.

THE "CONNECTICUT" COMPROMISE. The convention was
long deadlocked over the question of whether the states were
to have equal representation in Congress as under the New
Jersey Plan, or representation according to population, to

meet the demands of delegates from the most populous states. Finally, the Connecticut delegation proposed that there be equal representation for states in the upper house and a representation based on population in the lower, a compromise which was adopted.

THE "THREE-FIFTHS" COMPROMISE. The convention also found it difficult to reach an agreement as to whether slaves should be counted. The northern states wanted to count them for direct taxes but not for representation in Congress; the southern states wanted to count them not for direct taxes but for representation. It was finally agreed that three-fifths of the slaves should be counted both for direct taxes and for representation in Congress.

THE COMMERCE CLAUSE. The interests of northern and southern delegates clashed on the question of national regulation of commerce, the latter fearing an export tax and national interference with slavery. The compromise worked out provided that Congress should have power to regulate commerce and levy imposts, but that no tax on exports should be levied and the slave trade should not be interfered with prior to 1808.

OPPOSITION AND RATIFICATION

The proposed Constitution was transmitted to the Congress, which sent it to the state legislatures. The various states then enacted legislation authorizing the choice of delegates to attend state conventions for the purpose of ratifying the document. The nine states, necessary to make the Constitution operative, had ratified the new Constitution by June, 1788. New York and Virginia were not among them. The campaigns for and against ratification in these two states were very intense.

Federalist Papers. Alexander Hamilton, James Madison, and John Jay collaborated in writing a series of essays setting forth the arguments for ratification. These federalist papers won support for the Constitution in New York and have been considered a high water mark in political theory.

Opposition to the Constitution. The process of ratification gave the opposition its first opportunity to express hostility to the proposed change. In general, it may be said the forces opposed to ratification were the small farmers of the interior and the debtor classes. They made an impressive show of strength, and the Constitution was finally ratified only after definite concessions, which were the price of ratification, had been made.

Bill of Rights. The Constitution was accepted by such states as Massachusetts, Virginia, and New York upon the definite promise of the conservative leaders that a series of amendments guaranteeing individual rights would be speedily added to the original document. These constitute the first ten amendments to the Constitution. Thus the Constitution itself represents the fundamental political attributes of the revolution—the conservative aspect reflected in the body of the document, and the radical aspect in the first ten amendments.

FUNDAMENTAL PRINCIPLES

The Constitution thus adopted established several fundamental principles upon which the American governmental system has since operated.

Popular Sovereignty and Limited Government. The practically universal conviction that government rested upon a social compact supported the theory of popular sovereignty—that government was created by and was subject to the will of the people. As the preamble states, "We the people of the United States of America . . . do ordain and establish this Constitution for the United States of America." A natural corollary of this theory is the concept of a limited government, possessing only such powers as have been conferred upon it by the people. These two assumptions underlie the whole framework of American government.

Federalism. The transition of the Confederation into a federal union with both the national and state governments exercising sovereign power in certain particular spheres of activity was a logical one. This national-state dichotomy has been responsible for a large share of the complexity of our constitutional and political system and for no small share of its enduring virtues.

Government of Enumerated Powers.   Under the Constitution, the national government is one of enumerated powers only. "The powers not delegated to the United States by the Constitution, nor prohibited by it to the States, are reserved to the States respectively, or to the people" (Tenth Amendment to the Constitution).

Supremacy of the National Government.   The national government cannot be prevented by state action from exercising powers granted to it. (1) It is protected from taxation of its agencies and interference with its officers by the states. (2) The Supreme Court is final authority in all disputes between state and national governments involving the Constitution, and the laws and treaties made in accordance therewith.

Separation of Powers.   The Constitution set up a strict division or separation of powers, classifying governmental powers as executive, legislative, and judicial, and entrusting the performance of each to separate agencies. This feature, copied from what was mistakenly believed to be English precedent, is one of the often criticized characteristics of our system. It is alleged to bring diffusion, irresponsibility, complexity, confusion, and delay to the performance of governmental functions—rather than the checking of tyranny for which it was once designed. In order to prevent the undue expansion of one branch of the national government at the expense of the others, the Constitution provided for an elaborate system of checks and balances. (The First and Second World Wars as well as the great depression during the 1930's saw modifications in the traditional patterns of checks and balances.) Despite its complexities, however, the separation of powers is a deep-rooted and cherished American institution—for which no acceptable substitute has been found.

THE GOVERNMENT OF THE UNITED STATES

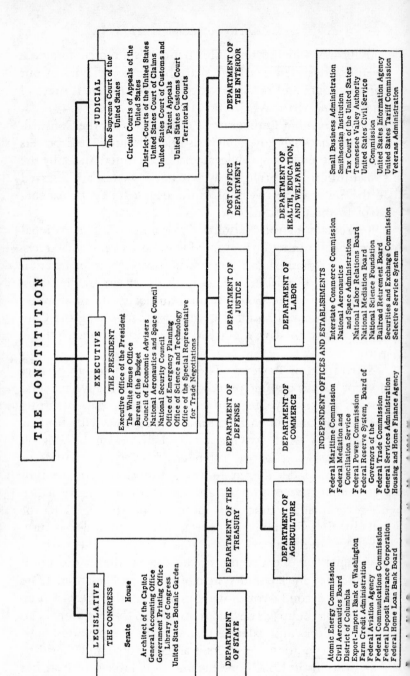

THE CONSTITUTION

LEGISLATIVE

THE CONGRESS

Senate   House

Architect of the Capitol
General Accounting Office
Government Printing Office
Library of Congress
United States Botanic Garden

EXECUTIVE

THE PRESIDENT

Executive Office of the President
The White House Office
Bureau of the Budget
Council of Economic Advisers
National Aeronautics and Space Council
National Security Council
Office of Emergency Planning
Office of Science and Technology
Office of the Special Representative
for Trade Negotiations

JUDICIAL

The Supreme Court of the
United States

Circuit Courts of Appeals of the
United States
District Courts of the United States
United States Court of Claims
United States Court of Customs and
Patent Appeals
United States Customs Court
Territorial Courts

DEPARTMENT OF STATE

DEPARTMENT OF THE TREASURY

DEPARTMENT OF DEFENSE

DEPARTMENT OF JUSTICE

POST OFFICE DEPARTMENT

DEPARTMENT OF THE INTERIOR

DEPARTMENT OF AGRICULTURE

DEPARTMENT OF COMMERCE

DEPARTMENT OF LABOR

DEPARTMENT OF HEALTH, EDUCATION, AND WELFARE

INDEPENDENT OFFICES AND ESTABLISHMENTS

Atomic Energy Commission
Civil Aeronautics Board
District of Columbia
Export-Import Bank of Washington
Farm Credit Administration
Federal Aviation Agency
Federal Communications Commission
Federal Deposit Insurance Corporation
Federal Home Loan Bank Board

Federal Maritime Commission
Federal Mediation and
Conciliation Service
Federal Power Commission
Federal Reserve System, Board of
Governors of the
Federal Trade Commission
General Services Administration
Housing and Home Finance Agency

Interstate Commerce Commission
National Aeronautics
and Space Administration
National Labor Relations Board
National Mediation Board
National Science Foundation
Railroad Retirement Board
Securities and Exchange Commission
Selective Service System

Small Business Administration
Smithsonian Institution
Tax Court of the United States
Tennessee Valley Authority
United States Civil Service
Commission
United States Information Agency
United States Tariff Commission
Veterans Administration

Supremacy of the Judiciary. As a corollary of the twin doctrines of limited government and the separation of powers, there has been developed, from arguments based on the Constitution, the doctrine of judicial review. Through this the courts exercise the power of annulling any legislative or executive acts which, in the opinion of the courts, go beyond the Constitution. This doctrine is defended by its friends as necessary to preserve the constitutional system and as producing a stable government by guarding against legislative precipitancy. This power logically belongs to the courts, they declare. The critics, on the other hand, declare that the courts thus infringe upon the legislative and executive functions, that they deny the operation of responsible representative government, and that they delay social and economic policy necessary to meet changing conditions.

GROWTH OF THE CONSTITUTION

The Constitution has shown a remarkable power of resistance to drastic change, but in many respects it has been sharply modified.

Amendments. A difficult amending process, requiring (a) proposal by a two-thirds vote in Congress or by a national convention and (b) ratification by three-fourths of state legislatures or by conventions in the states, has minimized the number of changes. All amendments, except the twenty-first, have been adopted after congressional proposal and ratification by the state legislatures. The first ten amendments were the price of ratification. The succeeding fourteen have made various alterations: the eleventh (1798) excluded from the jurisdiction of federal courts a suit against a state by a citizen of another state or of a foreign state; the twelfth (1804) changed the method of electing the President; the thirteenth (1865) forbade slavery throughout the United States; the fourteenth (1866) defined American citizenship, forbade abridgment of its privileges and immunities and placed the states under the limitations of "due process of law" in respect to life, liberty, and property; the fifteenth

(1870) forbade suffrage discrimination on account of race, color, or previous servitude; the sixteenth (1913) gave Congress power to levy an income tax without regard to population of the states; the seventeenth (1913) provided for the popular election of United States senators; the eighteenth (1919) prohibited the manufacture, sale, or transportation of intoxicating liquors; the nineteenth (1920) forbade suffrage discrimination on account of sex; the twentieth (1933) abolished the short, or "lame-duck," sessions of Congress and changed the date of the beginning of presidential and Congressional terms; the twenty-first (1933) repealed the eighteenth amendment; the twenty-second (1951) limited the President to two elective terms; the twenty-third (1961) extended voting rights to residents of the District of Columbia; and the twenty-fourth (1964) prohibits a poll tax as a requirement for voting in national elections.

Ratification Procedure. Congress designates the method of ratification to be used. A decision to ratify an amendment cannot be rescinded. Rejection by a state leaves it free to ratify the proposal at a later date. Congress may set a time limit for ratification, but if no time limit has been set, proposed amendments remain before the states indefinitely. Ratification by referendum is not acceptable.

Development by Statute. The Constitution has also developed into a living document as the result of the innumerable statutes which Congress has passed in order to complete the framework of government.

Development by Judicial Interpretation. The courts by their decisions have created a body of "constitutional law" which is a decisive factor in determining the course of government. The doctrines of implied powers, of inherent powers, of the sanctity of contracts, and other doctrines of the courts have virtually remade parts of the Constitution.

Influence of Political Parties. The persistent pressure of political parties within the framework of the constitutional system has resulted in many changes: the breakdown of the electoral college, the modification of the separation of powers, the growth of party institutions in Congress, and the party leadership role of the President.

Influence of the Presidency. The President construes the Constitution's provisions, makes many decisions based on his conclusions, and acts in accordance with his interpretations of the law. To a less significant degree the many department and agency heads take positions, or give orders, or act in accordance with their own interpretations of a particular constitutional provision. Such executive and administrative actions often result in giving parts of the Constitution an entirely new meaning.

Development by Custom. Finally, the Constitution has been modified by the growth of custom. The residence requirement for Congressmen, the development of the President's Cabinet, the Presidential nominating conventions, and the development of "senatorial courtesy" may be attributed in large part to custom.

Chapter 6

THE PRESIDENCY

The office of the President of the United States is one of the most powerful executive offices in the world. Its pre-eminence is to be understood not only from the generous terms of the Constitution but also from a consideration of the revolutionary changes which time has wrought in the original institution.

Term and Re-eligibility. The term of office for the chief executive in our presidential system is fixed at four years. The constitutional fathers placed no limitation on re-eligibility. In refusing to seek third terms as President of the United States, Washington and Jefferson established what came to be known as the two-term tradition. Although generally considered a part of our unwritten constitution, the anti-third-term precedent was broken by Franklin D. Roosevelt when he was re-elected not only to a third in 1940 but also to a fourth term in 1944. In 1947, Congress proposed a constitutional amendment limiting future Presidents to two elective terms. In 1951, this amendment was ratified by the required number of states and is now known as the Twenty-second Amendment. Prior to 1933, the President was obliged to take office on the March 4th following his election. Since the ratification of the Twentieth Amendment the President is required to take office on January 20.

Qualifications. The Constitution prescribes that the President must be at least thirty-five years of age, fourteen years a resident in the United States, and a native-born citizen.

Emoluments, Privileges, and Immunities. In addition to an annual salary of $100,000, the President receives special allowances for the White House, for travel expenses, and for other items. The President is immune from arrest for any offense, is not subject to the power of any court, and can be removed from office only by impeachment. After removal he is, of course, liable to arrest and punishment according to law.

Vice-President. The Vice-President must meet all the qualifications of the President, since he may succeed to the presidency. In recent decades some executive duties have been assigned to Vice-Presidents. His major function is to preside over the sessions of the Senate. In the event of a vacancy in the office of President, the powers and duties of that office devolve upon the Vice-President. Congress has by law provided that should both offices be vacant, the succession should go first to the Speaker of the House and then to the President pro tempore of the Senate. After the President pro tempore of the Senate the cabinet members (heads of the exectuive departments) succeed approximately in the order in which the departments were established by law. Seven Vice-Presidents have succeeded to the presidency.

CHOOSING THE PRESIDENT

Through the development of political parties, the election of the President has been changed from the original plan of indirect choice by a small group of electors to a system of nomination and election in which the whole country participates.

Electoral College. It was the intention of the Constitutional Convention that the President should be chosen apart from public influence and by a small select group of men. For this purpose they set up the electoral college, a system which provided that each state legislature should provide for the election of as many presidential electors as that state had senators and representatives in Congress; that these electors, at a designated time and place, should meet in each state and vote for two persons; that the result should be certified to the President of the Senate; that the votes should be counted in the presence of the House and the Senate, and the person receiving the highest vote, if a majority, should be declared President and the person receiving the second highest vote, if a majority, should be declared Vice-President; that a tie for the presidency should be decided by the House, voting by states (each state one vote), and a tie for the Vice-President should be decided by the Senate; that if there were no majority, the House should choose, by states, from the five highest.

After the election of 1800, the electoral system was modified through the Twelfth Amendment to require that each elector should name, on separate ballots, his choice for President and for Vice-President; in the event of no majority choice, the House should choose, by states, from the three highest on the list of those voted for as President; and the Senate, in event of no majority choice, should choose the Vice-President from the two highest names on the appropriate list.

Nomination of Presidential Candidates. The electoral college system as originally conceived hardly endured beyond Washington's administrations. The rise of political parties made it impossible to confine the choice of a President to the formal operation of such an indirect system. The determination of the political parties to capture the highly prized office of the presidency led them early to the nomination of a particular candidate for the office and to attempts to pledge electors to this candidate in advance of their choice as electors. The first nominating device was the Congressional caucus, but this was succeeded in 1831 by the nominating convention. The national convention of a political party meets for three purposes: to write a platform, to name candidates for President and Vice-President, and to set up a party organization for the ensuing four years. In the Democratic party, each state sends a number of delegates equal to twice its number of representatives and senators in Congress. In addition, a bonus of four delegates is allowed each state which was in the Democratic column in the preceding presidential election. In the Republican convention, each state has four delegates-at-large, plus one additional delegate for each state and Congressional district voting Republican in the preceding general election. Both conventions have representatives from the territories.

Delegates are chosen by state conventions, by state committees, by Congressional district conventions, by direct primary, or by combinations of these methods, as the rules of the party or the laws of the state may require. In some states a "presidential primary" gives the voter an opportunity to express his preference as to candidates, but his voice is usually ineffectual. In the Democratic convention, a two-thirds vote was necessary for nomination, until the 1936 convention voted to repeal this provision and substitute a majority. A majority vote has always been sufficient to nominate in a Republican convention.

Convention Procedure. The "keynote" address is given first by the temporary chairman. The four major committees of the convention are then set up, with one delegate from each state and territory on each committee: (a) the credentials committee decides who are the official delegates; (b) the committee on permanent organization prepares the slate of convention officers; (c) the rules committee proposes the rules of procedure for the meeting; (d) the committee on resolutions drafts the proposed party platform. The roll call is by states and the favorite sons are nominated with considerable fervor. The balloting is by states in alphabetical order. As might be expected, the views of the party's presidential candidates are a large factor in determining the choice of the nominee for Vice-President. Other considerations involved in the choice of a vice-presidential candidate include personality, geographical section, religion, prior commitments, and party loyalty.

Electing the President. In the months that intervene between the nomination by the convention and the choice of electors, each party expends every effort to insure the ultimate victory of its candidate. To meet the formal requirements of the Constitution a list of electors is prepared and placed on the ballot. The name of the presidential candidate usually appears at the top of the list. Every state now follows the general ticket system which provides that the party casting the highest number of votes in the state shall receive the entire electoral vote of that state. The electors cast their ballots, in form only, on the first Monday after the second Wednesday in December, for they are pledged to the party choice. To be elected candidates must receive 269 of the 537 votes.

Defects and Proposals for Change.   The system of nominating and electing the President is much criticized. In respect to nomination, it is maintained that the convention is: (a) irresponsible and its choice often runs counter to popular desires, (b) undemocratic in composition, and (c) hardly a conducive atmosphere to grave decisions concerning either the caliber of the candidates or the principles of the platform.

In respect to the election, it is pointed out that: (a) too much importance is given to "pivotal" states under the general ticket system, (b) a candidate may have a majority or even a plurality of the popular vote and may not be elected because presidential electors are not legally bound to vote for the presidential candidate receiving the highest popular vote.

The usual proposals for change are: (a) an extension of the presidential primary to include all the states, or (b) a national primary to choose presidential candidates; and (c) a direct popular vote for the President requiring election by plurality or majority, or (d) a return to the plan once used in several states by which two electors were chosen at large and one in each Congressional district in a state, or (e) a proportionate division of the electoral vote of the state, in accordance with the popular vote.

Executive Powers of the President

The first major group of powers exercised by the President are known as the executive powers.

Appointment.   By and with the consent and advice of the

Senate, or upon his own authority, the President appoints less than 3 per cent of the more than two million federal civil employees. While this proportion is small, the positions filled in this way include nearly all of the top level personnel of the executive branch. Practical restrictions or limitations on the President's power of appointment include the time-honored tradition of "senatorial courtesy," the need to placate a wing of the party and to keep members in line, the need to reward the party faithful, and the influence of interest groups.

Removal. The Constitution is silent in reference to the dismissal of the officers the President appoints with the advice and consent of the Senate. With the exception of judges and regulatory commissioners with quasi-judicial and quasi-legislative powers, who are protected by statutory limitations as to removal, one may assume that the President has unlimited power to remove any presidential appointee. Landmarks in the evolution of this principle include the Tenure of Office Acts, the Myers case, and the Humphreys case.

Supervision of Administration. The President has formal power to direct his subordinates in the performance of their duties. Furthermore, either by warrant of law or by virtue of the Constitution, he may promulgate executive orders which have the force of law and which must be obeyed.

Enforcement of the Law. In enforcing the law—not only acts of Congress, but treaties, court decisions, and all other national instruments backed by the authority of the Constitution—the President and his subordinates make use of the range of powers enjoyed by the President. These relate to war, foreign affairs, appointment, removal, legislation, and the broad authority that arises from the "execution of the laws" clause of the Constitution.

Military Powers. As commander-in-chief of the armed forces, the President has considerable authority over military policy. He shares the power over the military with Congress, which appropriates money, confirms appointments of high military officers, and declares war. The President has full power over troops and ships and has power to order intervention in other countries in time of peace. His actions may involve the country in a state of war, leaving Congress no alternative but to recognize the fact. During a war, the President directs the operations and may do the following: establish military governments, set aside constitutional guarantees, and use armed forces in the forcible execution of law and in the suppression of domestic violence.

Conduct of Foreign Relations.　As chief executive, the President is chief intermediary through whom all foreign relations are conducted. He receives foreign ambassadors and representatives, appoints our diplomatic representatives, and acts as the agency of recognition of foreign governments. He also possesses full initiative in treaty-making and may abrogate treaties or terminate the negotiation or confirmation of a treaty at any stage; and he may, on his own responsibility, enter into executive agreements which for all practical purposes may serve as treaties. For example, in 1940 President Franklin D. Roosevelt used an executive agreement to exchange fifty destroyers, belonging to the United States, for British bases in this hemisphere.

Pardon and Reprieve.　The President may, except in cases of impeachment, issue a pardon or reprieve to any person for any offense against national law. When issued in behalf of a stipulated group, the pardon is called amnesty.

LEGISLATIVE POWERS

The great powers exercised by the President as chief executive are equalled in importance by his powers as a leader of legislation.

Message.　The presidential message has grown from a formal requirement of the Constitution to a recognized and influential source of legislative action. Now, the President ordinarily outlines the course of his administration through his frequent messages to Congress. These constitute not only suggestions to Congress but significant appeals to the country as well. The major presidential messages sent to Congress are the annual "state of the Union message," the annual budget message, and the annual economic report. Indirect appeals to Congress are made through television, regional speeches, and, perhaps most important, the presidential press conference.

Following the examples of Woodrow Wilson and Franklin D. Roosevelt, Presidents in recent decades have enhanced their legislative leadership by appearing before the Congress to deliver their messages on the "state of the Union" and other special messages. In developing the New Deal program of legislation, President Roosevelt also inaugurated the method of a "must" list of legislation having presidential endorsement and which the President usually informs Congress must be disposed of before adjournment.

Veto. Through the use of the veto power the President is able to reject legislation unless Congress by a two-thirds vote of each house, shall overrule him. The President's position is further strengthened by his power to kill any proposed law through inaction if Congress adjourns within less than ten days after he has received the bill and before he has acted upon it. This is known as a "pocket veto." The President is not empowered to exercise the "item veto." The threat of having proposals vetoed is a factor of considerable import in deciding the ultimate scope and content of many bills.

Special Session. The President may call Congress back into a special session, but Congress cannot be forced to consider any particular question. In the summer of 1948, for example, President Harry S. Truman called the Eightieth Congress into a special session, urging it to deal with subjects which, he argued, needed attention, such as housing and civil liberties.

Budget. The Federal Bureau of the Budget, along with its job of assisting the President in the budget and the fiscal program preparation, gives considerable attention to the co-ordination of departmental proposals for legislation.

Ordinance-Making Power. Within the limits set by the Constitution, treaties, and statutes, the President has the power to promulgate rules and regulations having the effect of law. The Congressional delegation of discretionary authority to the chief executive reflects the growing tendency of Congress to establish the broad policies and leave the details to the President or his subordinates to fill in. The Supreme Court has established the general rule which requires that Congress set the standards and enunciate the policy under which the ordinance power is to be exercised by the President or his subordinates. In the NIRA (National Industrial Recovery Act) case, for example, the court found that Congress had given the President power without the required constitutional standard of policy.

Proposals through Cabinet Officers and Conferences. The President also directs the course of legislative action through reports and proposals to Congress issued by his Cabinet, and by frequent conferences with the leaders of Congressional committees.

Use of Party Agencies. In addition, the President very frequently resorts to the use of the pressure which may be exerted by the agencies of his party in Congress—the party caucus, the steering committee, and the floor leaders.

Proposals for More Direct Relations. The foregoing relations are often criticized as being incomplete and irresponsible. One of the frequent proposals for improvement is that members of the Cabinet should sit in Congress, without the power to vote but with power to submit proposals, to debate them, and to answer questions. Another suggestion is that we set up a Legislative-Executive Council for the formulation and effectuation of national policy. Other proposals include a question hour in Congress and presidential power to dissolve Congress and call a special election.

Chapter 7

THE NATIONAL ADMINISTRATION

The President and the Departments

The great growth of the national government during the past fifty years has produced an administrative system of unprecedented size and complexity. Civilian employees now number more than 2,000,000. The work done by these employees—ranging from tasks of greatest importance and difficulty to the significant but standardized work of carrying the mails and other relatively routine tasks—is organized in ten "cabinet" departments, about twenty-five separate permanent agencies, nine "regulatory" commissions or boards, and at least twenty temporary organizations. One of the cabinet departments, the Department of Defense, also directs the members of the armed services—military personnel now numbering about 2,600,000.

EXECUTIVE OFFICE OF THE PRESIDENT

To assist him in the general management of this large number of agencies, the President has a group of staff units organized into the Executive Office of the President, established in 1939. These units now include the White House Office, the Bureau of the Budget, the Council of Economic Advisers, the National Security Council (which supervises the Central Intelligence Agency), the Office of Science and Technology, the National Aeronautics and Space Council, and the Office of Emergency Planning.

White House Office. The White House Office, organized differently by each new President, includes several general assistants, special assistants assigned to Congressional relations, press relations, political party relations, and other continuing activities. In addition there are military aids, medical aids, and other staff assistants. The functions and importance of the White House staff have grown greatly in the twentieth century, especially since the pattern-setting administration of Franklin D. Roosevelt.

Bureau of the Budget. This agency, created in 1921 and placed under the President's direction in 1939, is not only a budget-preparing and budget-supervising agency, but is also an important general management arm of the President. Its duties include advice and assistance to the President on: the organization and management of all agencies, the review and analysis of all proposed legislation, the progress of the President's work program as it is carried out by the agencies, the general oversight of all activities upon the President's request.

Council of Economic Advisers. The Council of Economic Advisers was created by the Employment Act of 1946. At present it functions under Reorganization Plan 9 of 1953. It consists of three members appointed by the President by and with the advice and consent of the Senate. One of the three members is appointed chairman by the President. The activities of this council are as follows: analyzing the national economy and its many phases; advising the President on economic developments; appraising economic programs and policies of the government; recommending policies for economic growth and stability to the President; and assisting in the preparation of the President's economic reports to Congress.

National Security Council. Originally established in 1947, the National Security Council assists the President in the integration of foreign, domestic, and military policies and the development, co-ordination, and execution of national security policies. Mainly, these policies involve the State and Defense Departments, but almost all agencies of the federal government are affected in some degree.

Established under the National Security Council by the National Security Act of 1947, the Central Intelligence Agency co-ordinates intelligence activities in the interest of national security.

Office of Science and Technology. Established in 1962, this office under the direction of the President's science advisor co-ordinates the scientific and technological work of the executive branch and advises the President on science policy.

Office of Emergency Planning. In 1961, the Office of Civil and Defense Mobilization was retitled the Office of Emergency Planning. This office, headed by a director, his deputy, and three assistant directors, handles current industrial mobilization efforts and develops plans for use in future emergencies.

CABINET DEPARTMENTS

President's Cabinet. By long custom the secretaries of the major executive departments have been regarded as "The Cabinet." Cabinet members meet frequently with the President as a council of advisors. In more recent years, the heads of the majority of the staff agencies (e.g., the Bureau of the Budget) have also been included in cabinet meetings. The functions of this group are more formal than substantive, its power as an advisory body being whatever the President wishes to make it. As individual heads of departments, the secretaries are directly and fully responsible to the President. Although his appointing power is subject to the approval of the Senate, tradition gives the President practically a free hand in these appointments.

Powers and Duties of Department Heads. The heads of the departments and the responsible officers in charge of independent agencies supervise all the offices under their jurisdiction; exercise appointing and removal powers over subordinates, subject to law and civil service regulations; furnish information to the President and the Congress; issue regulations and ordinances in accordance with the authority of their departments; and decide upon all appeals from subordinates.

EXECUTIVE OFFICE OF THE PRESIDENT

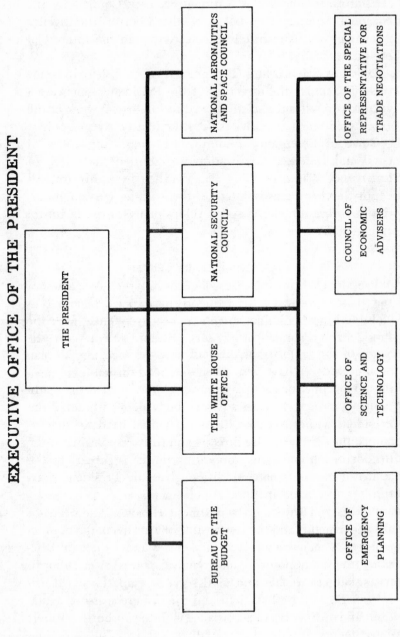

From the *U.S. Government Organization Manual, 1963–64.*

Department of State. This is the oldest of the executive departments and, as a result, the Secretary of State ranks first in the Cabinet. The functions of the department have always been important and difficult, but the emergence of the United States into the role of world leadership following the Second World War has given the department's assignments overwhelming significance. This new importance has resulted, in recent years, in several extensive reorganizations which have been necessary to adjust the administrative arrangements to new responsibilities. In 1949, and subsequently, the department was further overhauled and now has, under the direction of the Secretary and the Undersecretary, the following main subdivisions: the Deputy Undersecretary for Political Affairs; the Director of International Cooperation Administration; the Deputy Undersecretary for Administration; the Assistant Secretary for Congressional Relations; the Deputy Undersecretary for Economic Affairs; the Assistant Secretary for Public Affairs; the Assistant Secretary for International Organization Affairs; the Assistant Secretary for European Affairs; the Assistant Secretary for Near Eastern and South Asian Affairs; the Assistant Secretary for African Affairs; the Assistant Secretary for Inter-American Affairs; and the Assistant Secretary for Far Eastern Affairs.

Through these major units the Secretary of State and the Undersecretary conduct the foreign affairs of the United States. This department is responsible to the President for the direction of our ambassadors, ministers, and the Foreign Service staff overseas; it works with foreign ambassadors and ministers, negotiates treaties, represents the United States in international agencies, conducts an international information and cultural relations program, attends to our economic relations with the rest of the world, issues passports and visas, and carries in many ways the complex responsibilities of all our external affairs in world leadership.

Department of the Treasury. The Secretary of the Treasury, with the assistance of two Undersecretaries and three Assistant Secretaries, administers these main activities: the collection of customs, duties, and internal taxes; the engraving, printing, and minting of money; the supervision of expenditures and maintenance of federal accounts; the management of the public debt; the direction of the secret service, the narcotics squad, and the Coast Guard; the supervision of the national banks; the management of international financial matters.

Department of Defense. With the creation of the National Military Establishment in 1947, the long-recommended unification of the armed services began. The Departments of War (now Army) and Navy were made subordinate to the Secretary of Defense, and a new department, similarly subordinate, was organized as the Department of the Air Force. The secretaries of the three military departments do not have cabinet status, a rank reserved for the Secretary of Defense. A unified administration of the large and still jurisdictional-minded military forces has not been accomplished yet, but in 1949, and again in 1958, the President and Congress moved toward greater unification by conferring additional powers upon the Defense Secretary. His staff as well as his powers were enhanced, especially in the strengthening of his budgeting, accounting, personnel, research, purchasing, and other central controls.

The Secretary of Defense and the Undersecretary supervise the Joint Chiefs of Staff, and several other staff agencies, as well as the Departments of the Army, the Navy, and the Air Force. The subject will be discussed at greater length in Chapter 26.

Department of Justice. Under an Attorney General, a Deputy Attorney General, Solicitor General, and eight Assistant Attorneys General, the Department of Justice acts as the legal department of the national government. It includes a federal district attorney and a marshal in each of the eighty-eight judicial districts in the fifty states, Puerto Rico, and District of Columbia. Its main functions are to give legal advice to the President and other national officers, to conduct suits in which the United States is a party, to conduct investigations through the FBI, to prosecute offenses against federal laws, and to provide for the administration of federal prisons and the immigration and naturalization laws.

Post Office Department. The Postmaster General, a Deputy, and five Assistant Postmasters General direct the most extensive service of the federal government. Thirty-seven thousand post offices and more than 500,000 employees provide a service including letter-carrying, parcel post, air-mail, and postal savings.

Department of the Interior. The Secretary of the Interior, an Undersecretary, and five Assistant Secretaries direct varied functions of the Bureau of Land Management; the Bureau of Reclamation; the National Park Service; the Geological Survey; the Bureau of Indian Affairs; the Bureau of Mines; the Fish and Wildlife Service; the Office of Territories; and the three Power Administrations.

Department of Agriculture. The Secretary of Agriculture is assisted by an Undersecretary and four Assistant Secretaries in the direction of: The Agricultural Research Service (including the former bureaus of Agricultural and Industrial Chemistry, Animal Industry, Dairy Industry, Entomology, Human Nutrition and Home Economics; and Plant Industry, Soils, and Agricultural Engineering); the Agricultural Marketing Service; the Soil Conservation Service; the Forest Service; the Farm Credit Administration; the Extension Service; the Farmers Home Administration; the Commodity Exchange Authority; Rural Electrification Administration.

Department of Commerce. The Secretary of Commerce, assisted by an Undersecretary, an Undersecretary for Transportation, an Assistant Secretary for Administration, an Assistant Secretary for Domestic Affairs, and an Assistant Secretary for International Affairs, directs the following main activities: the Office of Business Economics, the Patent Office, the Bureau of Census, the Coast and Geodetic Survey, the Weather Bureau, the Bureau of Standards, the Bureau of Foreign Commerce, the Federal Maritime Board, and last but not least the Bureau of Public Roads.

Department of Labor. The Secretary of Labor, assisted by an Undersecretary and four Assistant Secretaries, administers a department organized into the following main bureaus: the Bureau of Labor Statistics, the Bureau of Labor Standards, the Wage and Hour and Public Contracts Division, the Veterans' Reemployment Rights, the Bureau of Apprenticeship, the Bureau of Employees' Compensation, the Bureau of Employment Security, the Bureau of International Labor Affairs, the Employees' Compensation Appeals Board, and the Women's Bureau.

Department of Health, Education, and Welfare. Reorganization Plan 1 of 1953 abolished the Federal Security Agency and transferred its functions to the Department of Health, Education, and Welfare. Its purpose is to improve the administration of those government agencies which promote general welfare in the fields of health, education, and social security. The Secretary, assisted by an Undersecretary and three Assistant Secretaries, supervises the affairs of the department: Public Health Service, Office of Education, Social Security Administration, Office of Vocational Rehabilitation, Food and Drug Administration, Saint Elizabeths Hospital.

Department of Housing and Urban Development. The Secretary is assisted by an Undersecretary and four Assistant Secretaries. The department was created in September, 1965. It is made up of several formerly independent agencies—the Housing and Home Finance Agency, the Federal Housing Administration, the Public Housing Administration, and the Federal National Mortgage Administration. Its purpose is to develop and recommend policies for promoting the orderly growth of urban areas; to coordinate federal programs relating to urban communities; and to encourage and assist in the solution of urban problems by state and local governments and private groups.

Chapter 8

THE NATIONAL
ADMINISTRATION
The Agencies and the Commissions

The growth of federal activities has been too great and too varied to be confined within the ten major departments discussed in the preceding chapter. Several administrative forms have been developed as alternatives, the most frequently used being the establishment of organizational units called "agencies," "administrations," "corporations," "authorities," "boards," and "commissions." The most important of these are described in this chapter.

AGENCIES

The agencies of the federal government which are discussed in this section are illustrative in organization, function, and activities of the wide-ranging variety of the whole array.

General Services Administration. The General Services Administration was established by the Federal Property and Administrative Services Act of 1949. It is responsible for assigning, regulating, or performing for executive agencies (as it finds advantageous in terms of economy, efficiency, or service) the functions pertaining to (a) procurement, supply, and maintenance of real and personal property and nonpersonal services, including transportation and traffic and public utility services management; (b) promotion of utilization of excess property; (c) disposal of domestic surplus property; (d) improvement of records management (within the limits set by the act of June 30, 1949) and related legislation; and preservation and administration of the permanently valuable noncurrent records of the government.

In addition, the agency is a "Home Office." As such, it receives, promulgates, and acts as custodian of laws passed by Congress and approved by the President. It also receives and preserves electoral college votes and supervises the official steps in amending the Constitution.

Housing and Home Finance Agency. Established in 1947, this agency provides a single organization for the federal housing programs. The enactment of a new and extensive housing program in the Act of 1949 expanded this agency into one of the most active in the executive branch. After further reorganization in 1955, the Agency's principal subdivisions were: Community Facilities Administration, the Urban Renewal Administration, the Federal Housing Administration, the Public Housing Administration, and the Federal National Mortgage Association. The Agency also aids the Voluntary Home Mortgage Credit Program. The Agency estimates the nation's housing needs and explores ways of meeting them. In 1965 the Agency and its functions were transferred to the Department of Housing and Urban Development.

Veterans' Administration. This agency, established in 1930, administers the laws providing the various benefits available to former members of the military and naval forces and for the beneficiaries and dependents of deceased members of these forces.

Atomic Energy Commission. Created by an act of 1946, this agency has charge of the atomic energy program of the national government. It exercises a government monopoly over the ownership, production, processing, and manufacture of fissionable materials, and it has charge of the production of atomic weapons. Most of its work is done by contractors. The development of atomic energy for industrial, medical, and other non-military uses is one of its major assignments.

National Aeronautics and Space Administration. Created by an act of 1958, this agency plans, directs, and conducts aeronautical and space activities (except activities primarily military); arranges for participation by scientists outside the government; and distributes information concerning space exploration. The agency inherited the staff, laboratories, and functions of the former National Advisory Committee for Aeronautics.

Federal Aviation Agency. This agency, created by an act of 1958, inherited the functions of the former Civil Aeronautics Administration and several other agencies. It controls the use of navigable airspace of the United States, maintains facilities, regulates air commerce for safety and development, conducts research for the advancement of air navigation development, and supervises the federal government grant-in-aid program for development of public airports.

Agency for International Development. This agency, established as a semi-autonomous unit in the State Department in 1961, has a long list of predecessors, beginning in 1948 with the Economic Cooperation Agency (ECA) to administer the European Recovery Program; it was followed by the Mutual Security Agency, the Foreign Operations Administration, and the International Cooperation Administration (1955–61). It is the central foreign aid agency for nonmilitary assistance to underdeveloped countries. Its programs include loans for economic development, contributions of food and agricultural supplies, and a great variety of technical and educational assistance.

Other Agencies. The responsibilities of the above agencies illustrate the type of work done by the executive branch outside the ten major departments. Agencies which were not discussed include: the Export-Import Bank, the Federal Mediation and Conciliation Service, the Railroad Retirement Board, the Selective Service System, and the U. S. Tariff

Commission. The Panama Canal is discussed in Chapter 15, *Territories and Possessions.*

REGULATORY COMMISSIONS

The regulatory commissions are used as the organizational method for exercising many of the regulations over the economic system, and are frequently described as mixed bodies exercising quasi-legislative, quasi-executive, and quasi-judicial powers. Their work is carried on in a controversial environment, rarely to the full satisfaction of those who advocate regulation or of those who are regulated. Consequently, there are persistent demands for reform. Currently popular is the recommendation for increased presidential control over regulatory commissions.

A defense of this type of organizational method has been made on the grounds that it (a) ensures independence in the exercise of quasi-legislative and quasi-judicial powers, (b) permits the securing of wide interest-group representation, (c) requires many minds to resolve the wide discretionary and policy-forming authority in order to rule and regulate, and (d) overlaps terms of members, thereby tending to increase continuity and expertness.

Interstate Commerce Commission.   The ICC is the oldest of the regulatory commissions. Established in 1887, the board consists of eleven members, appointed by the President, who select their own chairman, and whose main functions are to regulate the great common carriers—railroads, trucks, buses, water carriers—with respect to their rates, services, financial structure and records, and other matters related to public transportation policy.

Federal Trade Commission.   Established in 1914, this agency is charged with the task of promoting free and fair competition through prevention of price-fixing agreements, price discrimination, combinations in restraint of trade, boycotts, false advertisements, and other unfair methods. Composed of five members, including a chairman appointed by the President, the commission is also responsible for the formulation of policy in its field for recommendation to the President, the Congress, and the public. The members of the commission are appointed by the President, subject to the approval of the Senate, and serve seven-year terms.

Federal Reserve System.   Established in 1913, the system is directed by a board of governors which is composed of seven members appointed by the President and confirmed by the Senate. The board is responsible for the establishment of Federal Reserve Banks, and for the establishment and maintenance of an effective banking system. The reserve system, under the board of governors, comprises twelve Federal Reserve Banks, their twenty-four branches, and the member banks, including all national banks and such state banks and trust companies as make application and are accepted and are granted membership.

Civil Aeronautics Board.   As reconstituted in 1940, this board is composed of five members appointed by the President and confirmed by the Senate. The chairman and vice-chairman are designated annually from among the members by the President. Under the Federal Aviation Act of 1958, the board regulates the economic aspects of domestic and international United States air carrier operations and common carrier operations of foreign air carriers to and from the United States, participates in the establishment and development of international air transportation, and determines the "probable cause" of all air accidents (its findings being independent of the Federal Aviation Agency).

Federal Communications Commission.   Created in 1934, this commission is composed of seven members, appointed by the President with the consent of the Senate, who have responsibility for regulating interstate and foreign commerce in communication by wire and radio. It controls the rates and services of common carriers by wire and radio, licenses all radio broadcasting, and supervises the use of radio for safety at sea.

Federal Power Commission.   First established in 1920, the present commission was provided for in an act of 1930. There

are five commissioners, nominated by the President and confirmed by the Senate, one of whom is designated chairman by
the President. Their responsibilities include licensing the
users of power from federally controlled property, regulating
all electric utilities engaged in interstate commerce, requiring a uniform system of accounts among electric utilities, and
regulating those engaged in the transportation of natural gas
in interstate commerce.

National Labor Relations Board. Established in 1935
and modified by acts of 1947 and 1959, the National Labor
Relations Agency is headed by a board of five members nominated by the President and confirmed by the Senate. This
board is responsible for preventing unfair labor practices
specified by law, for ensuring the rights of employees to self-
organization and to bargain collectively through representatives of their own choosing, for designating appropriate units
for collective bargaining, and for conducting secret ballots to
determine the bargaining representative of employees.

Securities and Exchange Commission. Established in
1934, the commission consists of five members appointed by
the President with the advice and consent of the Senate; one
member is designated chairman by the President. Their as-
signment is to protect the interests of the public and investors
against malpractices in the securities and financial markets.

CORPORATIONS

Governmental Corporation. This is not a new administrative device; its use can be traced back to the Continental Congress and the Bank of North America. The First World War,
the depression of the 1930's, and the Second World War saw
the increasing use of the corporate form of organization for
the conduct of governmental activities. Some of the advantages of the corporate form are that (a) it has a large degree
of financial independence, (b) its employees need not be
under civil service, (c) it may sue and be sued, (d) it is possible to have a continuity of policy. Many of the arguments
in favor of this administrative device lose some of their sig-

nificance in light of the requirements of the Government Corporation Control Act of 1945. This act brought the government corporation under the same general type of budgetary, Congressional, and accounting control that is imposed upon other administrative units.

The Tennessee Valley Authority and the Federal Deposit Insurance Corporation are examples of federal government corporations.

ADMINISTRATIVE LEGISLATION

Each administrative organization—the department, the agency, the commission, and the corporation—exercises legislative and judicial powers in varying degrees. Claims for this Congressional delegation of discretion to the administrative officers (to formulate regulations) include: (a) Congress saves time that may be better used to consider broad questions of national policy, (b) administrators have the technical knowledge necessary to deal with the complex problems, (c) greater flexibility is permitted because rules may be changed more readily than statutes. In 1946, Congress passed the Administrative Procedures Act in answer, among other things, to charges that rules and regulations which vitally affect rights of persons and property were being promulgated, enforced, and adjudicated with little regard for due process of law. This act outlines the procedures to be followed by both the independent commissions and other administrative agencies which perform quasi-legislative and quasi-judicial functions. It also spells out the relations of both types of agency to the federal courts with respect to judicial review of administrative decisions.

Chapter 9

FEDERAL ADMINISTRATIVE REORGANIZATION

In the twentieth century, the growth of the executive branch both in size and complexity has produced a continuing interest in the possibilities and methods of administrative reorganization—a preoccupation shared by Presidents and Congress as well as by publicists and experts in administration and political science. Since 1901, when Theodore Roosevelt took office in the White House, no administration has failed to give attention to this problem, and there is general agreement that the full solution is still elusive. Expert consensus regards administrative reorganization as necessarily a continuous process.

EARLY EFFORTS

Theodore Roosevelt (1901–9). Although Congress in the 1890's had made some investigations into administrative structure and procedures, the problem was given its first presidential priority by Theodore Roosevelt when he established the Keep Committee to study the executive branch and make recommendations for its improved organization and operation. Perhaps the most tangible and enduring consequence of this committee's work was the transfer of national forests to the Department of Agriculture and the creation of the Forest Service under Gifford Pinchot, who was the committee's secretary.

Taft (1903–13). The appointment of the National Commission on Economy and Efficiency by President Taft set a new pattern for systematic appraisal of the executive branch. The chairman (Frederick A. Cleveland) and the other members were "experts" in administrative organization and methods. The major recommendation of the commission was that an executive budget system should be established, a proposal which Taft endorsed and attempted to install. The Congress resisted, in part because it was controlled by the opposition party after the 1910 elections. A decade later the plan was adopted.

Wilson (1913–21). Although President Wilson was in general agreement with the objectives of the administrative reorganization movement, he gave most of his attention in his first term to the legislative agenda of the New Freedom; in his second term he was wholly absorbed in the leadership of the government in World War I. One of the war powers acts (the Overman Act) gave the President extensive authority to reorganize executive agencies for purposes of the war effort, and Wilson used this act mainly to organize the newly created war agencies. At the end of the war he vetoed the proposed budget and accounting act, objecting to the autonomy of the General Accounting Office under the bill.

Harding and Coolidge (1921–29). The return of the executive branch to "normalcy" after World War I brought the Budget and Accounting Act of 1921, which Harding accepted despite the accounting features. The Bureau of the Budget began its significant work as a presidential agency. The Congress took the initiative also by establishing a committee to survey the executive branch. Harding, however, succeeded in making the committee a joint Executive-Congressional group by persuading it to accept his representative as chairman. The fruits of this survey were not great.

Hoover (1929–33). By experience, temperament, and connection President Hoover was strongly interested in administrative reorganization. The early onset of the economic depression, which began before he ended his first year in office, robbed Hoover of time or priority for such an effort. When Congress did give him authority in 1932 to reorganize the executive branch, his proposals were ignored, as Taft's had been in 1912–13.

FRANKLIN D. ROOSEVELT'S REORGANIZATION PROGRAMS
(1933–45)

Franklin D. Roosevelt shared Theodore Roosevelt's energetic interest in administrative reorganization and did more to reshape the executive branch than any other President in this century.

The Act of 1933. In this statute Congress gave Roosevelt almost unlimited power to reorganize agencies, bureaus, and departments for the purpose of meeting the problems of the economic depression. New agencies were created; old ones were reorganized, merged, or transferred. The reorganization was not, however, either comprehensive or systematic; the President lacked the staff to assist him in such an effort.

President's Committee on Administrative Management, 1937. This study, and its famous *Report,* gave Roosevelt a platform for his continuing program in administrative reorganization. The committee's *Report* made five major proposals: (1) Provide staff help for the President by creating an Executive Office of the President, including a strengthened White House staff of at least six professional assistants. (2) Transfer the Bureau of the Budget from the Treasury to the Executive Office, establish a Director of Personnel under the President (abolishing the Civil Service Commission), and also give the President a central planning office. (3) Extend the merit system upward, outward, and downward to include all except a few "policy-making" positions at the top level of the executive branch. (4) Overhaul, merge, and reorganize the more than 100 agencies, authorities, boards, and commissions, placing all of them (or almost all) within the following twelve major departments: State, Treasury, War, Justice, Post Office, Navy, Conservation, Agriculture, Commerce, Labor, Social Welfare, and Public Works. (5) Redefine the functions of the General Accounting Office (headed by an Auditor General responsible to Congress) to be the conduct of a financial postaudit of executive branch operations, restoring to the executive responsibility for accounts and fiscal transactions.

The Reorganization Act of 1939.   This act, which set the basic pattern for the subsequent series of reorganization statutes, gave Roosevelt the opportunity to carry out many of the recommendations of his 1937 Committee. The Executive Office was established, a White House staff was provided, the Bureau of the Budget became a presidential agency, and a liaison personnel officer was appointed to aid the President. Some new consolidated agencies were organized—for example, the Federal Loan Agency, the Federal Security Agency, and the Federal Works Agency. Some regulatory commissions were also reorganized. Of equal significance perhaps, the Bureau of the Budget was given the responsibility for continuous study and recommendation in the problem of executive branch organization.

The Legislative Veto Procedure.   One of the most important innovations of the 1939 Reorganization Act was a new method of accomplishing administrative reorganization. The President was authorized to submit to Congress reorganization plans which would go into effect unless, within sixty days, both branches of Congress voted against them. Subsequent reorganization plans (for example, the act of 1961) have somewhat strengthened the hand of Congress by providing that the plan may be rejected by a majority of all the members (not simply those voting) in either house, but the Presidents now have all the opportunities which go with possessing the initiative in administrative reorganizaton. Congress may debate, approve, or reject the plans, but it cannot amend them; nor delay the decision beyond sixty days.

World War II War Powers Acts.   During World War II Congress gave the President extensive reorganization authority, comparable to that given Wilson in 1917, Hoover in 1932, and Roosevelt in 1933. This authority was used in the organization of war agencies, including the transfer or merger of many of the regular agencies of the executive branch. Some of these changes became permanent; in other instances Congress insisted on, and Presidents agreed to, the restoration of prewar arrangements.

POSTWAR ADMINISTRATIVE REORGANIZATION

The First Hoover Commission, 1947–49. The Eightieth Congress reasserted Congressional interest in administrative reorganization by establishing the Commission on Organization of the Executive Branch (usually called the Hoover Commission, after its chairman, former President Hoover). The commission had twelve members: four appointed by the President, four by the President pro tempore of the Senate, and four by the Speaker of the House.

The Hoover Commission issued nineteen separate reports, each with accompanying recommendations. The more important of its proposals may be summarized as follows: (1) Strengthen the chain-of-command in the executive branch from President-to-Secretary-to-Bureau Chief-to-Field Office. (2) Establish an office of Personnel headed by a director who would serve the President directly. (3) Consolidate the State Department Civil Service staff and the Foreign Service into a single Foreign Affairs Service. (4) Strengthen the Secretary of Defense in his powers over the Departments of Army, Navy, and Air Force. (5) Make the Department of Agriculture primarily responsible for all forestry and land management, and the Department of Interior responsible for subsoil and water resources and major public works, transferring functions between the departments to accomplish this specialization of functions. (6) Create a United Medical Administration. (7) Transfer administrative functions of regulatory commissions to appropriate executive departments. (8) Create a new department of cabinet rank to include social security programs, education, and Indian affairs.

Results. The 1949 Hoover Commission Report was followed by the passage of the 1949 Reorganization Act, under which President Truman sent Congress almost forty reorganization proposals. Congressional reception was mixed. The new department for welfare activities was rejected; the Civil Service Commission was reorganized, but less drastically than recommended; the Secretary of Defense received some additional powers; and some regulatory commissions were reorganized to vest more power in the chairman. In 1953, under President Eisenhower, Congress agreed to the new department of Health, Education and Welfare.

The Second Hoover Commission, 1954–55. The Eisenhower administration sponsored a second organization survey of the executive by a similarly constituted commission, of which Herbert Hoover was again chairman. This commission devoted its main energies to identifying, and proposing the elimination of, governmental activities "in competition with private enterprise." Its administrative recommendations were few; but these included, importantly, the creation of a Senior Civil Service to include the high-ranking federal career positions, and the reorganization of the legal staffs and procedures of the executive branch (including the establishment of a Legal Career Service). Congressional reaction to the second Hoover Commission was not friendly, and the President did not pursue its proposals vigorously. The reorganization results were, in effect, not substantial.

Kennedy Task Forces, 1960–61. The committees and other groups assembled by President-elect Kennedy in November-December, 1960, in preparation for his assuming presidential responsibilities on January 20, 1961, were more concerned with policies and programs than with administrative structure, but their work did produce some organizational changes. The White House staff arrangements were overhauled, the foreign aid agencies were reshaped, and some regulatory commissions were modified in structure and procedure. Congress also received the President's reorganization powers in the Reorganization Act of 1961.

Enduring Patterns and Issues

Patterns. More than a half-century of administrative reorganization has now developed several recurrent features: (1) President and Congress accomplish some reorganization by special legislation—for example, the changes in the Department of Defense, 1958. (2) Most structural changes are effected by Presidents acting under reorganization acts, their plans being subject to the legislative veto procedure under such acts. (3) Both Presidents and Congress find special committees and commissions useful for periodic, comprehensive surveys of the executive branch. For most other proposals the Bureau of the Budget is relied upon for recommendations, resulting from its responsibility to analyze continuously the structure, operations, and performance of all executive agencies. In addition, Presidents Truman, Eisenhower, and Kennedy have sought advice from a small, continuing committee appointed by them to appraise executive branch organization dilemmas.

Persistent Problems. Some reorganization issues resist solution. The number of agencies still presents a dilemma, as it did in Theodore Roosevelt's day; old agencies are merged or liquidated, and new ones are needed each year to handle new priority programs. The chain-of-command in the executive branch is still fragile and is often broken by semiautonomous agencies. The question of presidential direction of agency personnel stands about where it did in 1939. The regulatory commissions are still in an administrative "no man's land," and the field offices of the major departments are often immune to central-office leadership. These persistent dilemmas serve to remind us that Congress, the political parties, and interest groups compete vigorously with Presidents for leadership and direction of the executive agencies, and the agencies themselves seek to maximize their own autonomy in governing themselves.

Chapter 10

THE CIVIL SERVICE

More than eight million people work in civilian jobs for the local, state, and national governments of the United States. Some of these are part-time or seasonal positions. In "full-time equivalents," there are about 7.5 million civilian employees. Of these, about 2.3 million work for the national government; the remaining 5.2 million are employed by state and local governments. In terms of the nation's total employment, governmental employees have quadrupled their share of the nation's jobs in the six decades since 1900.

FEDERAL PERSONNEL DEVELOPMENT

The Patronage Era. Beginning with the presidency of George Washington, appointments to federal jobs were largely determined by political party affiliation and endorsement. Removal and turnover for party reasons, the already prevalent pattern in state and local governments, did not become widespread, however, until President Andrew Jackson established that practice. Subsequently, Presidents of both parties followed the patronage system.

Civil Service Reform. Although Presidents and Congress made some efforts to reform the Civil Service in 1853 and 1871, it was not until the Pendleton Act of 1883 that the national government acquired a firm statutory base for a "merit" system of public employment. This act, patterned in general terms after the British civil service reforms, established a Civil Service Commission, provided for competitive and other types of examinations for entrance into the federal civil service, and limited patronage practices in other ways.

By subsequent presidential orders and by acts of Congress, the merit system has been gradually extended to include more than 90 per cent of federal employment.

CONTEMPORARY FEDERAL PERSONNEL SYSTEMS

Civil Service Commission Systems. The Civil Service Commission, composed of three members, not more than two of whom are "adherents of the same political party," is appointed by the President for six-year staggered terms and approved by the Senate. The Commission and its staff administer examinations, establish rosters of eligibles and certify eligibles to the agencies for appointment, classify positions in salary grades, supervise promotion and transfer of employees, make investigations of employee character and loyalty, and enforce the rules prohibiting party activity by civil servants.

The Commission, although it has a large staff, eleven regional offices, and several thousand local examining boards, has not been able to develop an integrated personnel system for its broad jurisdiction. Many special groups—for example, the postal service, the forest service, and others—have largely self-contained personnel systems under the wide umbrella of the Commission's general rules.

The Foreign Service. One of the largest personnel systems outside the Civil Service Commission jurisdiction is the Foreign Service, the main features of this personnel system being provided for in the Foreign Service Act of 1946 and its subsequent amendments. In the years since 1946, this personnel system has been much studied, criticized, and reorganized. One major event involved the 1955 merger of the State Department's civil service personnel system with the Foreign Service, a step called "Wristonization" after Henry Wriston, the chairman of the committee carrying out the action. The employees of the foreign aid and overseas information agencies operate under separate personnel systems, each of which is a special variation of the Foreign Service plan.

Other Special Personnel Systems. The Tennessee Valley Authority, the Atomic Energy Commission, the Central Intelligence Agency, the Public Health Service, the Federal Bureau of Investigation, and several other agencies also have separate and distinctive personnel systems. The legal staffs of the executive agencies are exempt from the examination process of the Civil Service Commission. Still other special groups—for example, the skilled trades—are the objects of special personnel legislation.

STATE AND LOCAL PERSONNEL SYSTEMS

Civil service reform in the states began in the same decade as it did in the national government. New York and Massachusetts led the way, but the remaining states were slow to follow. Today only a little more than half the state governments have a formal merit system. The larger city governments have a somewhat higher ratio; in county, town, and village governments it is considerably lower. The largest single group of state and local employees—the public school teachers—is for the most part under a personnel system which is defined in the state education laws. A professional license is required, tenure is protected in varying degrees, and salaries are usually standardized by law.

Constitutional Merit System. In several of the states, the merit system for state and local government employment is required by provisions of the state constitution. New York, California, and Michigan are important examples of this practice. In such states the merit system is protected against overt legislative or gubernatorial modification, although acts of omission cannot easily be remedied. Critics of constitutional merit systems charge that the systems encourage rigidity in personnel administration and that the courts are encouraged to intervene by civil service litigation, deciding managerial questions too often by the application of formal rules of law.

Statutory Merit Systems. Most state merit systems are statutory systems, based upon state laws of varying comprehensiveness and detail. In some states the responsibility for administering the personnel system is vested in a director appointed by the governor; in most states having merit systems, responsibility is entrusted to a semi-autonomous civil service commission, organized much as the federal commission is. In the view of many informed observers those state personnel systems are highly uneven in quality. Patronage is still extensively practiced in some; in others, it is alleged, the system has stopped partonage but is so elaborate in its rules that mediocrity, or even incompetence, is protected as much as competence.

Federal-State Merit Systems. State and local employees paid in whole or in part from certain grant-in-aid funds are required by federal law to be employed under a personnel system meeting federal merit standards. This requirement has introduced a limited merit system, even in those states where patronage is otherwise the rule.

Patronage Systems. Some states have resisted the civil service reform movement and are still characterized by patronage practices. The tendencies in these states, however, is increasingly to place some special groups under formal merit systems of their own—for example, the state police—or to permit the development of informal merit systems which protect employees against dismissal when there is a change of the party in power.

Local Government Personnel Systems. Merit systems have been adopted in most large cities, in many smaller cities, in quite a few countries, and in small units of government; the range in quality is, however, great.

Continuing Personnel Problems

Yesterday's solutions are often today's problems, and while there is a general consensus that merit systems are superior to patronage systems, there is also continuing concern about the shortcomings of merit systems. The contemporary debates on the improvement of public personnel systems include the following issues:

Executive Leadership. The Pendleton Act was ambiguous about the relationship of the Civil Service Commission to the President as chief executive. The ambiguity persists. The President's Committee of 1937 and the Hoover Commission of 1949 recommended that the President's leadership over the personnel system be strengthened. Studies of state and local personnel systems have usually also recommended that the governor, the mayor, the city manager, or the county executive, as the case might be, should have more direct control over the personnel system. The resistance to such change is very strong.

Legislative Influence. One of the sources of resistance to executive leadership is the desire of Congress, of state legislatures, and of local legislative bodies, to keep the influence which they have with civil service commissions. Resistance to executive leadership in personnel matters is a part of the normal tendency of legislative bodies to compete with chief executives.

Interest Group Opposition. Many interest groups also are allied with legislators in resisting executive leadership. Veterans' groups are prominent in this respect, and agricultural, labor, business, and professional groups often agree with them.

Organized Bureaucracies. Employee groups—for example, the postal unions, state employee unions, local police and fire organizations—often join with legislators and interest groups to resist executive leadership in personnel management.

"Closed" Career Services. Another issue raised by the merit system is the question of "closed" versus "open" career systems. In a "closed" system recruitment is to the entrance grades only in each service; advancement comes from the ranks, and seniority counts heavily. Employee groups, interest groups, and legislators favor this system. Chief executives, however, tend toward "open" career systems, feeling more often the need for "new blood" and highly trained specialists.

Chapter 11

THE ORGANIZATION
OF CONGRESS

The Congress of the United States exercises the legislative powers of the national government and is composed of two houses, the Senate and the House of Representatives. The former represents the states equally and the latter represents the population according to its distribution among the states.

Bicameral System.   The division of the national legislative body into two branches was the result of the following factors: (a) the English and colonial precedent favored the bicameral plan; (b) the demands of small and large states made it necessary to compromise; (c) the conservative opinion of the times, in nearly all the states as well as in the convention of 1787, demanded a check upon the "passion" and "haste" of the popular assembly; (d) the wide acceptance of the doctrine of limited government made two chambers seem desirable as checks and balances against each other.

House of Representatives

The House of Representatives in the Eighty-seventh Congress is composed of 437 members, plus a Resident Commissioner from Puerto Rico who may take part in the discussions but has no vote. Each state is guaranteed at least one representative. The remainder are apportioned among the states according to population. There is now, roughly, one representative for every 380,000 people, but no two Congressional districts have exactly the same population.

Method of Apportionment.   After each decennial census Congress is required to make a new apportionment. It failed to do so after the census of 1920. In 1929, Congress enacted a law which provided that the Census Bureau should calculate the number of representatives to which each state was entitled; unless Congress then made a different apportionment the one calculated by the Census Bureau should go into effect.

Congressional Districts. The actual division of the states into Congressional districts is made by the state legislatures. More than a century ago Congress required that members should be elected from districts composed of "contiguous and compact territory containing as nearly as practicable an equal number of inhabitants." This law, however, failed to stop gerrymandering, which is the practice of arranging districts so as to discriminate against the minority party in the legislature. Districts within the same state are often not compact and one district may contain two or more times as many people as another. Often, legislatures fail to make any reapportionment when one or more additional representatives are apportioned to the state after a census. The new representatives, called congressmen-at-large, are elected from the whole state.

Qualifications. A member of the House of Representatives must be at least twenty-five years of age, an inhabitant of the state from which he is elected, and seven years a citizen of the United States. He cannot, during his term as representative, hold a military or civil office under the government of the United States. Custom has added a further qualification. It is almost impossible, except in urban centers (for example, New York City), for an individual to be elected to the House of Representatives unless he is a resident of his district.

Elections. Each house of Congress judges the election returns and qualifications of its members. On rare occasions the House of Representatives has extended the meaning of the word "qualifications" to permit exclusion of persons whose opinions it disapproves, e.g., Brigham Roberts and Victor Berger. In closely contested elections the majority

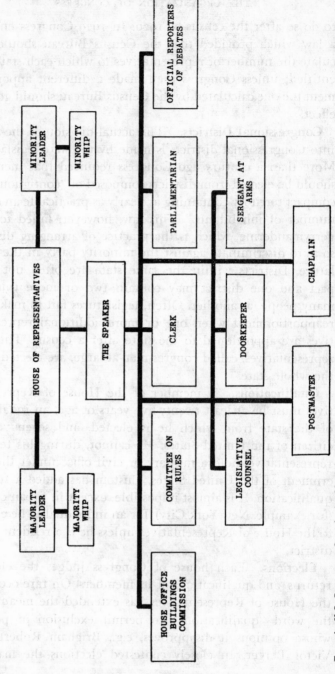

HOUSE OF REPRESENTATIVES

- HOUSE OF REPRESENTATIVES
  - MAJORITY LEADER
    - MAJORITY WHIP
  - MINORITY LEADER
    - MINORITY WHIP
  - HOUSE OFFICE BUILDINGS COMMISSION
  - COMMITTEE ON RULES
  - THE SPEAKER
    - PARLIAMENTARIAN
    - SERGEANT AT ARMS
    - CHAPLAIN
    - CLERK
    - DOORKEEPER
    - POSTMASTER
    - LEGISLATIVE COUNSEL
    - OFFICIAL REPORTERS OF DEBATES

From the *U.S. Government Organization Manual, 1963–64.*

party of the House has shown the disposition to seat the contestant belonging to its own party.

Term of Members. Members of the House of Representatives serve for two years. They take office on January 3 of the odd-numbered years.

Vacancies. In case of the death, the disqualification, or the resignation of a member of the House, the governor of the state calls a new election to fill the vacancy. The successful candidate serves the remainder of the unfinished term.

SENATE

The Senate of the United States is composed of one hundred members, two being elected from each state.

Qualifications. A senator must be at least thirty years of age, an inhabitant of the state from which he is elected, and a citizen of the United States for nine years.

Elections. The ratification of the Seventeenth Amendment transferred the election of senators from state legislatures to the people of the states. Senators are elected for a term of six years, one third being elected every two years. The Senate also excludes or expels members for irregular election, but it has not yet excluded or expelled any member because of his opinions.

Vacancies. In case of a vacancy a new state election may be called. Until it is held, the state legislature may empower the governor to make a temporary appointment.

COMPENSATION

Members of Congress receive $30,000 per year. Of this amount up to $3,000 may be claimed as a tax-exempt expense if the member maintains a residence both in his state and in Washington, D. C. Members also have a fixed annual allowance for office staff, travel to and from sessions, and franking privilege for official business.

PRIVILEGES OF MEMBERS

By virtue of their office the members of Congress enjoy special privileges. They are free from arrest except for

UNITED STATES SENATE

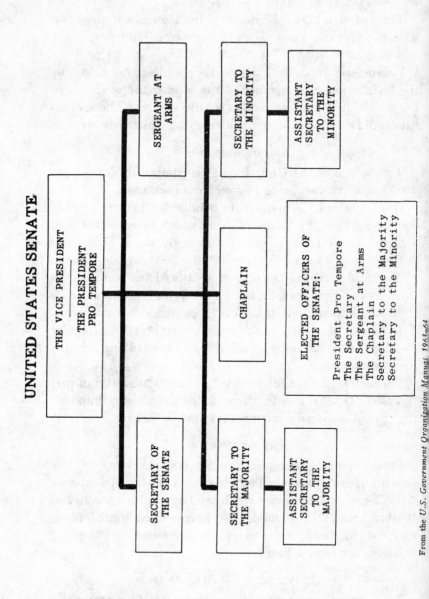

THE VICE PRESIDENT

THE PRESIDENT PRO TEMPORE

SECRETARY OF THE SENATE

SERGEANT AT ARMS

SECRETARY TO THE MINORITY

CHAPLAIN

SECRETARY TO THE MAJORITY

ASSISTANT SECRETARY TO THE MINORITY

ASSISTANT SECRETARY TO THE MAJORITY

ELECTED OFFICERS OF THE SENATE:

President Pro Tempore
The Secretary
The Sergeant at Arms
The Chaplain
Secretary to the Majority
Secretary to the Minority

From the U.S. Government Organization Manual 1963–64

treason, felony, or breach of peace, during attendance on sessions of Congress, or while going to or returning from sessions. They cannot be questioned or held responsible in any other place than in their respective houses for any speech or statement on the floor of Congress, in committees, or in official publications. Such immunity does not apply when a member of either house quotes, outside his house, words spoken there. A member may be punished by his own house, even to the point of expulsion which requires a two-thirds vote. Congressmen may send official mail under postal frank (free of charge). Many Congressmen use this privilege for the sending of political speeches and "extensions of remarks," from the *Congressional Record,* to constituents.

SESSIONS

The Constitution, under the Twentieth Amendment, adopted in 1933, provides that "Congress shall assemble at least once in every year, and such meeting shall begin at noon on the third day of January, unless they shall by law appoint a different day." Special sessions may be called by the President at any time after the close of the regular session.

CONGRESS AT WORK

The methods by which Congress attempts to meet the numerous demands upon its time and energy reveal both its virtues and its shortcomings.

Business of Congress. The business confronting Congress, as the national legislative assembly, is enormous. Its mass is so great that before it an unorganized membership would be helpless. Not only must the great machinery of the national government be kept going, but also emergencies must be met and the national interest and the local constituency cared for. Thus, organization is essential.

House and Senate Leadership. The Speaker of the House of Representatives is the leader of the majority party in that body. After the election of their presiding officer the members of the House elect a clerk, a sergeant-at-arms, a doorkeeper, a postmaster, and a chaplain. Of these, only the Speaker is a member of the House.

In the Senate the Vice-President of the United States serves as the presiding officer. A President pro tempore is chosen by the Senate after nomination by the majority party caucus. He presides over the Senate in the absence of the Vice-President, and succeeds to the Presidency of the United States in the event of the death or disability of the President, Vice-President, and Speaker of the House. The other officers of the Senate correspond to those of the House of Representatives.

Legislative Committees. Under the pressure of business, Congress has set up systems of standing committees: sixteen committees in the Senate and twenty in the House. Each committee corresponds broadly to a branch of legislation. For instance, the Senate Finance Committee has charge of all financial legislation coming before the Senate. The membership of these committees is determined by an agency (the "committee on committees") in each political party. The committees are the gateways of legislation because every bill is referred to them. Without the approval of the committee to which it is referred a bill has little chance of being passed.

Work of Committees. After a bill is referred to a committee, it is printed and put on the committee calender. The proposed law may be referred to a subcommittee for study, and hearings may be held on it. Often, the discussions in subcommittee and later in committee lead to amendments to the bill. The next step involves a decision of whether or not to report the measure to the house. The committee may "report" the bill to the house or pigeonhole it. There is a discharge rule by which a committee can be forced to report a bill to the floor of the house. However, it is so difficult to put into operation that the legislative body is rarely able to compel a committee to report on a measure.

Rules of Procedure. One of the major differences between the two houses of Congress is in their rules of procedure. In the House the rules vest great power in the organization and its leaders, but in the Senate the rules allow a wide scope of freedom to the individual member. The Speaker of the House may refuse dilatory motions, withhold recognition of members arising to speak, and count as present any member who, being present, refuses to answer the roll-call. Also, the rules of the House provide that no member may speak more than one hour except by unanimous consent, and a special rule may at any time be introduced which restricts debate to a few minutes for each member and sets a definite hour for ending all debate. The five-minute limitation in the House is not by special rule but is a regular rule for the consideration of proposed amendments in the committee of the whole. The House makes great use of the committee of the whole for legislation, but the Senate does not use the device at all. The Senate rules, on the other hand, limit the freedom of members only when the closure rule is adopted. This requires a two-thirds vote and any senator is then allowed to speak for one hour before a vote is taken.

Committee on Rules in the House.   After the body of rules have been readopted at the start of a Congress, all proposals for amendment are referred to the Rules Committee. This body may obtain the passage of "gag rules" limiting debate, prescribe or prevent the amendment of specific measures, prevent the consideration of particular measures, facilitate the consideration of favored legislation, and introduce the rules which move up certain bills on the calendar.

Filibusters and Closure in the Senate.   In the Senate, a member is permitted to talk as long as he pleases, subject only to the restrictions of the closure (or cloture) rule. The efforts to block legislation may take the form of speech-making, roll-calls, and other time-consuming tactics. The closure rule which was adopted in 1917 provided for closure on any measure. It has been invoked only four times. The 1949 rule provides for closure on any measure, matter, or motion but must be voted by two-thirds of all Senators duly chosen and sworn. No closure rule is possible on a motion to change the regulations.

Course of Legislation. The legislative process for all ordinary acts may be summarized as follows: A bill is introduced by any member of the House or Senate and is referred to an appropriate committee by the presiding officer. The committee reports, favorably or unfavorably, the original or amended bill. It is debated, amended, and approved in the house of its origin. At this point it is sent to the other house, referred to a committee, and reported as approved, amended, or disapproved. It is debated, amended, approved this time by the second house. Conferees of both houses are named and meet to resolve differences. The conferees report, and the bill is finally approved in both houses and goes to the President for his signature. Upon being signed by the President and promulgated by the Secretary of State the bill becomes a law.

Conference Committees. Since both houses of Congress must approve every law passed, it is often necessary to seek a basis of agreement when differences arise. The usual method of resolving these differences between the two houses is for the presiding officer of each to designate a certain number of members to serve on a conference committee which attempts to work out a compromise. The report of the Conference Committee is then accepted or rejected as a whole by each house.

PARTY AGENCIES IN CONGRESS

The description of the organization and procedure of Congress is incomplete without notice of the control exercised over the legislative machinery by party agencies.

Party Caucus. The basic party agency is the caucus, which is a closed meeting of the members of a political party in the House or Senate. The caucus selects the party candidate for the presiding officer (in the House, the Speaker; in the Senate, the President pro tempore), and appoints the several caucus agencies (to be described later). In the House the caucus determines the party attitude upon important legis-

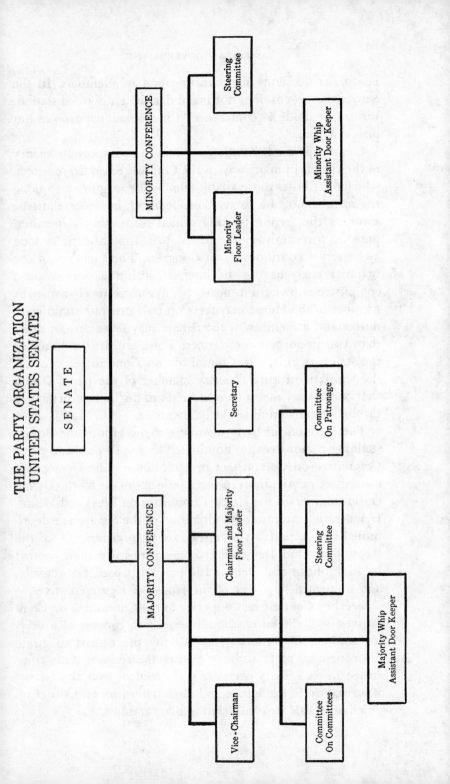

THE PARTY ORGANIZATION
UNITED STATES SENATE

SENATE

MAJORITY CONFERENCE

MINORITY CONFERENCE

Vice-Chairman

Chairman and Majority Floor Leader

Secretary

Minority Floor Leader

Steering Committee

Committee On Committees

Steering Committee

Committee On Patronage

Majority Whip Assistant Door Keeper

Minority Whip Assistant Door Keeper

lation; its decisions are binding upon its members. In the Senate the caucus does not make decisions upon legislation; instead, it holds a "conference" for discussion purposes but does not vote.

Committee on Committees. The most important agency of the caucus in many ways is the Committee on Committees which distributes the available committee assignments among the members of the party. Consideration, however, must be given to the "seniority rule" which insists that a member, once on a committee, is entitled to reappointment as long as he serves continuously in Congress. The member of the majority party having the longest continuous service on a committee is by custom nearly always made its chairman. A member of the House may serve on only one important committee and a member of the Senate may serve on not more than two important committees. Thus, within the limits of the seniority rule, the Committee on Committees controls the legislative future of every member of the party. It is a well-known fact that a member rises to distinction primarily through good committee assignments.

The Republican party members of the House and Senate standing committees are nominated by the Republican party Committee on Committees in each house. The Democratic committee nominations in the House are made by the Democratic members of the House Committee on Ways and Means. Democratic committee nominations in the Senate are determined by the party's Committee on Committees. All of the Republican and Democratic nominations are then ratified by Republican and Democratic party caucuses, respectively, and confirmed by a vote of the House of Representatives.

Steering Committee. Superior to the Committee on Committees is the Steering Committee, which consists of a varying number of leaders designated by the caucus to guide the course of party strategy during the session. This committee in each party exercises great control over the course of legislation in the House and often determines the order in which proposals are considered in that chamber.

THE PARTY ORGANIZATION
UNITED STATES HOUSE OF REPRESENTATIVES

HOUSE OF REPRESENTATIVES

Speaker[1]

MAJORITY CAUCUS

- Committee On Committees*
- Committee On Patronage
- Steering Committee
- Majority Whip
- Majority Floor Leader

MINORITY CAUCUS

- Committee On Committees*
- Minority Whip
- Minority Floor Leader

[1] The speaker is in fact the choice of the Majority Caucus, though formally selected by a vote of the whole House.

* Members of the Ways and Means Committee in Democratic Organization.

Floor Leader. Each party caucus designates a member to act as party leader during the session. His duty is to keep the party membership "in line," to guide the course of debate, and to determine when the formidable pressures of the party shall be brought to bear to secure passage of party measures or to accomplish defeat of opposition measures. The floor leader is aided by a lieutenant called the whip.

The Whips. Under the direction of his floor leader, the whip ascertains the sentiment on a given question and secures the attendance of members of his party for votes on important matters. He also keeps in touch with the legislative program and advises members when certain bills are expected to be considered.

CRITICISMS OF CONGRESS

An institution as important as the national Congress, with its enormous amount of business, has not escaped criticism or suggestions for improvement.

Major Criticisms of Congress. The major criticisms of Congress as a legislative body may be summarized as follows: (a) Congress is unrepresentative, the Senate being undemocratic in its equality of representation for all states whether populous or sparsely inhabited and the House being subjected to the evils of "gerrymandering" as well as denying representation to the minority in each district; (b) Congress is the victim of delay and complexity, particularly in reference to the relations between the two houses; (c) Congress occupies an irresponsible position in the governmental system and internally is the victim of an autocratic and irresponsible partisan machine.

Suggested Improvements. The above criticisms are accompanied by a series of suggested improvements which are summarized here in the same order: (a) the members of the House of Representatives should be elected by proportional representation from plural member districts; (b) the delays and complexities of relations between the two houses could be minimized, if not avoided, by a system of joint committees replacing the present separate committee systems; (c) the irresponsible position of Congress and its subservience to partisan agencies could be overcome by the Cabinet-in-Congress or the Council plans described in Chapter 6, *The Presidency.*

Congressional Reorganization Act of 1946. Throughout the 1930's and early 1940's the criticism of Congress for what were described as its outmoded methods increased. In 1944 Congress began to take notice of these attacks and shortly thereafter established a Joint Committee on the Organization of Congress, with Senator La Follette as chairman and Congressman Monroney as vice-chairman. During the time that this committee was at work, the American Political Science Association and the National Planning Association each published carefully developed recommendations.

In the Legislative Reorganization Act of 1946 the Congress adopted many of the recommendations of its joint committee. The number of committees in each house was sharply reduced: from 48 to 19 in the House of Representatives and from 33 to 15 in the Senate. In addition, the staffs of these committees were made more adequate; the Legislative Reference Service was strengthened significantly; and tort claims were transferred to administrative and judicial settlement. Other improvements in facilities and procedures were adopted, including registration of lobbyists, higher salaries for congressmen, and elimination of many time-wasting bills.

The reforms, while salutary and important, have not greatly altered the Congressional institution. Seniority in determining committee leadership, the vulnerability of party leaders in both parties and both houses, and resistance to the President continue as major characteristics.

Chapter 12

THE POWERS OF CONGRESS

Congress is generally known as the lawmaking branch of the national government, but, in practice, it is considerably more. As in the case of the President who exercises many powers of a legislative and judicial nature, the Congress performs many time-consuming non-legislative functions. Whether legislative, judicial, or executive, the powers of Congress are the principal powers of the national government.

CLASSIFICATION OF POWERS

Congressional powers, legislative or non-legislative, can be considered in terms of these seven classifications.

Constituent. The Congressional power which allows participation in the amending process is called constituent, and is among the non-legislative powers of Congress. All amendments to the Constitution involve some form of congressional action, but Congress does not have the authority to make fundamental changes in the Constitution. The initiative rests with Congress; each of the twenty-three amendments to the Constitution have been proposed by a two-thirds vote of both houses. In addition to the initiation of proposals for the alteration of the Constitution, Congress determines the manner to be used, and designates the time limit for ratification.

Electoral. The participation of the Congress in the electoral procedure, for President and Vice-President of the United States, is another non-legislative function. The Constitution provides that when the presidential electors have cast their ballots "they shall make distinct lists of all persons voted for as President and all persons voted for as Vice-President, and of the number of votes for each; which lists they shall sign and certify and transmit sealed to the seat of government of the United States, directed to the President of the Senate; the President shall in the presence of the Senate and the House of Representatives open all the certificates and the votes shall then be counted." Failure of the electoral college to elect a President through the lack of a majority vote for any candidate, throws the election into the House of Representatives. Under similar circumstances the Senate chooses the Vice-President.

Judicial. Among the judicial powers of Congress are those concerned with impeachment, and the organization of the federal court system. In reference to impeachment, the Constitution states, "The President, Vice-President, and all civil officers of the United States shall be removed from office on impeachment for, and conviction of, treason, bribery, or other high crimes and misdemeanors." The "articles of impeachment" (or charges) are the result of action in the House of Representatives. The Senate sits as a court to hear the case; and a two-thirds vote of the Senate is necessary to convict.

The organization and establishment of the courts fall within the congressional judicial functions. The Constitution provides that the judicial power of the United States be vested in one Supreme Court and in inferior courts as Congress ordains. Even the Supreme Court is not completely established by the Constitution; and the number of courts and judges is determined by the Congress. *The Federal Judicial System* is discussed in Chapter 13.

Executive. The Senate shares, with the President, the powers to appoint government officials and to make treaties. Through the practice of "senatorial courtesy" the Senate's power of confirming appointments, which is executive in nature, has been greatly increased. In addition, the Congress enjoys certain supervisory powers over the executive, and, as a result, may determine the extent of authority of the executive and administrative branches of the government in many situations.

Control over Administration. Congressional control over administration is effectuated in part through the statutory creation of departments and agencies for specific functions, and through the supervision of appropriations. Congress decides what new functions are to be undertaken and determines by law the agencies and organizations to be established to perform these functions. Generally, Congress defines the activities of these agencies, departments, and organizations in great detail in order to catalogue and limit their powers. Through these measures, Congress attempts to control or influence the policies to be carried out by these administrative agencies. The necessity of an annual request for funds enables the appropriations committees of the Congress to review the programs of the administrative units and to decide whether or not to continue, curtail, or abolish the functions of one or more of the units. The President is, of course, an influential participant in these lawmaking processes.

Investigative Powers. Another function through which Congress attempts to maintain partial control over administration is that of investigation. This inquisitorial power, as it is sometimes called, belongs to Congress (and state and local legislatures), and it empowers the investigation of judicial branch and executive branch activities and of economic, social, and political conditions when they warrant it. Congressional inquiries may be directed at securing information about draft legislation, at shaping governmental policy, at spotlighting a particular activity to mold public opinion, or at holding the executive and administrative units to rigid accountability. Congressional investigating committees may subpoena witnesses and records and may hold witnesses in contempt for noncompliance.

Legislative Powers. The major function of Congress is legislation. According to the Constitution, Congress is the only national lawmaking authority; it must assume the responsibility for this function and cannot delegate legislative powers to any other arm of the government. Every exercise of legislative power must be based upon constitutional authorization, that is, it must rest upon the many express and implied forms.

ENUMERATED. The Constitution provides Congress with a clear mandate of authority to legislate on a long list of subjects including taxation, appropriations, borrowing, payment of debts, currency, regulation of commerce, postal power, foreign affairs, declaration of and termination of war, copyrights, inferior federal courts, and others.

IMPLIED. Congress also possesses powers which, though not expressly granted, may be reasonably inferred or implied. The "implied powers" clause of the Constitution gives Congress the authority "to make all laws which shall be necessary and proper for carrying into execution" the powers placed by the Constitution in Congress or in the executive branch of the government. The carrying of an express power beyond its phraseology was accepted in Marshall's decision in the case of *McCulloch* v. *Maryland*. Many of the major functions performed by the federal government have their basis in "implied" powers.

RESULTANT. Congressional power to act in a particular field, while not traceable to a specific grant of power, can be justified on the grounds that it may be deduced from several enumerated powers taken collectively, or from all of them combined. Powers derived in this manner are known as "resulting powers." For example, Congress has the power to decide on the punishment for the violation of national laws, although the power is not inferred or expressly granted by the Constitution.

EMERGENCY. Congress does not have explicitly defined emergency powers. During wars or depressions the so-called emergency powers of Congress have represented new applications of existing powers or the implementation of powers or the rarely used broader interpretation of the enumerated powers. For example, the control of prices and rationing of scarce goods is accomplished under a provision of the "emergency powers."

MANDATORY AND PERMISSIVE.   Many of the powers granted to Congress under the Constitution either are not exercised or are exercised only in part. Such powers are permissive in that Congress is free to make use of them or not, in whole or in part. Those powers Congress is duty bound to employ are called mandatory powers. For example, Congress is bound to take a regular decennial census, and to reapportion seats in the House of Representatives after each of these censuses. But if Congress fails to perform these mandatory functions, there is no simple way in which the national legislature can be forced to act. The only resource the people have is to elect men to Congress who will observe these mandates.

EXCLUSIVE AND CONCURRENT.   In all cases in which the states are denied the power to legislate upon the particular matters which the national legislature may act on, the Congressional power is considered exclusive. Concurrent power refers to the authority of the Congress and the state legislatures to enact laws relating to the same subject. For example, both state and national legislatures levy income taxes.

Delegation of Legislative Powers.   The Constitution prohibits the delegation of Congressional legislative powers to the states, or to the people. However, Congress may delegate legislative power to the executive. In this case, Congress sets forth the general policy in the statute and, within the scope of such provisions, gives discretionary power to a federal officer or commission.

Limitation of the Powers of Congress.   The Tenth Amendment limits the power of the national government. Thus, the Constitution gives Congress, as a policy-determining agency, certain powers and denies others. The limits placed on the power of Congress include: (a) the system of checks and balances which denies Congress sovereignty in the field of legislation; (b) the prohibitions upon the national government set down in the Constitution primarily for the purpose of preventing the national government from infringing on the rights of the people or the states; (c) the reserved powers of the states. In the past years, as economic and social ties have knitted the United States closer and closer together, the people have, consciously and unconsciously, directed that the national government assume more powers.

Relative Importance of the Senate and the House. In evaluating the relative importance of the two houses of Congress it is necessary to bear in mind that (a) all bills to become laws must pass both houses of Congress; (b) the Senate's influence on foreign affairs is matched by the House's influence on money bills; (c) the Senate's increased role in the building of a postwar world is more than offset by the fact that money (the House's influence) is required to effectuate most of the postwar world programs; (d) the Senate is a smaller body, the term of office is longer and, as a result, the members tend to be more experienced and more widely known and to enjoy greater prestige.

Chapter 13

THE FEDERAL JUDICIAL
SYSTEM

The Constitution is brief and explicit in its provisions for this organization of a federal judiciary: "The judicial power of the United States shall be vested in one Supreme Court, and in such inferior courts as the Congress may from time to time ordain and establish." The federal judiciary is responsible for the trial of cases involving federal laws. Each state also has its own judicial system.

Supreme Court. The Supreme Court, composed of a Chief Justice and eight Associate Justices, stands at the head of the system of federal courts. This court has original jurisdiction in "all cases affecting ambassadors, other public ministers and consuls, and those in which a State shall be a party." The Supreme Court has appellate jurisdiction, only, in all other cases coming before it. Involving questions of law and constitutionality, these cases come to the Supreme Court from the inferior federal courts or from the state courts on appeal or by writ of error or by writ of certiorari.

Circuit Courts of Appeals. There are eleven circuit courts of appeals, including the District of Columbia, one for each of the eleven judicial circuits into which the United States is divided. The number of judges in each circuit varies from three to nine. These intermediate appellate courts consider appeals in cases originally decided by the federal district courts within the several circuits, and review all final decisions and certain interlocutory decisions of circuit courts, except those where the law provides for a direct review by the Supreme Court. These courts of appeal are also empowered to review and enforce orders of federal administrative bodies. In most cases the decisions of the circuit court of appeal are final, but the Supreme Court may call up on writ of certiorari any case involving an important constitutional or legal point.

The Judicial Conference of the United States is the annual conference of the Senior Circuit Court judges with the Chief Justice as chairman, meeting as a judicial council for the federal courts to modify the rules in order to expedite business. In 1939, Congress established the Administrative Office of the United States Courts. This office is subordinate to the Judicial Conference of the United States and the Supreme Court, and is the central agency for the administration of the rest of the judicial system.

Federal District Courts.   District courts are the trial courts of both law and equity and hear cases under general federal jurisdiction. At the present time, there are eighty-six district courts in the fifty states plus the district courts in Puerto Rico and the District of Columbia, making a total of eighty-eight federal district courts. Each state has at least one district court and the larger and more populous states have two, three, or four districts. There is at least one judge for each district, and the districts with large amounts of litigation may have more than twenty. Usually only one judge is required to hear and decide a case in district court, but in some types of cases three judges are called together to comprise the court. In all there are now about 320 district judgeships.

Courts of the District of Columbia.   According to the provisions of the Constitution, Congress has exclusive sovereignty over the District of Columbia. Therefore, Congress established two courts for the District of Columbia: a court of appeals and a district court, with nine judges in the former and fifteen judges in the latter. These courts determine within the usual federal jurisdiction and decide on many local issues (such as divorce and local crimes) and review decisions of the federal administrative agencies; decisions may be appealed to the Supreme Court of the United States.

Special Courts. In addition to the "constitutional courts" and in order to determine matters not within the scope of Article III of the Constitution which authorizes this system, Congress has found it necessary to create what are known as "legislative courts": the U. S. Court of Claims, the U. S. Court of Customs and Patent Appeals, the U. S. Customs Court, Territorial Courts, and the Court of Military Appeals which operates within, but not under, the Department of Defense. These courts differ from the constitutional courts in that they are special courts created to aid the administration of laws enacted pursuant to the powers delegated to Congress.

U. S. COURT OF CLAIMS. Consisting of a chief judge and four associate judges, the Court of Claims decides the validity of certain kinds of claims including suits filed with it against the United States and claims referred by Congress and the executive departments, except pension claims. It hears cases *en banc,* with all judges present.

U. S. COURT OF CUSTOMS AND PATENT APPEALS. Consisting of a chief judge and four associate judges sitting *en banc,* the Court of Customs and Patent Appeals decides questions arising under customs laws. In addition, it reviews certain trade-mark and patent cases, and decisions which the Customs Court hands down on classifications and duties on imported merchandise, decisions of the Patent Office on applications and interferences as to patents and trade-marks, and legal questions in the findings of the Tariff Commission concerning unfair practices in import trade.

U. S. CUSTOMS COURT. This court reviews appraisals of imported merchandise and the decisions of customs collectors, including liquidation of entries, orders on rate of duty, and exclusion of merchandise. The Customs Court is made up of nine judges—one of whom the President names chief judge—who hear cases in three divisions of three judges each. An interesting limitation imposed on this court is that no more than five judges may be members of the same political party.

TERRITORIAL COURTS.   Based on its authority to govern the territories, Congress established district courts in Puerto Rico, the Virgin Islands, and the Canal Zone. The district court of Puerto Rico has the same jurisdiction as similar courts in the United States. In addition to this jurisdiction, the other territorial district courts hear and decide local cases which in the states are decided by state courts. There are four territorial judges—one each in Puerto Rico, the Virgin Islands, the Canal Zone, and Guam.

COURT OF MILITARY APPEALS.   This court, which functions for administrative purposes in the Department of Defense, was established to review cases of courts martial in which the sentence, affirmed by a board of review, affects a general or flag officer or extends to death; to review all cases which the Judge Advocate General orders forwarded to the court; and to grant reviews on petition of the accused where good cause is shown.

Appointment of Judges.   The provisions of the Constitution specify the manner of appointment of judges of the Supreme Court and, on this basis, Congress has extended, by law, the same method of appointment to the other federal judgeships. All federal judges are nominated by the President, and approved, or confirmed, by the Senate.

Removal of Judges.   By provision of the Constitution, all federal judges hold office during good behavior and can be removed only by impeachment. Their compensation cannot be diminished during their continuance in office. At seventy years of age federal judges, with ten years of service, may resign or retire at full salary for life.

JURISDICTION OF FEDERAL COURTS

Chief Justice Marshall defined the jurisdiction of the federal courts and divided it into two broad classes. "In the first, their jurisdiction depends on the character of the case, whoever may be the parties. . . . In the second class, the jurisdiction depends entirely upon the character of the parties."

Jurisdiction over Subjects. Four classes of cases fall under Marshall's first division, the jurisdiction of the subject: (1) cases in law and equity arising under the Constitution; (2) the laws of the United States involving treaties made under the authority of the United States; (3) admiralty cases; and (4) maritime cases. In this jurisdictional division the nature of the controversy, or subject of the suit, is of prime importance.

Jurisdiction over Parties. Marshall's second division, jurisdiction of the parties, embodies cases affecting foreign ambassadors, public ministers, and consuls; controversies to which the United States is a party; controversies between citizens of different states, between a state and a citizen of another state, and between a state or a citizen of the United States and a foreign citizen or state.

Nature and Jurisdiction of Federal Courts. The jurisdiction of the federal courts is both exclusive and concurrent. They have *exclusive jurisdiction* in (a) cases involving crimes against the laws of the United States; (b) suits for penalties brought under laws of the United States, suits under admiralty and maritime jurisdictions, or under patent and copyright laws; (c) proceedings at bankruptcy; (d) suits to which a state is properly a party; (e) suits against ambassadors or other public ministers and consuls. In all other cases in which the federal courts exercise jurisdiction it is *concurrent jurisdiction*. State courts may also exercise it.

FEDERAL COURT WRITS

In the exercise of the national judicial power granted by the Constitution, the federal courts have the authority to use the important writs of habeas corpus, mandamus, injunction, and certiorari.

Writ of Habeas Corpus. This historic writ is used by the courts to prevent the detention of persons without due cause and within the provisions of law. The Constitution provides "The privilege of the writ of habeas corpus shall not be suspended, unless when in cases of rebellion or invasion, the public safety may require it." The writ is an order to any person detaining another person to bring the person detained into court and justify the detention. It is issued by the federal courts in behalf of any petitioner held under federal or state authority for violation of a federal law. It may be used against private persons as well as public officers to determine the legality of a detention. In the case where it is used against a police officer, the proper authorities bring the prisoner before the court, where, after a summary inquiry, the court either orders the prisoner released or held in custody or on bail to await regular trial.

Writ of Mandamus. By using this writ the courts can command public officials, private persons, and corporations to perform the duties required of them by law. The writ of mandamus is a court order, ordinarily, to a public officer instructing him to perform a legal duty. It cannot be issued to force public officials to act when the duty involves the exercise of judgment or discretion; it affects compliance only when the duty is clearly ministerial. The federal courts use this power sparingly and issue the writ only when the legal duty is clear, and when performance cannot be accomplished in any other way.

Writ of Injunction. Used by the federal courts in proceedings at equity, the writ of injunction can be enforced by arrest of the person of the defendant. An injunction may be a restraining order forbidding the performance of certain acts specified in the writ as unlawful, or it may be an order to perform a legal duty, the completion of which can be accomplished only by the defendant's action. In every case the requirement of equity jurisdiction, that the remedy at law be inadequate, must be met. The use of the writ of injunction has been frequently criticized, particularly as it has been used in labor disputes. Congress has attempted to regulate the use of the writ of injunction through the Clayton Act and the Norris-LaGuardia Act, but it is still a controversial implement when applied to the field of industrial relations.

Writ of Certiorari.   The need and purpose of the writ of certiorari arises from the fact that in certain cases the losing litigant has an unquestionable right to an appeal; in others the Supreme Court exercises its discretionary power in deciding whether or not to review the findings of the inferior court. In the latter case, the litigant petitions for a writ of certiorari and if the Court decides that good reason has been shown for it to review the proceedings it instructs the inferior court to submit its record of the case for review.

FEDERAL COURT PROCEDURE

The federal courts operate under the procedures defined in the Constitution, in the laws of the United States, and in the rules and precedents of their own making.

How Cases Appear before Federal Courts.   Cases reach the dockets of the federal courts by virtue of the concurrent and exclusive jurisdiction previously described, by removal from state courts on the grounds of "diverse citizenship" of the parties or the "federal question" involved, by appeal from state courts on the basis of a right claimed under the Constitution, the laws, or the treaties of the United States.

Procedure in Criminal Cases.   Federal courts have jurisdiction over those criminal cases defined in the Constitution and those cases which result from the delegation of power to Congress.

CONSTITUTIONAL JURISDICTION.   Criminal cases defined in the Constitution include: piracies and felonies committed on the high seas, cases under international law, counterfeiting coins and currency, treason against the United States, and offenses committed in places under the direct control of the United States (such as in the District of Columbia).

CONGRESSIONAL JURISDICTION.   Criminal cases which result from the delegation of power to Congress include: mail robberies (Congress has the power to establish post offices), liquor traffic violations (the power to regulate liquor traffic was given to Congress by the Eighteenth Amendment), interstate crimes of automobile theft and kidnaping.

GUARANTEES IN CRIMINAL ACTIONS. The manner in which federal courts are required to try offenses against the laws of the United States is defined in considerable detail in the Fifth and Sixth Amendments. The major guarantees are: that in all cases, except misdemeanors, there shall be indictment by a grand jury; that an exact copy of the indictment shall be furnished the defendant; that he shall not be required to testify against himself, nor be deprived of life, liberty, or property without due process of law. Trial must be public and by jury, and in the vicinity of the alleged crime. The accused must be given the assistance of counsel and may subject witnesses to questioning. Bail, pending trial, must be reasonable. No person may be twice subjected to trial for the same offense. It is under these rules, and with the privileges of the individual in mind, that the federal district attorneys conduct criminal prosecution.

Procedure in Civil Cases. The civil cases tried in federal courts may be divided into three groups: cases at law, cases in equity, and admiralty and maritime cases.

CASES AT LAW. Civil suits at law are mainly actions arising out of civil wrongs or torts, or actions based upon contracts. These cases are brought before the court in certain forms of action: assumpsit, replevin, trespass, or trover. In common law cases, the Constitution requires that wherever the amount in controversy exceeds twenty dollars a jury trial shall be had.

CASES IN EQUITY. Briefly, cases in equity deal with controversies for which there is no remedy at law. Equity was once an elastic judicial process, but has been reduced to forms which are inflexible and often overlap common law. In putting this procedure to work, the courts follow a highly technical set of rules drawn up by the Supreme Court. Often, equity is carried out by using the writs of injunction and mandamus, violations of which are punishable in contempt of court proceedings.

ADMIRALTY AND MARITIME CASES. The admiralty and maritime law of the United States is founded, largely, on the admiralty code inherited from older countries but modified by Congress for its use by the federal courts. However, international law is "our law," according to the Supreme Court, and the federal courts are constantly being called upon to apply it. Before treaties become effective, Congress must act on them. Cases which involve public and private rights and fall under treaties made under international law are heard in federal courts.

JUDICIAL REVIEW

The most controversial power of the Supreme Court is its prerogative of reviewing the constitutionality of legislation. No other power exercised by the Supreme Court has been so surrounded by criticism as the judicial review of legislation. Many critics believe that the Constitution does not give this power to the court, that it only exercises it. However, in a federal system of government the Constitution can draw only a general separation of power between national and state governments, which results in the prevalence of situations constantly in need of interpretation.

Judicial Review of Federal Legislation. In the celebrated case of *Marbury* v. *Madison* (1803) Chief Justice Marshall declared that the courts possess the power to declare null and void any legislative act which, in the opinion of the courts, was "repugnant to the Constitution." This opinion has since been questioned by both friends and critics. The main steps in Chief Justice Marshall's argument were: (a) the Constitution is superior, paramount law, binding all agencies of government; (b) it is the essence of judicial duty to declare what the law is; (c) the courts are, therefore, obliged to declare when a law is in conflict with the Constitution and to refuse to be bound by such law. By virtue of this precedent the court has repeatedly set aside acts of Congress as null and void.

Judicial Review of State Legislation by Federal Courts. Of a different nature, but exercised in much the same manner, is the review of state legislation by the Supreme Court on the grounds of "constitutionality." The most numerous cases in this respect arise under the "due process of law" and "equal protection of the laws" guarantees of the Fourteenth Amendment. Social and economic legislation by the state legislatures has been so frequently overruled by the court on these grounds that the impartial quality of judicial review has been questioned more and more.

Modification of Judicial Review. The courts, however, do not have unlimited power to pass on the constitutionality of legislation. The Supreme Court, itself, and the Constitution have enforced limitations on the judicial veto in respect to legislation. These restrictions on the veto power are: (a) the court concerns itself only with the unconstitutional parts of an act, and rarely reviews the whole legislative act; (b) litigated cases, only, are reviewed by the judiciary; (c) before the court will stamp an act unconstitutional, it must be clearly so beyond a doubt; (d) political questions have been consistently refused review by the court; (e) usually, the court and the judges do not consider the wisdom of legislation, but merely the constitutionality of legislation.

"FIVE-TO-FOUR" DECISIONS. The increase in the number of important decisions, during the 1930's, in which the court set aside legislation by a majority of one member of the court gave the opponents of judicial review a fresh opportunity to offer proposals for reform. The invalidation of the Agricultural Adjustment Act, as well as the narrow margin by which the Tennessee Valley Authority Act was upheld, was made a focal point for the renewal of attempts to curb the powers of the Supreme Court. The following are solutions which have been proposed: (1) Abolish the power of judicial review by constitutional amendment. (2) Provide that Congress may repass a law which has been set aside by the court in the same way it may override a presidential veto. This, too, would require a constitutional amendment. (3) Provide that the concurrence of seven of the nine justices of the Supreme Court shall be required in exercising the power of judicial review. Some are of the opinion that the latter could be accomplished by an act of Congress, but it is more likely that a constitutional amendment would be necessary.

Roosevelt Proposal of 1937. In February, 1937, President Roosevelt proposed a plan described as a statutory solution for the problem created by the refusal of courts to uphold legislation on social and economic problems. In brief, the plan permitted the retirement of judges at seventy years of age, on full salary, and empowered the President to appoint one additional judge (up to a maximum of fifteen for the Supreme Court) for each judge failing to retire at seventy.

This plan was submitted to Congress and defeated. One of its results, however, has been a new trend in the decisions of the court. This was greatly facilitated by the occurrence of several vacancies in the Supreme Court, to which President Roosevelt appointed men sympathetic with his social and economic legislative programs.

Judicial Review in the 1950's. The Supreme Court again became a center of controversy in the 1950's, largely as a consequence of a series of "civil rights" decisions affecting the segregation of Negroes in public schools and other public facilities, the rights of the accused in criminal proceedings, and legislation or regulations designed to prevent or punish subversive acts. In 1958–59 conservative Congressional critics of the Court made strong efforts to limit its jurisdiction or discretion. These efforts failed by a narrow margin, but the critics have some ground for feeling they have made an impression on the Court.

Chapter 14

FOREIGN AFFAIRS

The determination of the foreign policies of the United States and the conduct of the relations resulting from these policies is shared in varying degrees by the President, the Senate, the Department of State, and the House of Representatives.

President and Foreign Affairs. The President, undoubtedly, occupies the most important position in the determination and the conduct of the foreign relations of the U. S. He controls the diplomatic representatives of the United States through the power of appointment and removal. His power includes the negotiation of treaties. The latter are subject to a two-thirds vote of approval by the Senate. He enjoys the power, based on his general control of foreign affairs, to enter into executive agreements with foreign countries without the consent of the Senate. The distinction between executive agreements and treaties lies in the matters handled through them. The former is used primarily for business relations or administrative adjustments with foreign states.

Senate and Foreign Affairs. The Senate shares with the President the power of appointment of diplomatic, consular, and State Department personnel. The great power of the Senate in foreign affairs rests historically upon the constitutional provision that it may approve or reject treaties negotiated by the President and the Department of State on behalf of the United States; a two-thirds vote of the senators present is required for ratification of a treaty. Thus, the Senate may effectively repudiate the negotiations entered into by the President or his agents. To what extent the Senate is entitled to consultation during the actual course of negotiations is a moot question; experience seems to indicate that the President must at least informally consult with the Senate or certain senators during the negotiations. The most successful Presidents have appointed members of the Senate to the group of agents conducting negotiations. Once a treaty draft is laid before the Senate, it may be approved, amended, or rejected. If a treaty is amended by the Senate, the President may either reopen negotiations with a foreign power or allow the treaty to die. If the Senate approves the treaty it is usually ratified by the President and the foreign powers involved and becomes legal upon proclamation. It is possible, however, that the President may indeed fail to ratify the treaty.

Department of State and Foreign Affairs. The power of the State Department in foreign affairs is derived from its character as the formal organ of communication between the President and foreign countries. It follows such directions as the President may give it, and in general its power is sharply determined by the extent to which the President assigns discretion and power to it. Some presidents have been extremely active in the administration of foreign affairs, but others have left a large part of the formulation of foreign policy or the conduct of negotiations to the Secretary of State and his aides. The department is also important for its direction of the diplomatic and consular staffs. All routine and most of the important foreign business is transacted through the Department of State.

House of Representatives and Foreign Affairs. The power of the House of Representatives to control foreign relations is an indirect but frequently an important one. One is manifested in control over financial expenditures—by which the House of Representatives can influence the President's activities in foreign affairs. Evidence of the power of the House to influence foreign affairs is exhibited in those instances in which an act of Congress is necessary to give effect to some part or all of a treaty. The House can, in such instances, withhold its approval. The House has also joined the Senate on occasion in its resolutions designed to influence the course of our foreign relations.

Requiring annual legislative authorization for foreign aid and foreign information programs has been a favorite Congressional method of influence over foreign policy since World War II. Just as Congressional legislation may repeal or modify privileges granted by a treaty, a treaty may have the effect of repealing a Congressional law. The most recent in point of time prevails. Treaties, and statutes passed to enforce them, have been upheld by the court even when they infringed upon the reserved powers of the states.

BASES OF FOREIGN POLICY

Although American foreign policy, in any instance, depends largely upon the interplay of immediate and material factors, the language and to some extent the substance of a specific policy is profoundly influenced by a number of generally well-established historic precedents.

Policy of Isolation.   No American foreign policy has been so lasting in influence as isolationism. Gaining a foothold in political thought during the first hundred years of national existence, the policy of isolation became almost traditional. Through it, American foreign relations were based on the theory that America was a self-contained nation and should "steer clear of permanent alliances with any portion of the foreign world." Actually, the United States was isolationist only to the extent of being concerned with problems within the nation rather than without; the United States was almost always influenced, in some respect, by the prestige of a few European countries in foreign affairs. The rise of America to the position of a leading world power has nullified any sound basis for isolationism, but it is still a factor of considerable importance in the formulation of United States foreign policy.

Monroe Doctrine.   Second only to the policy of isolation in its wide acceptance is the broad theory called the "Monroe Doctrine." Named after President James Monroe, who proclaimed it in 1823, it has been variously followed, extended, or modified by succeeding presidents. Originally, it set forth these ideas: (a) the American continents are no longer subjects for colonization by foreign powers; (b) the United States will not take part in wars concerning European powers; (c) the United States will not interfere with existing colonies and dependencies of European powers in the Western hemisphere; (d) interference with the countries of the Western hemisphere, who have declared and maintained their independence, will be regarded as an unfriendly act by the United States. In later practice, the Monroe Doctrine was assumed to mean: (a) the powers of the Eastern Hemisphere are forbidden to acquire territory in the Western Hemisphere; (b) the smaller Latin-American states must maintain order and meet their financial obligations, or the United States will intervene to secure them; (c) the Caribbean region is within the "sphere of national supremacy" of the United States; (d) American economic interests in Central America will be fully protected, if need be, by armed intervention; (e) "Pan-Americanism," within the limits of the dominant interests of the United States, will be encouraged.

"Good Neighbor" Policy. At the beginning of his administration President Franklin D. Roosevelt extended the Monroe Doctrine in order to assume protective duties for the Western Hemisphere. But, in a later term of office, he radically transformed the imperialistic trends of the Monroe Doctrine into a "good neighbor" policy. Although the United States has not surrendered its dominant position, it has withdrawn its armed forces which were previously stationed in certain Latin-American states, and has partially renounced its rights to intervene therein. The Pan-American Peace Conference (December, 1936) adopted specific measures for preserving peace in the Western Hemisphere and for preventing intervention in any American republic by a non-American power. The Lima Conference of December, 1938, marked an intensification of this program and resulted in even closer Pan-American ties to prevent foreign intervention.

In 1948, an important step in Pan-American relationships was taken when the Charter of the Organization of American States, a regional agency within the United Nations, was adopted. The Pan-American Union, with main offices in Washington, D. C., is the general secretariat for the organization; the council is composed of one representative from each of the twenty-one republics of the Western Hemisphere.

U. S. World Leadership.   The interdependence of the nations of the world is a reality of the twentieth century which has progressively weakened the eighteenth- and nineteenth-century bases of American isolation. The Spanish-American War brought the United States the problems and opportunities of overseas possessions. The First World War involved us even more heavily in the future of Europe and the European world. At its close, through President Woodrow Wilson, we took a prominent part in the establishment of the League of Nations, but our traditional isolationism reasserted itself in our refusal to join the League. Throughout the 1920's and 1930's our basic foreign policy remained ambivalent: we multiplied our instances of co-operation with the League and promoted the Kellogg Peace Pact of 1928, but our Neutrality Acts of 1937 and 1939 were isolationist in temper. Despite the latter, the Second World War immediately reached out to involve us in world affairs. President Franklin D. Roosevelt gradually shook off the restraints of isolationist policies, before Pearl Harbor and our total involvement in the war, and the United States began again the direct exercise of world leadership.

United Nations.   Again the United States, in the midst of a world war, became one of the main architects of a world association. This time our commitment was almost without opposition. The preparatory conference for a United Nations organization was held at Dumbarton Oaks, in Washington, D. C., and the United Nations Conference to draft a charter met in San Francisco in 1945. The United States was the first nation to ratify the Charter of the United Nations, with but two dissenting senators. The permanent headquarters of the

United Nations is located on American soil, in New York City. In addition to being a leading member of the United Nations, the United States belongs to and is a leader in all the specialized international agencies set up in concert with the UN: the International Labor Organization, the Food and Agricultural Organization, the World Bank, the International Monetary Fund, the World Health Organization, the International Civil Aviation Organization, and many others. The United States seems now largely free of the phantom of isolation.

Cold War.   Following quickly upon the defeat of the Germans and the Japanese, the United States found itself in growing disagreement with its former ally, Russia. These differences rapidly intensified into hostile relationships so closely approaching armed conflict as to be universally described as "the cold war." Although Russia has remained within the United Nations, her use of the veto over actions requiring unanimity has been frequent, and her membership in the specialized agencies has been, on her own choice, almost zero.

European Recovery Aid.   The major prize in the cold war between Russia and the United States is the friendship and support of Europe. The United States recognized its obligations to preserve Europe as part of the democratic world by extending unprecedented aid to western Europe. Economic assistance was provided through the Marshall Plan (administered by the Economic Co-operation Administration). The alliance of the United States and Canada with ten nations of western Europe was declared in the Atlantic Pact of 1949 and was mainly an effort to maintain peaceful co-operation in the North Atlantic. Special aid was also extended to Greece and Turkey.

Far Eastern Dilemmas.   The cold war has spread from Europe and Eurasia to the Far East. The conquest of China by the Communists from the north, despite heavy American aid to the Republic of China, presented the United States with unresolved dilemmas to complicate our future course in the Far East. Our problems in this area are intensified by the lack of a solid base for counteraction with which the democracies of Western Europe and Britain provide us in the Atlantic area. The invasion of South Korea by the North Koreans in June, 1950, resulted in UN military action. The United States played a large role in the defense of South Korea, contributing the major proportion of troops and equipment to the fighting forces serving under the UN flag in Korea.

Foreign Policy Toward the Far East. Traditionally, the United States built its foreign policy toward Asia around the "open door" declaration of friendship for China as a counterpoise to European and Japanese intervention on the Asiatic mainland. The end of the Second World War brought, first, the United States occupation of Japan and, second, a treaty of friendship and alliance with the Japanese in 1952. At the present time, United States policy in the Far East is built around the necessity to slow down and contain the Communist advance by (a) military assistance to Korea, (b) alliance with Japan and the Philippines, (c) strongly expressed friendship with India, Indonesia, Vietnam, and other non-Communist nations and economic and military assistance to the Chinese Nationalists based on Formosa, and (d) strong military bases in the Pacific. These specific points are the major features of the new United States foreign policy in the Far East, but the enduring form of the new policy is still a matter of national debate.

The uneasy truce which characterizes present policy is illustrated by the extended negotiations, begun in 1960, over the frontiers and internal stability of Laos and by the recurrent difficulties concerning the islands in the Formosa Strait, especially the defense of Quemoy and Matsu against the Communist Republic of China which seeks the transfer of these islands to its jurisdiction. A more recent example is the program of economic and military aid to South Vietnam in its protracted conflict with the pro-Communist Viet Cong assisted by support from the north.

Chapter 15

TERRITORIES AND POSSESSIONS

Closely related to foreign affairs is the problem of acquisition and government of territories, possessions, and other special jurisdictions.

Inherited and Acquired Territories. All the territory which has, from time to time, been governed under the Constitution was either inherited or has been acquired. The "inherited" territory was the Northwest Territory which was surrendered by the states to the national government under the Articles of Confederation. The "acquired" territory is all of the remainder, beginning with the Louisiana Purchase in 1803 and extending down to the acquisition of the Virgin Islands in 1917. Prior to 1867, all of the territory acquired by the United States was contiguous and eventually was divided up into states. The other American acquisitions represent noncontiguous possessions and are not necessarily assured of admission to statehood in the future. The principal American territories were acquired in the following manners: Alaska by purchase in 1868; Hawaii by agreement in 1898; Puerto Rico, Guam, and the Philippines by war and treaty with Spain in 1898; Panama Canal Zone by lease in 1902; the Samoan Islands by treaty in 1904, and the Virgin Islands by purchase in 1917.

The Constitution was explicit about the Northwest Territory, but other territories have been acquired and governed by implied powers. It is now a generally accepted fact that the United States may acquire territory by implied powers from the admission of new states, the making of treaties, or through the waging of war and the concluding peace.

Power to Govern Territories. The Constitution vests in Congress the power to "dispose of and make all needful rules and regulations respecting the territory or other property belonging to the United States." This authority, thus conferred, was for many years regarded as unlimited, but the Supreme Court imposed a number of limitations upon the Congressional exercise of this power beginning with the Dred Scott decision. In that case, the Court established that the Congress, in legislating for "incorporated" territories, is bound by all the limitations in the Constitution not clearly inapplicable, and in legislating for "unincorporated" territories it is bound by the "fundamental" but not by the "formal" limitations of the Constitution. The "fundamental" and "formal" aspects of the Constitution have not yet been fully defined by the Supreme Court.

Incorporated and Unincorporated Territories. Both Alaska and Hawaii, before they were admitted to statehood in 1959, were considered, as incorporated territories, a part of the "United States," and their citizens enjoyed the same personal rights as the people in the states. The District of Columbia is the only remaining incorporated territory. The unincorporated territories—Puerto Rico, Guam, the Virgin Islands, American Samoa, and the Canal Zone and Panama Canal—belong to the United States. The people of the unincorporated territories cannot claim the rights which are considered "formal" limitations under the Constitution. Generally speaking, statehood for this type of dependent is a remote possibility.

Organic Acts. Through the various Organic Acts, each of which specifically concerns a territory, Congress has supreme legislative control over all dependencies. Congress can deny all of a territory's local legislative freedoms, and act itself as the legislature, or it can provide for a locally-elected legislative body, with whatever degree of power it chooses. The basic laws or constitutions of the United States possessions are in the form of Congressional acts which Congress may change or revoke entirely. If Congress should fail to legislate, the President may provide the necessary laws.

GOVERNMENTS OF THE TERRITORIES

The Congress, the President, and the Department of the Interior are variously concerned in the governments of the possessions of the United States. In a similar capacity, Congress also governs the District of Columbia.

Commonwealth of the Philippines. On March 24, 1934, the Congress provided (in Public Law 127) for the estab lishment of the Commonwealth of the Philippines as the first step toward the eventual independence of the islands. Under the authority conferred by this act, the Philippines adopted a constitution and inaugurated a new government. The latter follows the general outlines of the American pattern: the president is directly elected by the people, serves a six-year term, and cannot serve two consecutive terms; the national assembly holds all the legislative power and is composed of ninety-eight representatives elected from the provinces according to the distribution of the population (the number of members is never to exceed 120) to serve three-year terms; the judicial power is vested in a supreme court and such inferior courts as are created by law. During the ten years which preceded the complete independence of the Philippines, certain restrictions were exercised by the United States: acts affecting currency, coinage, imports, exports, and immigration had to be approved by the President of the United States; foreign affairs were directly controlled by the United States; all acts of the national assembly were reported to the Congress of the United States; the United States maintained armed forces in the islands and called the Philippines' armed forces into service; the laws of the Commonwealth were subject to review by the United States Supreme Court; and the United States maintained a high commissioner in the Philippines, and the Philippines sent a resident commissioner to the United States.

Since July 4, 1946, the Phillipine Commonwealth has been completely independent. From the United States the Philippine state receives special tariff concessions and the maintenance of naval bases there. Due to the form that the American defense system has taken, and as a result of former relations, the United States maintains close ties, almost a protectorate relation, with the Philippines.

Government of Puerto Rico. Until 1950, Puerto Rico was governed under the Organic Acts of 1900 and 1917. The latter act extended citizenship to the residents of the island and included a bill of rights. In 1947, Congress made the governor an elected official and provided him power to appoint heads of all departments of Insular Government. The legislature is popularly elected and consists of a senate of nineteen and a house of thirty-nine members. Acts are not only subject to the territorial governor's veto but also must be submitted to the President and may be annulled by Congress. Judges of Puerto Rico's supreme court and the federal district court, the latter having an attorney and marshal, are appointed by the President. Other judges are appointed by the governor and Puerto Rican senate. A resident commissioner, elected for four years, sits in Congress but has no vote. In 1950, Congress enabled Puerto Rico to draft its own constitution and it is now called a Commonwealth, though its structure is still the same.

Governments of the Virgin Islands and the Panama Canal Zone. The governor of the Virgin Islands is appointed by the President and the Senate and exercises such authority as the President confers in addition to the veto power. The islands are composed of two municipalities, each having a legislative council which meets jointly at least annually to form a legislative assembly in order to enact legislation for the Virgin Islands. Congress extended American citizenship to the residents of the Virgin Islands in the Organic Act of June, 1936. The Department of the Interior exercises jurisdiction over the islands.

The Canal Zone is a government reservation administered by the Canal Zone government. Both the Panama Canal Company and the Canal Zone government are headed by one individual, bearing the titles of president and governor simultaneously, appointed for four years by the President and the Senate of the United States.

Minor Territories and Military Bases.   As a result of our emergence into world leadership in the twentieth century, the United States has acquired a series of island possessions and military bases for which patterns of local government have just begun to emerge. In 1947, the United Nations Security Council extended the trusteeship of the 625 Pacific islands, formerly held by Japan, to the United States. The Carolines, Marianas, and Marshalls, which were included in this group, were transferred from the jurisdiction of the Department of the Navy to the Department of Interior for administration in July, 1951.

After 50 years' rule by the United States Navy, Guam began a transition to a system of civil government on September 1, 1949. Under the Organic Act of Guam approved August, 1950, Congress placed Guam under the administration of the Department of the Interior and conferred United States citizenship upon the inhabitants.

In July, 1951, the Department of the Interior also took over the supervision of American Samoa from the Navy Department. Baker, Jarvis, and Howland have been under the jurisdiction of the Interior Department since May, 1936. Midway and Wake are still under the administration of the Department of the Navy.

Government of the District of Columbia.   The Constitution in a special provision vests in Congress the power "to exercise exclusive legislation in all cases whatsoever over such district . . . as may . . . become the seat of the Government of the United States." By virtue of this authority Congress makes all the laws for the government of the District of Columbia, vesting executive authority in a commission of three members, two of whom are residents of the District appointed by the President and the Senate for three years, while the third, selected from the army engineers corps, is designated by the President for an indefinite term. Although there are no local government elections, the citizens' advisory council wields considerable power through its representations before Congressional committee hearings. The Twenty-third Amendment to the Constitution (1961) gave residents of the District the right to vote in the election of the President and the Vice-President.

Chapter 16

THE STATES AND THE FEDERAL GOVERNMENT

The governments of a federal system present many problems in regard to the proper relationship with each other. Perhaps the most important is the relationship between the central government and the units called "states."

Nature of the Federal System.   The national government possesses only those powers specifically delegated to it, or reasonably to be inferred from the Constitution. As for the states, the Tenth Amendment provides that "the powers not delegated to the United States by the Constitution, nor prohibited by it to the states, are reserved to the states respectively, or to the people." The delegation of a particular power to the national government does not deny to the states the right to exercise the same power within their respective spheres, unless the power is clearly prohibited to the states or is such that it can be exercised only by the national government. Of the body of powers thus reserved to the states, some are distributed by the respective state constitutions to the executive and judicial branches of the state government. The remaining governmental powers are exercised by the state legislatures, subject to federal and state constitutional restrictions. The major residual power exercised by the state is the police power, which is the power of the state to enact legislation to protect and promote the health, safety, and welfare of the people.

Admission to the Union.   Of the fifty states, only thirteen are members of the Union by virtue of ratifying the Constitution. Of the remaining thirty-seven, four states—Vermont, Kentucky, Maine, and West Virginia—were formed by separation from other states. At the time of its admission, Texas was an independent republic. The remaining thirty-two were admitted from territorial status. Congress is given general powers to make admissions subject only to the limitations that "no new states shall be formed or erected within the jurisdiction of any other state; nor any state to be formed by the junction of two or more states or parts of states, without the consent of the legislatures of the states concerned." The process of admission to the Union involves: (a) the territorial petition to Congress, (b) the passage of the enabling act by Congress, (c) the calling of a constitutional convention, (d) the drafting of the tentative constitution in the territory, (e) the Congressional acceptance of the territorial constitution, (f) an act of admission through Congressional resolution. Congress can impose upon the territory any conditions it sees fit before passing the resolution admitting it to the Union as a state. However, once the territory is a state it can revoke all such conditions with the exception of those involving compacts on property rights.

Legal Equality of States.   Notwithstanding any differences in area and population, the states are equal in their constitutional and legal status: no special powers or privileges in law accrue to any one of them; no one of them can exercise any direct coercion upon another.

Federal Guarantees to the States.   The federal government is required, by the Constitution, to respect the territorial integrity of the states, to protect each state against invasion and domestic violence, and to guarantee each state equal representation in the Senate and a republican form of government. A "republican form of government" has never been clearly defined. The Supreme Court has declared the question to be political in character and hence to be decided by the President and Congress.

Limitations on the States.   The Constitution either expressly or by implication imposes certain limitations upon the states. (1) "No state shall enter into any treaty, alliance, or confederation"; nor, except with the consent of Congress, "keep troops, or ships of war in time of peace, enter into any agreement or compact with another state, or with a foreign power, or engage in war, unless actually invaded, or in such imminent danger as will not admit of delay." (2) No state may levy, without the consent of Congress, any imposts or duties on imports or exports except such as are necessary for inspection laws, nor any tonnage duty. Neither may a state tax any federal instrumentality. (3) No state may "coin money; emit bills of credit; make anything but gold and silver coin a tender in payment of debts." (4) No state may pass any law "impairing the obligations of contract." (5) No state may pass any ex post facto law nor any bill of attainder; nor may any state "make or enforce any law which shall abridge the privileges or immunities of citizens of the United States; nor . . . deprive any person of life, liberty, or property, without due process of law; nor deny to any person within its jurisdiction the equal protection of the laws." (6) No state may deny or abridge the right of citizens to vote, on account of sex, race, color, or previous condition of servitude.

Obligations of States

In their relations with each other the states are required to operate under certain specific conditions imposed by the Constitution.

Full Faith and Credit. First, the Constitution requires each state to recognize and, if need be, accept and enforce the civil judgments and decrees of another state.

Privileges and Immunities of Citizenship. Second, the Constitution also provides that the "citizens of each state shall be entitled to all privileges and immunities of citizens in the several states." This is taken to mean that citizens in moving from one state into another shall be subjected to no special and arbitrary discriminations. Natural citizens are usually compelled to wait a year before being permitted to exercise the suffrage for national and other officers; artificial persons (corporations) may not be admitted at all unless engaged in interstate commerce or a kind of activity covered by some other national power.

Rendition of Fugitives from Justice.   Third, under the terms of the Constitution the states are obliged to deliver up any persons, accused of crime, who have fled from one state into another. Whether or not such a person shall be returned, however, lies within the discretion of the governor of the state harboring the accused.

Federal Grants-in-Aid

Perhaps the most interesting recent development in the relation of the states with the national government is the growth in federal grants-in-aid to the states.

Grant-in-Aid.   A conditional grant of federal funds to the states to be used for a specified purpose is known as a grant-in-aid. Congress has made extensive use of this device under its power to levy taxes for the general welfare and its practically unlimited appropriation power. The conditions attached to the federal grant usually include: (a) the money must be spent for purposes specified, (b) the necessity for conformance to standards fixed by a federal supervising agency and submission to federal inspection and control, (c) the states, alone or together with their local governments, must contribute a designated proportion of the total cost of the function or project, and (d) civil service stipulations.

Federal policy since the beginning of 1933 has greatly magnified the grants-in-aid system. These federal programs are illustrative of the extensive applications of the grants-in-aid system: public assistance, housing, vocational rehabilitation, social security, highways, urban renewal, education, and public health. The magnitude of the grant-in-aid program since 1933 has greatly altered the realities of the federal system and prepared the way for even more powerful inclinations toward shared powers.

Centralization.   The expansion of national powers into fields long considered the sole jurisdiction of the states has taken place as a result of the growing complexity of social and economic conditions. The extension of national authority has been accomplished in some instances through constitutional amendments, more often by the courts' liberal interpretations of the enumerated powers conferred by the Constitution on the national government.

Co-operation between State Governments. Some observers argue that "centralization" might be slowed down to some extent if the states made more effective use of the existing means of co-operative effort and at the same time experimented with additional devices to help solve mutual state problems. The Council of State Governments is the co-ordinating body for most of the agencies engaged in voluntary co-operation across state lines. Along with its extensive research activities, this council serves as a clearinghouse for many bodies of state and local officials, such as the Governor's Conference and the National Association of Secretaries of State. A device that is being used more and more by the states, as a means of collective action, is the interstate compact. This is a formal agreement among states to handle a particular problem that transcends state lines and requires Congressional consent. Examples of problems handled recently by interstate compacts include the Colorado and Columbia Rivers and the Port of New York Authority.

The "Politics" of Federalism. Federalism is a political problem more than a constitutional or administrative one. The argument is usually in fact over the merits of a particular governmental program rather than over the abstract legal or ideological issues around which the public debate is conducted. Grants-in-aid, for example, probably strengthen state governments instead of weakening them. The opposition to them is based fundamentally upon resistance to the policies represented by the grant-in-aid program itself, not primarily upon concern with the role of states as such in the federal system. A half-century of experience with grants-in-aid and related national government programs indicates we have entered an era of federalism in which shared powers, "co-operative federalism," is the dominant theme.

Chapter 17

CITIZENSHIP, CIVIL RIGHTS, AND SUFFRAGE

"All persons born or naturalized in the United States, and subject to the jurisdiction thereof," says the Fourteenth Amendment, "are citizens of the United States and of the State wherein they reside." Citizenship of the United States is by this provision made paramount and state citizenship made incidental.

Citizenship Acquired by Birth. Persons may acquire citizenship in the United States by virtue of being born here (the right of place), which is closely associated with the ancient legal tradition of England and known as the *jus soli* principle; or by virtue of the fact that their parents are citizens (the right of blood), which is described by Roman civil law as *jus sanguinis*. Thus, a person of any race, creed, or color, regardless of the fact that his parents may be aliens, if born here, is a citizen; and the children of American citizens born while the parents are resident abroad or travelling outside the country are also citizens. The latter right is not described in the Fourteenth Amendment, but from 1802 Congress has, by law, extended citizenship in these cases.

Citizenship Acquired by Naturalization. Naturalization is the legal process by which an alien becomes a citizen. It has been, at times, and may be collective; that is, a group of persons may be given the status of citizens by an act of Congress, by treaty, or by joint resolution. The process is, however, usually individual and, as outlined by present law, takes at least two years to complete. For a long time, only white persons and those of African descent were eligible. However, recent changes in the naturalization law permit many Asiatics to obtain citizenship. The system is administered by the Immigration and Naturalization Service in the Department of Justice, and partly by specified courts, federal and state, having jurisdiction over the place where the alien resides. The process consists of three main steps. (1) Any non-enemy alien, 18 years of age and a legal resident of the United States, is eligible if he or she files a declaration of intention to become a citizen before a court of competent jurisdiction; at the completion of this step the candidate receives his "first papers." (2) Not less than two nor more than seven years, thereafter—following at least five years of residence in the United States and after having reached the age of twenty-one —he formally petitions for citizenship showing that: he lawfully entered the United States; he can read and write English; he has knowledge of the history, principles, and form of government of the country; he does not, nor has he within ten years prior to the date of application, advocated the overthrow—individually or as a member of an organization—of the government by force, the illegal destruction of property, or the doctrines of communism or totalitarianism; he is in favor with the order of the United States; he is of good moral character; he renounces his allegiance to his former country. This petition must be accompanied by the affidavits of two American citizens, testifying to the moral character and legal residence of the candidate for citizenship. (3) Then the petition is checked by the Immigration and Naturalization Service of the Department of Justice. If, after investigation, the judge is satisfied that the candidate meets all the requirements of citizenship, he gives the oath of allegiance and issues a citizenship certificate.

CIVIL RIGHTS

One of the fundamental attributes of constitutional government is a body of private rights which, while never absolute, guarantee a certain measure of personal freedom. These rights are nowhere fully enumerated in the American constitutional system, but the most important ones find express or implied support in the Bill of Rights and other guarantees.

Guarantees of Personal Liberty. In both national and state constitutions, the individual finds important guarantees, which include: the right to be free, the right to be equal, the right to property, freedom of religion, freedom of expression, the freedom of assembly and the right to petition, the right to citizenship and its privileges, immunity from bills of attainder and ex post facto laws; and the guarantee that "due process of law" is essential for any conviction of a crime or misdemeanor, "due process" ordinarily guaranteeing an indictment, a jury trial, immunity from double jeopardy, and protection against cruel and unusual punishment. To what extent these guarantees exist as against the several states is determined by the state constitutions and the decisions of the Supreme Court.

SUBSTANTIVE RIGHTS. The following civil liberties are considered to be of a substantive nature.

Freedom from Slavery and Involuntary Servitude. The individual's foremost privilege under a democratic government is the right to freedom. However, the Constitution was in effect almost fourscore years before this obvious right was added to the law of the country. The Thirteenth Amendment expressed the fact that the United States was to be a society of free men: "Neither slavery nor involuntary servitude, except as a punishment for crime whereof the party shall have been duly convicted, shall exist within the United States or any place subject to their jurisdiction." This amendment was an outgrowth of the Civil War. Conscription is not considered involuntary servitude.

Freedom of Religion. "Congress shall make no law respecting an establishment of religion or prohibiting the free exercise thereof," states the First Amendment. The Supreme Court has considerably expanded the scope of this clause by developing the doctrine of separation of church and state.

Freedom of Expression. This right concerns the freedom of speech, press, and other forms of communication. It is a relative concept, in that no one is free to slander or libel another and during times of emergency it has been considerably curtailed. Even under normal conditions the right of free speech and press is limited by standards of decency and morality. Holmes's "clear and present danger" rule is still a guiding yardstick in cases involving this basic right.

Freedom of Assembly and the Right to Petition. The First Amendment forbids Congress to restrict the "right of people peaceably to assemble and to petition the government for redress of grievances." This right is not absolute. The right of assembly can be restricted by police power to guarantee the health, the safety, and the morals of the community. In many communities a permit for holding meetings is required. This requirement may serve as a barrier to particular purposes, if the authorities abuse their use of the police power.

Right to Keep and Bear Arms. The Second Amendment states: "A well-regulated militia, being necessary to the security of a free State, the right of the people to keep and bear arms shall not be infringed." This does not prevent the state from exercising its police power through a licensing system, requiring a permit for the possession of particular weapons.

Conviction of Treason. This crime is one of the most difficult to prove under American laws. The citizen is protected against being judged a traitor by a Congress acting on insufficient evidence or with political purpose. Article Three of the Constitution states: "Treason against the United States shall consist only in levying war against them, or in adhering to their enemies, giving them aid and comfort. No person shall be convicted of treason unless on the testimony of two witnesses to the same overt act, or on confession in open court." As a result, there have been very few citizens named as traitors in the history of the United States. Actions against the United States which fall short of treason may still be punishable as espionage. In these situations, Congress defines the nature and punishment for acts of espionage.

Equal Protection of the Laws. According to the Fourteenth Amendment a state cannot "deny to any person within its jurisdiction the equal protection of the laws." This right is second only in importance to the right to be free. It is not concerned with equality in the possession of goods, but rather with the equality of persons under law and the equality of opportunity. In other words, the concern is the enjoyment of the cultural, the social, and the economic advantages of a free society and the opportunity to contribute to the society and its progress. The interpretation of the "due process" clause of the Fifth Amendment also deals with this right. But the state is permitted, for legislative purposes, to set up a reasonable classification of people. In 1950, the Supreme Court handed down decisions tending to make discrimination against people of color on railway trains illegal and the segregation in educational institutions more difficult to practice. Since the Brown and Bolling cases in 1954, a succession of decisions and orders by the Supreme Court has made segregation in all forms increasingly difficult to practice.

Only a citizen enjoys the advantages of full membership in a society, such as running for office, holding public office, voting, etc. It is obvious, therefore, that this right is axiomatic in a democratic society. The Fourteenth Amendment provides a firm basis for citizenship and naturalization. Although, the right to vote is regarded as an essential characteristic of citizenship in a democratic society, securing it for every mature citizen of the United States is still a problem confronting the country.

PROCEDURAL RIGHTS. The various methods by which our freedoms and rights are insured are known as procedural liberties. They include the following.

Freedom from Ex Post Facto Laws. Section Nine of Article One of the Constitution provides that "No bill of attainder or ex post facto law shall be passed." Thus Congress cannot legislate to make something a crime which was not defined as a crime at the time of commission. This applies only to criminal justice, not to retroactive legislation on civil matters.

Freedom from Bills of Attainder. As defined by the Supreme Court, "A bill of attainder is a legislative act which inflicts punishment without a judicial trial." Quoted in the preceding paragraph, Article One of the Constitution denies Congress the power to pass legislation imposing punishment by legislative rather than judicial procedure.

Right to Indictment by Grand Jury. The first clause of the Fifth Amendment to the Constitution provides that the individual, accused of a capital or infamous crime, has the right to a presentment or indictment of a grand jury. Unless an indictment is returned by a grand jury, the judiciary cannot continue the prosecution of the individual.

Right of Habeas Corpus. This writ was designated to prevent arrest or unlawful imprisonment without bringing charges against, or granting a trial to the individual. The suspension of the writ of habeas corpus has always caused a great deal of controversy. The ninth section of Article One of the Constitution provides that the writ may be suspended "when in cases of rebellion or invasion the public safety may require it."

Right to Trial by Jury. The Constitution contains three statements providing for jury trial: Section Two of Article Three, and the Sixth and Seventh Amendments. These clauses establish the right of a jury trial; the Supreme Court has established the necessary features of the federal system. These guarantees extend to criminal, as well as civil, cases, but the accused may waive the right of trial by jury and select to be tried before a judge.

Right to Defense. The Sixth Amendment of the Constitution provides "In all criminal prosecutions the accused shall enjoy the right to a speedy trial, . . . and to be informed of the nature and cause of the accusation; to be confronted with the witnesses against him; to have compulsory process for obtaining witnesses in his favor, and to have the assistance of counsel for his defense." Federal criminal procedures have observed these rights with little question. However, it has been necessary for the Supreme Court to rule that the

Fourteenth Amendment demands that the states provide an individual accused of murder, where the penalty for conviction may be capital punishment, with counsel if he is unable to do so himself.

Freedom from Excessive Bail. The first clause of the Eighth Amendment states that "Excessive bail shall not be required." Again, this right is relative because it does not prohibit the denial of bail in capital crime cases. However, if an accused person believes that his bail is too high, he is allowed to have the amount reviewed. Wide discretion is used by the courts in fixing the bail of an individual. The severity of the offense must be taken into account, as well as the financial status of the person, and the fact that he may forfeit the bail and fail to appear at trial if released.

Freedom from Unreasonable Search and Seizure. The Fourth Amendment to the Constitution places obstacles in the way of the police forces, to prevent them from acquiring unreasonable powers. The search warrant procedure was directed against "general warrants," which were related to the "writs of assistance" of colonial times. The latter allowed general searching expeditions to private homes in the hope of discovering evidence. In relation to the same amendment, the Supreme Court recently declared that evidence acquired, by government agents or private individuals, through wire tapping could not be used in federal criminal cases.

Freedom from Double Jeopardy. The Fifth Amendment to the Constitution provides that no person may be tried twice for the same crime. A trial by federal and state jurisdictions for an act which violates both federal and state laws is not double jeopardy. Nor is it a violation of the double jeopardy clause if the act committed violates two federal acts and the resulting offenses can be judicially established.

Right of Due Process of Law. The Fifth Amendment to the Constitution protects the citizen against arbitrary action on the part of the federal government. The Fourteenth Amendment protects persons against arbitrary action on the part of the state government. Due process not only protects the people against arbitrary action, but against arbitrary regulation of private rights. It is important to note that "due process" clauses afford protection beyond that provided by the Bill of Rights.

GUARANTEES TO PRIVATE PROPERTY. So traditional to our way of life is the right to acquire and hold property that it is almost part of American political and economic processes. The Fifth Amendment, addressed to the federal government and the Fourteenth Amendment, addressed to the states, protect this right. Each extends the far-reaching guarantees of "due process of law" and the limitations on the power of eminent domain. However, this right, like all others, is relative and is not spoken of as a civil liberty.

Civil Rights Laws of 1957, 1964.   Beginning with President Truman's Committee on Civil Rights (1946), the national government has increased rapidly its role in the protection of minority groups, especially the Negroes. Executive orders by Presidents Truman and Eisenhower were followed by the progressively sweeping Civil Rights Acts of 1957 and 1964, the first Congressional actions since 1871. These statutes extended national government protection of civil rights by (1) raising the civil rights functions of the Department of Justice to the level of a major unit under an Assistant Attorney General, (2) establishing a Civil Rights Commission to investigate and evaluate civil rights legislation and enforcement, (3) strengthening federally guaranteed rights in public accommodations, voting, and education, and (4) increasing the powers of the Department of Justice to act upon its own initiative in the civil rights field through injunction and other enforcement proceedings.

EXERCISE OF THE SUFFRAGE

No other privilege traditionally belonging to citizens is of greater ultimate importance than the exercise of the suffrage. The extent to which it is exercised and under what conditions determine to a large degree the democratic or undemocratic character of the government.

Constitutional Basis of the Suffrage. The national Constitution makes only a few references to the exercise of suffrage in the United States. Voters for members of the House of Representatives must have "the qualifications requisite for electors of the most numerous branch of the state legislature." The Fifteenth Amendment forbids denial of the vote "on account of race, color, or previous condition of servitude." The Nineteenth Amendment forbids denial "on account of sex." The Twenty-fourth Amendment forbids denial of the vote in federal elections "by reason of failure to pay any poll tax or other tax." Beyond these requirements, the states are free to fix, in their constitutions and laws, any conditions or restrictions they wish so long as they do not abridge the terms of the Fourteenth Amendment guaranteeing equal protection of the laws to all citizens.

Extension of the Suffrage. In the beginning there were considerable restrictions surrounding the suffrage, particularly property and religious qualifications, but the American states have gradually democratized the suffrage. White manhood suffrage was established under the influence of the democratic frontier and was practically complete before 1860. Negro suffrage was, at least in law, established as a result of the Civil War; and woman suffrage, after a gradual movement in the states, was established in 1920 by the Nineteenth Amendment.

Present Suffrage Requirements. While it is impossible to generalize about all the suffrage regulations in the fifty states, standard qualifications are: (a) the minimum voting age is twenty-one in all states except Georgia and Kentucky, eighteen; Alaska, nineteen; and Hawaii, twenty; (b) all states set up some residence requirement, ranging from one to two years in the state, three to six months in the county, and usually thirty days in the election district; (c) all states require the voter to be a citizen; (d) all states deny to certain groups—the insane, the idiots, paupers, criminals, public charges, and others—the exercise of the suffrage, the disqualifications being specified by statute; (e) many states employ literacy tests to prevent voting by the illiterate, but the use of these tests has been curtailed by federal legislation. The Voting Rights Act of 1965, aimed at eliminating racial discrimination in voting, suspended the use of literacy and other qualifying tests in states and counties which had them in effect on November 1, 1964, and where less than 50 per cent of the voting age population was registered or voted in that election. State and local poll taxes have been eliminated through state legislation and, finally, Supreme Court decision. In March, 1966, the Supreme Court declared Virginia's poll tax unconstitutional on the grounds that it violated the "equal protection of the law" clause of the Fourteenth Amendment. This decision was considered broad enough to invalidate the other existing poll tax requirements in Alabama, Mississippi, and Texas.

Chapter 18

THE POLITICAL PARTY SYSTEM

The most far-reaching and influential of governmental institutions is in most respects an extra-legal one: the political party. The nature and composition of each party will vary greatly with time and place, but it may be said that it is an organization of persons who have combined to control or influence both the policies and the personnel of government. The membership of any political party will be determined by several more or less tangible factors.

Economic Factors. Perhaps the most important factors determining the composition of political parties are the economic interests of the groups making up the membership. Banking, manufacturing, mining, agriculture, and labor are among the groups influential in determining the character of political parties.

Social Factors. In addition to economic factors, race, religion, and social classes are often important in determining allegiance to political parties.

Traditional Factors. The economic and social factors are reinforced by the very great influence which hereditary party allegiance and the traditions of each party have upon the voter.

Sectional Factors. When the factors mentioned above are combined in a distinct geographical region we have what is called "sectionalism" as an element in political party composition. The "Solid South" is one of the strongest expressions of the sectional factor in the United States.

NATIONAL PARTY ORGANIZATION

NATIONAL PARTY CONVENTION

NATIONAL COMMITTEE
Chairman chosen by presidential nominee

One man and one woman from each state, and from District of Columbia, Alaska, Hawaii, Puerto Rico, Philippines and (in Democratic Party) the Canal Zone; nominated as laws of the states require and ratified by the National Conventions.

CONGRESSIONAL CAMPAIGN COMMITTEE
Republican Party: one member from each state with Republican representation in House, chosen by caucus of state delegation.

Democratic Party: one member from each state having Democratic representation in House, chosen by caucus of state delegation; in addition, one man and one woman from states without representation, designated by chairman of caucus.

Management of campaign activities in behalf of party candidates for U.S. House of Representatives.

SENATORIAL CAMPAIGN COMMITTEE
Republican Party: 7 Senators, appointed by Chairman of conference for two year term.

Democratic Party: 6 Senators, appointed by conference for two year term.

Management of campaign activities in behalf of party candidates for U.S. Senate.

ADVISORY COMMITTEE
Democratic Party only, consisting usually of ten or more national figures.

EXECUTIVE COMMITTEE
A select executive organization varying in membership, but usually fifteen in Democratic and twenty-five in Republican Parties. Chairman of National Committee is usually chairman of executive committee.

EXECUTIVE DIRECTOR
Designated by executive committee to direct activities of National headquarters.

BUREAU OF PUBLICITY
Empowered by executive committee to conduct editorial and publicity activities.

National Party Organization

The American political party organization is a loosely co-ordinated system of national, state, and local organizations. The relations between the three divisions are based more upon informal agreements and "understandings" than upon permanent official connections. The national organization consists of three separate agencies.

National Committees. Each party has a National Committee, consisting of one man and woman from each state and certain executive officers—a chairman, an executive secretary, a treasurer, and others. The state representatives are nominated by the state delegations to the National Convention and the nominations are formally ratified by the convention. The chairman is named by the presidential candidate, and the remaining executive members are chosen by the National Committee. The functions of the committee are to conduct the presidential campaign, to raise funds for the party, to exercise general supervision over the affairs of the party, to select the convention city, and to maintain party morale through favorable publicity and through the individual efforts of the committeemen in each state to guide all party activity.

Senatorial Campaign Committees. Each party also maintains a national agency concerned with the campaigns of party nominees for the United States Senate. The Republicans maintain a Senatorial Campaign Committee of seven senators, named by the chairman of the Republican conference in the Senate. The Democrats have a similar committee of five members chosen in the same manner. These committees co-operate with the National Committees, give all their attention to the campaigns of candidates aspiring to the Senate, and raise and distribute funds for that purpose.

Congressional Campaign Committees. Finally, each party maintains national agencies to aid the campaigns of party nominees for the House of Representatives. In the Republican party, the committee consists of one member from each state having Republican representation in Congress. The Democrats do likewise, but also allow the chairman to appoint a woman member from each state and to appoint a member from each state which has no Democratic member in the House. In both parties, nominations to the committee are made by state party delegations in the House and are ratified by the party caucus.

State and Local Organizations

The national party organizations described above depend to a very great extent upon the support and co-operation of the more elaborate state party organizations. In each state the parties are organized not only to capture state and local offices but to participate in national contests as well.

State Central Committees.   In each state each party maintains a central committee, varying in size from 11 members in Iowa to 811 in California and chosen usually by state conventions or party primaries, which serve as agencies to link the numerous local organizations with the national system. The committees may often exercise very great power by fixing the qualifications for party membership, but their usual function is to conduct state campaigns. The chairman and his executive committee quite frequently are able to dominate the entire party system of the state.

County Committees.   One of the most important units of American party organization is the county committee which is maintained by each party in most every county in the United States. Of varying size and chosen by varying methods, its main purpose is to manage local party affairs, using the considerable patronage of the local government to weld the party into a victorious combination. Such committees are often the nuclei of powerful "political machines"—for example, the Tammany Hall organization, whose control is centered in the executive members of the New York County Democratic Committee.

City Committees.   In important populous urban centers, a separate organization frequently manages party affairs in connection with the city government. The organizations of Philadelphia and Chicago are examples of this type.

Precinct or Election District Organization. All party organization rests ultimately upon the "unit cell" of the precinct or election district. Although the precinct committee is often mentioned, in practice the organization is usually composed of a single committeeman or captain. This individual is the routine agent of the party organization in its contacts with the voters and is frequently no more than an employee of the county or city committee.

Informal Organization. This formal hierarchy of committees is rarely the actual repository of power. In the party system power is informally distributed among officeholders, industrialists, labor leaders, publicists, lawyers, "bosses," who make up the "informal organization."

FUNCTIONS OF PARTIES

The political party is the primary agency through which the citizen attempts more or less successfully to control his government. In meeting this demand the party performs a number of significant functions.

Selection of Candidates. The political party is the most important agency in determining what names shall appear on the ballots in general elections as candidates for office. Originally, the party organization, through a party convention, named the candidates. However, these party conventions were openly criticized because they were often controlled by "machines" and "bosses." In order to make party selections more democratic, the *direct primary* was adopted by many states. The primary system, as such, allows every member of the party the right to vote on party selections in a primary election. The party convention system of selecting candidates still survives in a few states.

Conduct of Campaigns. No less important is the function performed by the political party in conducting the campaigns which precede an election. Through the party organization, issues are formulated and discussed, candidates

TYPICAL STATE AND LOCAL PARTY ORGANIZATION
Utah Party Committee Organization

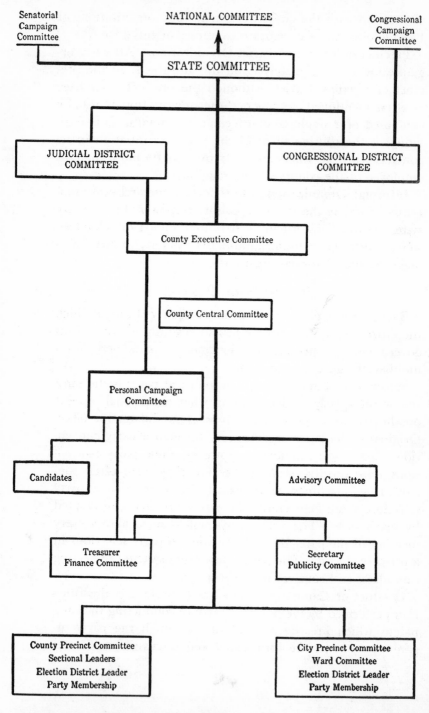

are presented to the public, and the voters are rallied to the polls in behalf of one set of candidates or another.

Control of Government. The political party imparts a unity to our loosely organized government by co-ordinating its separate branches; the party brings the executive and legislature together on party policies.

DEVELOPMENT OF PARTIES

American political parties in their historical development have shown a remarkable continuity in policies and sources of strength. As would be expected, their development parallels the economic, political, and social history of the country.

Federalist-Republican Alignment (1789–1830). From the very beginning of the national government there was discernible a division into two major political groups. One—the Federalists—was led by Hamilton and dominated the government until 1800, and promoted, in general, measures designed to favor the investors, the merchants, the manufacturers, and associated groups. The other—the Republicans—was led by Jefferson and constituted an opposition group until 1800, when it came into power. Its power was based upon the farming population, with some support from urban centers, and its governmental policies were, in general, designed to meet the demands of the agricultural groups. With the disappearance of the Federalist party in 1816, a period of party fusion began in which the Republican leaders became more conservative but by 1828 signs of revolt were apparent.

Democratic-Whig Alignment (1830–1860). With the election of Andrew Jackson to the presidency in 1828 a new alignment, though along familiar lines, appeared. Jackson welded the farmers of the West and South, and the masses of the East, into the Democratic party, which revived the left-wing policies of the Jeffersonian movement by destroying the National Bank, reducing the tariff, and democratizing the administration. Henry Clay and others marshalled into the Whig party the groups who had originally formed the

bulk of the Federalist party. The winning presidential candidates in 1840 and 1848 represented the Whig party. However, the Whigs never rose above the status of an opposition
party and were eventually undermined by the slavery
question.

Republican-Democratic Rivalry (1860–1932). The events
leading up to, and consummating in, the Civil War effected
a realignment of parties which has continued with more or
less stability to the present day. The Democratic party
emerged from the Civil War as the party of the South and
has since gradually recruited strength in the urban centers
of the East and West, particularly among the immigrant
groups. The Republican party was originally a fusion of the
industrial and financial interests of the East with the anti-
slavery farmers of the Northeast and of the West, but leadership of the party is usually considered to have crystallized in
the former group. The policies of the two parties had been
shaped to fit the interests of the groups composing each. In
the 1920's each party revealed a rift in its own ranks, look-
ing toward an impending realignment. The Democrats were
divided into the hostile camps of a conservative leadership
in the South and in the northern cities, and a growing revolt
of the left-wing urban and agrarian groups. In the Republican party, finance and industry was faced with the increasing hostility of western agrarianism.

New Deal Democratic Ascendancy (1932–1952). The
great depression which began in 1929 intensified these forces
in the major parties and in 1932 the Democratic party, having under the leadership of Franklin D. Roosevelt become
the party of the left-wing urban and agrarian groups, cap-
tured the erstwhile Republican and insurgent strongholds of
the West and Middle West. Its sweep was repeated in the
Congressional elections of 1933 and the presidential contest
of 1936. Some reversals of this trend were indicated by the
Congressional and state elections of 1938. President Roosevelt
obtained a third term in 1940 and a fourth term in 1944,
maintaining his previous support among urban and labor

groups, but receiving a smaller portion of the middle-class vote than previously. In 1946, President Harry S. Truman and his party lost control of Congress to the Republicans, but the 1948 elections saw the victorious resurgence of the Democratic party, capturing both Congress and the presidency.

Republican White House, Democratic Congress (1953–1961.) The great popularity of Dwight D. Eisenhower as Republican presidential candidate brought the Republicans back to the executive branch in 1952, with a small majority in Congress also. Despite Eisenhower's victory in 1956, the Democrats won Congress in elections in 1954, 1956, and 1958.

Democratic Resurgence (1961–   ). In 1960 John F. Kennedy defeated Richard Nixon in a close contest and the Democrats retained Congress. In the 1962 Congressional elections the Democrats gained a larger majority. In 1964, Lyndon B. Johnson won over Barry Goldwater in a Presidential and Congressional landslide for the Democrats.

Minor Parties. Throughout its history and particularly since the Civil War, the United States has had a number of minor parties, most of which have been left wing in character. The Greenback party, the Populists, the Progressives, the Socialists, and others have all contributed important policies, among them the popularizing of social reforms, to our major parties. Up to the present time, the minor parties have called attention to issues which the major parties have ignored. In this way, they have expressed political discontent and forced the major parties to attend to controversial and touchy issues.

REGULATION OF PARTIES

So important an agency of government as the political party has not completely escaped governmental regulation, although the steps taken have usually been regarded as insufficient.

Regulation of Campaign Funds. The most familiar field for the regulation of party activities is the attempt to control campaign expenditures. Congress has, by a series of acts, prescribed that party organizations concerned with campaigns for national office must file statements of receipts and expenditures prior to and after the election. Candidates for Congress are also required to file statements of expenditures, and are limited to the amount fixed by the state or in any case to $10,000 for the senatorial candidates and $2,500 for candidates to the House (or three cents per voter if the total is less than $25,000 for the former and $5,000 for the latter). Other acts forbid contributions by federal employees or by corporations. The states have added to this regulation with similar legislation which in general: (a) requires itemized statements of receipts and expenditures both from candidates for office and from party committees; (b) fixes the amount which may be expended in campaigns for various grades of offices; (c) prescribes the purposes for which funds may be expended; (d) limits those who may contribute. Enforcement has proved to be difficult in national and state elections.

Regulation of Nominating Procedure. The second field into which regulation has entered is that of nominations. The most extensive form of regulation requires that nominations be placed under a direct primary system in which a preliminary election, with all the safeguards of a regular election, is provided and the party members select nominees from the field of candidates. State laws often define party membership and provide for the election of party committeemen at various levels. The full success of this system awaits three corollary reforms: the adoption of a short ballot, the establishment of a merit system for the civil service, and the establishment of responsible government now denied by a complex separation-of-powers system.

Primary. The caucus, the legislative caucus, and the convention have in many states been superseded by the direct primary. When a primary is limited to party members it is called a "closed" primary; party membership is checked in several ways. The "open" primary doesn't require any statement of party affiliation. Particular problems arise when the primary is tantamount to an election as it is in many one-party areas.

Chapter 19

THE STATE CONSTITUTIONS

Each of the fifty states is governed under a state constitution which is the supreme law of the state except as it conflicts with the Constitution, laws, and treaties of the United States.

CONSTITUTIONAL PROVISIONS

The state constitutions, unlike the national Constitution, have undergone marked changes since 1776, when the first ones were formed.

Prior to 1900. The most significant changes had been: (a) a constant tendency to increase in length; (b) an increase in electoral offices; (c) the extension of the suffrage; (d) a tendency to impose detailed restrictions upon the legislature in both its powers and its procedures; and (e) a steady increase in the power of the governor.

Since 1900. The most significant changes have been: (a) the continued rise in the power of the governor; (b) the expansion of the merit principle; (c) the adoption of the short ballot; (d) the increasing use of the executive budget; (e) the expansion of state services; (f) an increase in the power of the electorate through such devices as the initiative, the referendum, and the recall; (g) the rise of administrative reorganization. At present, the typical state constitution may be said to consist of the sections which are described in the following paragraphs.

Preamble. Following very closely the preamble of the national Constitution, this section usually states the general

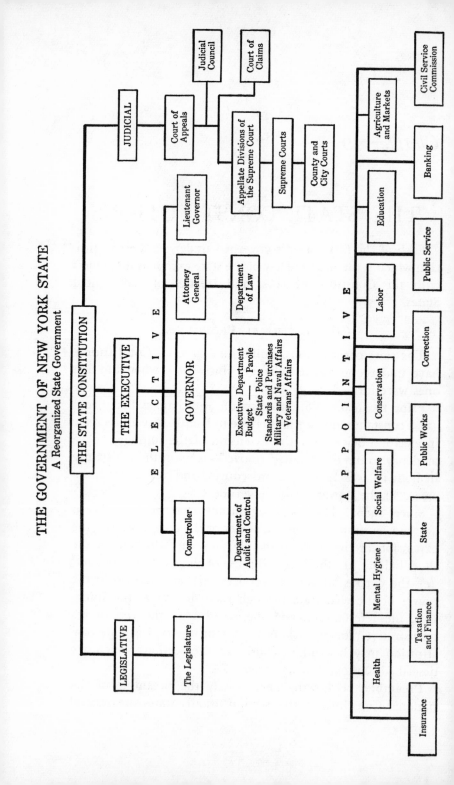

THE GOVERNMENT OF NEW YORK STATE
A Reorganized State Government

THE STATE CONSTITUTION

LEGISLATIVE

The Legislature

JUDICIAL

Court of Appeals

Judicial Council

Court of Claims

Appellate Divisions of the Supreme Court

Supreme Courts

County and City Courts

THE EXECUTIVE

ELECTIVE

Comptroller

Department of Audit and Control

GOVERNOR

Executive Department — Parole
Budget
State Police
Standards and Purchases
Military and Naval Affairs
Veterans' Affairs

Attorney General

Department of Law

Lieutenant Governor

APPOINTIVE

Insurance

Health

Taxation and Finance

Mental Hygiene

State

Social Welfare

Public Works

Conservation

Correction

Labor

Public Service

Education

Banking

Agriculture and Markets

Civil Service Commission

principles upon which the American government is based and the purpose which the constitution is designed to accomplish for the state.

Bill (or Declaration) of Rights. This heritage of individualistic democracy lists in great detail the individual rights of life, liberty, and property. Just as the federal Bill of Rights protects us from arbitrary action by federal officials, the state bill of rights protects the citizens from arbitrary acts on the part of the state. The broad interpretation given by the court to the due process clause of the Fourteenth Amendment has tended to lessen the relative importance of these state constitutional guarantees. For many years the state courts' interpretations of these rights served as a major barrier to social legislation. Even today several state courts take a dim view of the legislature's constitutional ability to deal with social and economic problems.

Framework of State Government. Each state constitution describes at length the structure and powers of the three departments, legislative, executive, and judicial. It also defines the powers and relationship of state and local governments.

Suffrage Provisions. Each constitution also fixes the general and special qualifications for the suffrage or defines the limits within which the legislature may do so. The general conduct of elections may also be prescribed.

Special Provisions. There is a growing tendency to regulate leading problems by constitutional provisions, such as taxation, finance, banking, public utilities, public and private corporations, and others. These are so numerous and of such varying character that it is impossible to generalize about them.

AMENDMENT AND REVISION OF STATE CONSTITUTIONS

An essential provision in any state constitution is the method of constitutional change. There are usually four ways in which a state constitution may be modified.

Popular Initiative and Referendum. About one-fourth of the states provide for amendment by popular initiative of proposals (by a specified number or percentage of voters) and submission to a popular referendum in which the proposal must receive at least a majority and in some states a specified percentage of the votes cast upon the proposal.

Legislative Proposal and Popular Referendum. Every state except New Hampshire allows amendment of its constitution by legislative proposal which becomes part of the constitution when ratified by a majority or other specified percentage of the votes cast in a popular referendum. In thirty-six states only a single session is required to act on a proposal. The remaining states require approval by two successive legislatures. In Delaware, action by two successive sessions completes the amending process without popular referendum.

Constitutional Conventions. While seldom used, the state constitutional convention is the agency through which a thorough revision is usually effected. It is used, or has been used, by all states except Rhode Island. It must be used to amend the constitution in New Hampshire. The convention may be called in some states by legislative provision, in others by a legislative proposal ratified in a popular referendum, and in still others by popular initiative and referendum. A few state constitutions have become operative upon the calling of a convention alone, but the more usual process is to submit the proposals of the convention, separately or in entirety, to a popular referendum for ratification. The revision of the New York State Constitution in 1938 is an interesting example of the problems involved in adopting a new constitution and how they might be resolved. The work of the convention was greatly aided by a state constitutional convention committee which, preparatory to the convention, undertook the tremendous job of research concerning the problems with which the convention was to be confronted. Its reports were compiled and published for the delegates' use. New York's convention recommendations were submitted to the voters as a series of nine proposals. Three were rejected. In 1947, New Jersey submitted its recommendations for a new constitution as a single proposition and the people ratified the change. The New Jersey Convention of 1947 was a "limited convention" in the sense that it had no power to propose changes in legislative representation in that State.

Commission. Constitutional change by commission is a comparatively recent method of revising state constitutions. The legislature establishes a special commission to prepare a revision and report it to the legislative body. The legislature may submit the report, as is or with changes, to the voters.

Model State Constitution. For almost thirty years the National Municipal League has been working on the problem of securing more effective state constitutions. Through its Committee on State Government the League has published four revised editions of a model state constitution. This model meets many of the criticisms of contemporary state constitutions with progressive recommendations representing the conclusions of expert opinion.

Chapter 20

THE STATE LEGISLATURES

The position of the state legislatures, as one of the main policy-determining agencies of the states, is basic and primary in representative government. The state legislatures are nevertheless practically everywhere denied the organization and powers essential to an effective discharge of their responsibilities. They are hampered by constitutional restrictions; they are of an unwieldy size; they are ineffectively organized; their procedure is unduly complicated; their representative character is nullified by poor methods of selection; and they lack opportunity for responsible and effective relations with the executive on important matters.

Bicameral v. Unicameral

Every state legislature, except that of Nebraska, is organized in two separate houses. This bicameral system, whose origins are similar to those of the bicameral plan for the national Congress, has long been a target of academic critics.

Criticism of Bicameral System.. The major criticisms of the bicameral system for state legislatures are that (a) it no longer serves any useful purpose; (b) it unduly complicates the legislative process; (c) it serves as a convenient device for control by irresponsible minorities and party machines, and for an unrepresentative system of "rotten boroughs."

Nebraska's Unicameral Legislatures. Nebraska's adoption of the unicameral legislature in 1934 is the only step yet taken toward a unicameral system. For it, the advantages of a smaller body with improved personnel and greater opportunities for deliberation, plus increased responsibility, are claimed. The greater proportion of large American cities, the Canadian provinces, and several new governments of Europe have found the system superior. Several other states have, in popular referendum, failed by a very small margin to adopt the unicameral form. Nebraska's experience of over twenty years with a unicameral body is often cited as an argument that other states should follow her example and discard the second legislative chamber.

CRITICISMS OF STATE LEGISLATURES

Our present state legislatures are practically all of an unwieldy size, and there has been an increasing body of criticism directed at the basis and abuses of the system of representation.

Criticism of the Present System. The criticisms levelled at the present method of selecting state legislators are that the election of members by geographical districts (a) increases the number of "rotten boroughs," (b) denies representation by population, (c) deprives the minority in each district of representation, (d) intensifies rural-urban discrimination, and (e) provides opportunities for "gerrymandering."

The Supreme Court Acts. In 1962 the Court reversed a long history of holding legislative apportionment to be a "political question" outside court jurisdiction. In *Baker* v. *Carr* the Court held the issue to be justiciable, and in a series of 1964 decisions ordered the states to provide, in both houses of state legislatures, systems of legislative apportionment which would meet the new criterion of "one man, one vote"— that is, each legislator should be elected from a district as nearly equal in population as possible to every other district in the state for his house of the legislature. The result of this major new court policy is that almost every state legislature is now undergoing a basic change in its district system, under the close supervision of the federal courts. Urban-suburban electorates are gaining more representation; rural areas and small towns are losing seats.

LIMITATIONS ON LEGISLATURES

The state legislatures, unlike the national Congress, are not dependent upon an enumeration of powers in the Constitution, but are in theory entitled to exercise any and all legislative powers not prohibited by the national and state constitutions. The exercise of judicial review by state and federal courts has sharply limited the application of this theory, however. Because of this confusion it is perhaps most profitable to arrive at an idea of the extent of legislative power by a review of the limitations that are placed upon the powers of state legislatures.

Limitations on Financial Powers. The limitations in financial matters usually include the requirements that taxes must be for a public purpose and of a uniform rate; that appropriations must also be for a public purpose and in some cases must follow a prescribed procedure; and that the public debt of the state shall not exceed a fixed limit.

Limitations on Special Legislation. Most state constitutions limit special or local legislation by state legislatures by requiring one or more of the following: that no special law shall be passed if a general law is possible, that on certain specified subjects there shall be no special legislation, and/ or that an extraordinary majority of two-thirds shall be necessary for approval of special laws.

Limitations on Legislative Procedure. The most usual constitutional restrictions on legislative procedure prescribe the frequency and length of sessions, fix a quorum for business, require the printing and reading of all bills before passage, define the way in which money bills may originate, provide for yea and nay votes, and require that every legislative act embrace but a single subject.

Limitations Prescribed by Judicial Review. Perhaps the most considerable body of restrictions upon state legislatures has been developed by the state and federal courts through their frequent reversals of legislative acts as infringing upon the guarantees of "due process" in respect to "life, liberty, or property"—with greatest emphasis upon the latter.

Qualification, Terms, and Compensation. The usual constitutional prescriptions for membership in the state legislature relate to age, citizenship, and residence. The average minimum age requirement in the lower house is twenty-one, in the upper house twenty-five. All state legislators must be citizens of the United States. One year's residence in the district just prior to election is a usual requirement. Members of the lower house are usually elected for a term of two years. Senators are elected for a term of four years in the majority of the states; the salary for legislative service is extremely low. The turnover in legislative personnel is very high.

Legislative Sessions. The majority of the states have biennial sessions. Seventeen states, including New York, hold an annual session. In the majority of states, sessions are limited, most frequently, to sixty days, but the governor may call a special session. In several states the legislature itself may call a special session.

STATE LEGISLATIVE PROCEDURE

While state legislatures in general follow the procedure of the national Congress, it is to be emphasized that freedom of debate is much more limited and partisan rule much more pronounced in the legislatures.

Presiding Officer. The speaker of the lower house of a state legislature is even more powerful than the Speaker of the national House of Representatives. He has full power of recognition, of ruling on questions of procedure, and in all but two states the power to appoint the committees to which he refers bills. The presiding officer of the upper house does not always exercise the latter power. In general, then, it may be said that state legislatures are practically ruled by the presiding officers who are party leaders.

Committee System. State legislatures do much of their work through a system of committees similar to that used in

the national Congress; that is, they are partisan in composition and each is entrusted with almost complete power
over the bills which come within its province. The system is
criticized on the grounds that the committees are too
numerous and of unwieldy size, that they overlap and duplicate each other, that too little publicity attends their activities, and that they are too powerful and irresponsible. The
joint-committee system of Massachusetts, Maine, and Connecticut is often suggested as a solution. Through this system
delay and duplication are avoided, and it is also easier to
place responsibility.

Legislative Rules of Procedure.   In state legislatures rules
of procedure generally achieve the acme of futility. So
archaic, involved, and tedious are the rules that they serve
only to place the leadership groups more definitely in control and to so delay the passage of bills that most of the
legislative business must be accomplished near the end of a
session by a suspension of the rules—a practice which en-
courages ill-considered and hasty lawmaking.

Legislative Council.   One of the most promising proposals
for improvement in the work of the state legislature is the establishment of a legislative council in which certain members
of the legislature are entrusted with the task of formulating
major policies which are then to be presented to and defended before the legislature. Over two-thirds of the states
have adopted this plan since 1933.

Legislative Information.   Another promising development is the improvement in the extent and quality of legislative information furnished by the legislative reference
bureaus, which now gather material and give expert aid in
the drafting of laws. The efforts of these bureaus are also
being increasingly supplemented by reports of special commissions, by reports from special legislative inquiries, and
by information furnished by executive departments. The attempt to regulate the lobby, through registration of lobbyists
and financial accountancy is another step in the direction
of legislative improvement.

Model State Constitution Proposals. The Model State Constitution of the National Municipal League recommends that state legislatures should: (a) be unicameral, or, if this is not accepted, that each house be reduced in size, with more equitable apportionment, and with joint committees; (b) require committees to keep more complete records, release bills not reported on, issue agenda of committee meetings one week in advance; (c) establish a legislative council of seven to fifteen members, chosen by and from the legislature, which would be in continuous session and which would provide central leadership for the legislature; (d) be elected for two years and be a continuous body, meeting at least quarterly.

Direct Legislation. Nearly half of the fifty states make provision for initiative or referendum. The initiative is a device which enables a specified number of voters, by petition, to propose a law and secure its submission to the electorate for approval. The referendum permits the voters, by petition, to ask that a statute or ordinance enacted by a representative legislative body be submitted to the electorate for a final decision on whether or not it shall take effect.

Chapter 21

THE GOVERNOR AND STATE ADMINISTRATION

The office of governor in the American states has developed from an indirectly selected executive with few powers to an elected executive exercising an increasing range of powers.

Term of Office. The term of office of the governor ranges from two years in twenty states to four years in thirty states.

Qualifications, Re-eligibility, and Compensation. United States citizenship is required of all governors. The minimum age requirement is usually thirty years. The residence requirement is usually five years preceding election. About half of the states with a four-year term make the governor ineligible for a second consecutive term. Some of the states limit an incumbent to two or three consecutive terms. The annual salaries of governors range from $10,000 to $50,000. Some states also provide the governor with an official residence.

Removal from Office. With the exception of one state (Oregon) the governor may be removed from office by process of impeachment. Removals resulting from impeachment charges include Governor Sulzer of New York (1913) and Governors Walton and Johnston of Oklahoma (1923 and 1929). In twelve states the governor may be removed by popular recall. This is a device whereby a petition signed by a specified number of people secures a special election to determine whether a designated officer shall continue in office. Only one officer has been removed by popular recall— Governor Frazier of North Dakota in 1921.

Powers of the Governor

The powers of the governor may, like those of the President, be discussed under several divisions.

Legislative Powers. Although the state governments are organized along the traditional lines of the separation of powers, the governor has become a highly important source of legislative proposals. His position of leader of legislation arises from a number of associated powers: the delivery of regular and special messages to the legislature; the power to summon special sessions of the legislature; the power of veto over legislation, further strengthened in most states by the item veto; the concentration of budget control in the hands of the governor in certain states. The practice of passing skeletal bills has grown with the governor or other officers having power to fill in details. Through an energetic exercise of these powers the governor may become in reality the source of legislation.

Executive Powers. The governors of the states are not equipped with the powers of the chief executive in the degree to which the President is endowed. The power of appointment is greatly limited by the practice of electing heads of state administrative departments and the power of removal is limited by a number of constitutional and statutory requirements. The trend is toward strengthening the governor's authority to hold his subordinates responsible to him. In addition to the limited power of appointment and removal, the governor has the power to grant pardons, paroles, commutations, and reprieves; and he is the head of various boards and commissions. In general, he is the military as well as the civil head of the state.

Model State Constitution Proposals. The model state constitution prepared by the National Municipal League would greatly increase the powers of the governorship, making it more nearly like the presidency. It would empower the governor to appoint an administrative manager, limit the number of departments to not more than twenty, and empower the governor to appoint and remove all heads of departments. The governor, his administrative manager, and heads of departments would sit in the legislature as full members but without vote. The governor could order a referendum on any bill failing to pass the legislature. He would prepare and submit the budget and revenue and appropriation bills, and exercise an item veto or reduce items in appropriation bills.

STATE ADMINISTRATION

The administrative systems of the various states, extensive in their range, reflect the increasing necessity in an industrialized civilization for governmental agencies to regulate social and economic activities. They reveal also a process of growth which has failed to adapt itself to the principles of effective organization.

Units of State Administration. Most state administrative systems have certain offices in common: a lieutenant-governor, who presides over the senate and is legal successor to the governor; a secretary of state, who is keeper of state records and sometimes issues certificates of incorporation and supervises elections; a treasurer, who keeps and pays out the moneys accruing to the state; an auditor or comptroller, who audits all financial records; an attorney general, who is legal agent of the state government but seldom has the power to supervise locally elected prosecuting attorneys; a superintendent or commissioner of education, who supervises the educational system of the state. These officers are usually elected; they are generally independent of the governor, preventing centralization of responsibility. In addition to these agencies, there are in most states from ten to one hundred separate agencies: tax agencies, civil service commissions, public works agencies, charities and health offices, and a number of agencies dealing with agricultural and industrial questions—farm boards, insurance and banking commissions, public utilities boards, labor offices, agencies for supervision of corporations. Many of these agencies and boards have overlapping terms, often longer than the term of the governor. The selection and control of these agencies varies; it may rest with the governor or with the legislature or with both.

Financial Administration. The financial management of most states reveals a similar lack of centralized responsibility. Aside from certain constitutional limitations on debts, the states have found that the most satisfactory financial control is through budget systems which organize the revenues and expenditures of the state under the responsibility of the governor. Reorganization suggestions usually require that the tax base be shifted to the tax on income as the major source of revenue and that the budget be more thoroughly organized with the responsibility resting clearly with the governor.

Personnel Administration. When local governments are included, the states employ more than half of the civil servants in the United States. About half the states have adopted a merit system for the selection of employees. Approximately one-half of the employees, those in the public education system, are chosen by a professional licensing system.

ADMINISTRATIVE REORGANIZATION

The preceding description of state administration is sufficient to establish its generally unsatisfactory character. Several states have undertaken a series of steps to reorganize their systems on a satisfactory basis.

General Defects of State Administration. The major defects of state administration may be summarized as: (a) decentralization in selection, appointment, and removal of state officers of administration; (b) duplication of agencies in a widely scattered system; (c) lack of co-ordination between the separate agencies; (d) consequent waste and inefficiency.

Proposed Reorganization. The basic principles of reorganization in state administration are that the agencies, commissions, and departments be consolidated into a few major departments over which department heads, appointed and removed by the governor, shall have full supervisory powers. The governor is thus invested with the full responsibility essential to efficient administration.

Since Illinois adopted a plan of reorganization in 1917, reorganization plans of one kind or another have been adopted in more than thirty states. New York state has reduced the number of elective state officers to four: the governor, comptroller, lieutenant-governor, and the attorney general. The governmental activities of New York state are vested in nineteen departments. Prior to 1927, the work of administering the affairs of the state was spread among 187 branches of the government.

New Jersey (as a result of constitutional revision in 1947), Alaska, and Hawaii now represent the most integrated state administrative systems.

Chapter 22

THE STATE JUDICIAL SYSTEMS

The state courts have a wider range of jurisdiction than the federal courts and consequently carry a greater share of the administration of justice. Just as Congress has only delegated powers of legislation, the federal courts have only that jurisdiction conferred upon them by the Constitution; and just as legislative power not delegated to the federal government is reserved to the states, all judicial power not delegated to the federal courts remains with the state courts.

Functions of State Courts. The state courts not only determine the guilt or innocence of persons accused of the violation of state laws, but also serve as guardians of constitutional rights, adjust civil disputes, settle matters of property transfers, and appoint receivers to temporarily manage property in dispute. They may also exercise the power of judicial review, and in some states give advisory opinions.

Hierarchy of State Courts

The organization of state courts resembles the familiar pyramid plan of the federal system: that is, lower courts of limited jurisdiction, courts of general jurisdiction, and a high court of appellate jurisdiction. Some states have intermediate appellate and special courts as well.

Justices of Peace. At the base of the state judicial systems are the courts presided over by justices of the peace. These courts exercise a limited jurisdiction and are customarily restricted to trial of petty crimes and civil cases involving a small amount of property. The justice may hold preliminary hearings in cases involving more serious crimes. They also act in an administrative capacity in solemnizing marriages and attesting various legal documents. The justice of the peace is usually paid by the fees he collects. In certain cities, municipal courts and police courts, with similar jurisdiction, have replaced the justice courts.

General Trial Courts. Next in rank above justices of peace courts are the intermediate trial courts variously called the courts of common pleas, the county courts, the district courts, the circuit courts, the superior courts, or the supreme courts. They have original and appellate jurisdiction in both civil and criminal cases, because cases are appealed from the justices' courts. Their jurisdiction is general and extensive.

Appellate Courts. Every state has a high court of appeals, usually called the supreme court of the state, which exercises appellate jurisdiction over cases appealed from the lower courts. About one-third of the most populous states have established intermediate appellate courts which hear appeals in particular types of cases and thus reduce the burden of work upon the highest court.

State Judicial Administration

The major aspects of state judicial organization include the selection, tenure, and removal of judges; the jury system; the prosecuting staff for criminal cases; and the trial procedure.

Selection, Tenure, and Removal of Judges. The judges of state courts are selected by three methods: by popular election, which is the most widely used method; by the legislature; by the governor, with the approval of the upper legislative chamber. None of these methods has been completely satisfactory, but the latter has produced the best results. The tenure of judges in state courts ranges from four years to life, with an increasing tendency to lengthen the terms. State judges are removed by impeachment, by the governor upon an address of the legislature, by concurrent resolution of the legislature, by the recall, and of course, by failure to be re-appointed or re-elected.

Jury System.   The tradition of trial by jury is one of the strongest of our judicial system. All state constitutions guarantee trial by jury in criminal cases and all but two (Utah and Louisiana) extend the privilege to civil cases. The system consists of two parts, the grand jury and the petit jury. The grand jury performs only a preliminary function: that of beginning criminal proceedings with an indictment. The grand jury consists of from seven to twenty-three members, and the concurrence of from five to twelve members is required for an indictment. It proceeds upon its own initiative, or upon suggestions of the prosecutor or the court. The grand jury returns an indictment drawn up by the prosecutor and makes a presentment if it acts on its own motion. The petit, or trial, jury consists of from six to twelve members; unanimous concurrence is required in capital cases in all states and in felony cases in all but Louisiana. In misdemeanors and civil cases certain states allow a verdict by two-thirds or three-fourths votes.

Public Prosecutor.   In criminal cases, an essential part in the administration of justice is played by the public prosecutor. He is an elective officer whose jurisdiction extends over one county. State supervision by the attorney general is casual and ineffective. This leads to a decentralized and uneven system of law enforcement.

Judicial Procedure.   State courts perform their work under a set of procedural rules laid down in large part by legislative acts and supplemented by rules of the courts themselves. These rules regulate in great detail such things as the admission of evidence, the selecting and instructing of jurors, the handling of witnesses, and the status of motions by the attorneys. The state courts operate under three elaborate procedures. They are called civil, criminal, and equity. Generally, it is upon an actual or alleged violation of the rules of these procedures that most appeals are based.

JUDICIAL REORGANIZATION

The complex structure of the state judicial system, with its slow and cumbersome operation, has been the object of persistent criticism and over a period of years there has been developed a definite plan for reorganization which, it is claimed, will give the administration of justice efficiency and dispatch.

Judicial Reorganization. The first item in reorganization of state courts is the creation of a Judicial Council which will have full administrative authority over a consolidated court system; its powers are to include central direction of the unified courts, the supervision and transfer of judges, the relief of crowded calendars, and, in the most thorough plans, the power to appoint all subordinate judges. It is sometimes argued, however, that the governor should exercise the appointing power.

The second item of reorganization is that trial by jury should be made optional and the jury system itself improved by better methods of selection.

The third item is that the present complicated procedure be replaced by rules drafted and periodically modified by the Judicial Council rather than by the legislature.

Since the first edition of the Model State Constitution recommended, in 1921, the creation of state judicial councils, more than three-fourths of the states have adopted them in some form. Most of these councils possess only investigatory and advisory powers. A few actually adopt rules and transfer judges from court to court to ease the clearing of the docket. The need for improvement in judicial administration has been recognized and is beginning to gain acceptance along with the principles of the unified court plan. New Jersey, California, and Missouri have provided for a considerable degree of unification in their judicial systems, as do the new constitutions of Alaska and Hawaii.

Chapter 23

COUNTY AND LOCAL GOVERNMENT

There are approximately 102,000 units of local government in the United States. Of these units more than 3,000 are counties and 16,000 are incorporated places. The towns and townships number 20,000, and school and other districts total close to 60,000. The county is the most prevalent unit in the sense that all the area of the United States is included within some county and that it exists in all states (though called a parish in Louisiana). It serves both as an administrative division of state government and as a means of local self-government.

Characteristics of the County. The number of counties in each state ranges from three in Delaware to 254 in Texas, the average being from sixty to one hundred. The areas average about one thousand square miles, and the population from about ten to thirty thousand. The county has the power to acquire, hold and dispose of property, and to sue and be sued in the courts of the state.

COUNTY FUNCTIONS

The county, in its dual capacity, performs two classes of governmental functions.

Functions as State Administrative Unit. As part of the government of the state, the county through its agents, enforces and administers the state laws, collects taxes, conducts criminal prosecutions, supervises elections, and performs a multitude of specific functions assigned to it by state law.

Functions as Unit of Local Government. No less important are the numerous functions performed by the county in its own right as a local government. These include the administration of the educational system, the health and welfare activities, highway construction, highway maintenance, local elections, and many additional functions.

COUNTY ORGANIZATION

The organization of county government varies from state to state, but certain features are typical.

Board of Supervisors. The county board of supervisors, sometimes called the county court, is the chief governing agency. It is an elective body, usually large in size, and its powers ordinarily include the levying of taxes for county and sometimes for township purposes, the issuance of bonds, the equalization of assessments, and the supervision of expenditures; it is also custodian of county property, has power to build highways, to provide for and control local elections, and to appoint and remove certain county officers.

County Officials. The other county officials usually include the sheriff, the public prosecutor, the county clerk, the auditor, the superintendent of schools, the coroner, the assessor, the county treasurer, and the recorder of deeds. They are usually elective and are, therefore, independent of the board of supervisors. The sheriff is the officer of the courts of record in the county, keeper of the county jail, and conservator of the peace. The coroner holds inquests to determine the cause of deaths caused by violence or under suspicious circumstances. The county clerk serves as secretary to the county board. In some states he is charged with the issuance of licenses and permits. The auditor examines claims against the county, and the assessor is concerned with assessing property for the purposes of the property tax.

COUNTY REORGANIZATION

No other unit of our government has been more subject to criticism than our county governments, and there is already under way a recognized program for reorganization and reconstruction.

Defects of County Government. The voluminous criticism of county government may be summarized under these points: (a) as a form of government, it is loosely organized, without a responsible head, and its offices are without a clear definition of functions; (b) as a unit of the state administration, its offices lack co-ordination with centralized bureaus and their activities are inadequately organized; (c) as a unit of local government, it has become unnecessary in urban areas where city governments perform all necessary functions, and it covers too small an area in nonurban sections.

Reorganization of County Government. The reorganization of county government proceeds along the three major lines of criticism. First, it proposes for county government a small elective council clothed with full legislative power, including the power to select, supervise, and remove a county manager who would in turn have the power to select, supervise, and remove county administrative officials. An alternate plan provides for an elected county executive rather than an appointed manager. Employees would be under the merit system. Second, it proposes the consolidation of all activities, which are not essentially local, under state rather than county government. Third, it proposes that counties be abolished in all urbanized areas, their functions being assumed by the city governments, and that in nonurban areas several counties be consolidated into one economical governing unit.

County Home Rule. The most significant advance in the reorganization of county government has been the adoption of the home rule principle for counties in seven states. In New York, under a constitutional amendment granting home rule to counties, the legislature adopted an enabling act in 1936, and the people in 1937 adopted as part of the new state constitution even more extensive provisions for home rule in the reorganization and simplification of county government. Several populous suburban counties have been reorganized under this plan. Improved management has been achieved in the Los Angeles and St. Louis areas under the principle of county home rule. The most recent step forward in the movement has been the adoption of a constitutional amendment in Florida in 1957, which permitted home rule for Dade County and which subsequently established a modernized metropolitan county government.

Municipalities or Incorporated Places.   In most states a community with a specified minimum population, within a given area, is permitted by general statute to organize as a municipal corporation. The procedure followed by such a community seeking incorporation involves a petition followed by a referendum vote of the residents. In every state the larger municipalities are legally known as "cities," the "lesser" municipalities are designated as "villages" or "towns" and differ from cities in that theirs is a simple governmental structure with considerably less extensive powers than cities exercise.

Towns and Townships.   In the New England states the town is the chief unit of local government. Most villages are under the jurisdiction of the town government. Towns vary in population from less than 500 to over 25,000 residents, and in geographic size from twenty to forty square miles. In the northeastern and north central regions of the country the township is a unit set up for governmental purposes. It is subordinate to the county in its functions, which are primarily rural in nature.

County Districts.   In the South and West the counties are divided into units known differently as civil districts, precincts, and magisterial districts. These administrative units are subordinate to the county and their authority is limited.

Special Districts.   These units of local government are established for the performance of a single governmental function. They include such familiar types as school districts, sanitary districts, fire protection districts, and water supply districts. Most special districts have, within constitutional limits, some form of financing power.

Consolidation of Local Units

There has long been a well-organized movement for the consolidation or abolition of many local government units and the unification of their poorly organized functions into larger units and under more effective administrative·control. Some of the measures proposed, and to some extent adopted, with a view to correction include: geographic consolidation, county consolidation, school consolidation, city-county consolidation, township coalition, reorganization, transfer of functions, and functional consolidation.

Chapter 24

MUNICIPAL GOVERNMENT
AND ADMINISTRATION

The city is in many ways the special problem of our complex, industrialized society. In its governmental aspects, it is a special form of local government developed to meet the complex problems of urban centers. In law, the city is a municipal corporation possessing corporate and governmental powers: to acquire, hold, dispose of property, enact ordinances, raise money by taxation, exercise right of eminent domain, sue and be sued. The powers granted to a city are strictly construed and the city is liable for torts in connection with its business enterprises but not in connection with its governmental functions, unless expressly made so by statute.

CITY CHARTERS

Cities are governed under charters granted by the state legislatures. These charters are of several types and may grant power in general terms or in minute detail.

Charter Systems. The five charter systems in use in the states are: (a) the special charter system, through which every city is given a special charter by the legislature; (b) the general charter system, under which all cities have identical charters; (c) the classified charter system, under which cities are classified in population groups, and cities in the same group are given a standard charter; (d) the optional charter system, by which several standard charters are provided by state law and the cities in popular referendum select their choice among these; (e) and the home rule charter.

Home Rule for Cities.   In twenty-six states, the cities are allowed to exercise considerable freedom in choosing their form of government under legislative or constitutional provisions for "home rule." More than 200 cities operate under this system. The "home rule" charter is usually adopted in a popular referendum. Its provisions as to form of government are usually not subject to review but none of its provisions may be in contradiction to the general laws of the state.

State Administration Control.   The failure of "home rule" as a panacea, as well as the modern tendency toward centralization, has led to increasing state administrative control over cities. The control is variously exercised: (a) through advice and information; (b) through supervision over subsidies; (c) through direct administrative participation; (d) through legal coercion.

Forms of City Government

Whatever the charter system, the form of city government will be one of the following, or a variant of one of them.

Mayor-Council Type.   The oldest form of city government is the mayor-council type, and it is still used in the majority of American cities. The general features are: (a) a mayor, elected for a term of from one to five years, and endowed with the usual executive powers of enforcing laws and ordinances, of appointments and removals, and in some cities the power to draw up the budget; (b) a city council, sometimes bicameral, the members frequently elected from small single-member districts, exercising the legislative power of passing ordinances for governing the city and frequently approving or disapproving the mayoral appointments. An extensive administrative organization is common to all forms of city government.

Commission Plan.   The first reorganization in city government was the transfer from the mayor-council form to the commission plan. The commission, usually consisting of five members, replaced the mayor and the council, thus concen-

A MODERN CITY GOVERNMENT

The Organization of the Government of the City of Cincinnati

THE COUNCIL

Nine members, elected at large by proportional representation

MAYOR

VICE-MAYOR

CITY MANAGER

City Auditor

Board of Health

Sinking Fund Trustees

Board of Park Commissioners

Board of Directors University of Cincinnati

Department of Law

Department of Safety
- Police
- Fire
- Welfare
- Buildings

Department of Public Utilities

Department of Public Works

City Treasurer

Superintendent of Water Works

Superintendent of Hospitals

Purchasing Agent

Personnel Officer Secretary to Civil Service Commission

SPECIAL COMMISSIONS

Civil Service Commission
3 Members: 1 Appointed by Mayor; 1 by Board of Directors; University of Cincinnati; 1 by Board of Education

City Planning Commission
7 Members: City Manager, a Member of Council, 5 Appointed by Mayor

Public Recreation Commission
5 Members: a Member of the Board of Park Commissioners, a Member of the Board of Education, 3 Appointed by Mayor

The Mayor and Vice-Mayor are chosen by the Council from its own membership; the City Manager may not be chosen from the Council. The Mayor's appointments are made "with the advice and consent of the Council"; the City Manager's appointments are not subject to Council approval, but his appointment of the Superintendent of Hospitals is subject to the approval of the Board of Directors of the University of Cincinnati.

trating the legislative and executive authority in one body. Each commissioner was in charge of one or more administrative departments. Although this plan represented an advance over the mayor-council form, it was soon replaced as a model reform by a third plan.

Council-Manager Plan. To remedy the major defect of the commission plan—the absence of administrative centralization—the council-manager plan was devised. Its chief feature is the selection by the council of a city manager—an expert in administration—who is given full power of appointment and supervision over the city's administrative system. The manager is directly and fully responsible to the council. This plan has had considerable success, but experience early suggested the advisability of a still further modification.

Proportional Representation—City Manager Plan. This form claimed the primary advantage of providing a more representative council than any other plan. It established a small commission or council elected at large or by plural-member districts by proportional representation, hence, its name. The provision for proportional representation was designed to break the power of the political machine by destroying its monopoly of the council, for under the proportional representation provision there is at least a strong opposition group within the council. In all other respects it is similar to the council-manager plan.

Strong Mayor-General Manager Plan. The resistance of the large cities to the city manager plan has led in recent years to a new formula. The mayor is strengthened as the city's chief executive by granting him greater powers of budget preparation and administration, of personnel management, and of managerial supervision over city agencies; but, even more importantly, a general manager, appointed and removable by the mayor, is provided. Boston, New York City, Newark, Philadelphia, New Orleans, Los Angeles, and San Francisco are among the large cities using this plan.

Municipal Administration

Municipal administration represents in many ways the most intense application of governmental activities. The range of municipal functions is extensive. Since these are primarily "line" functions, the administrative machine is a complex one.

Staff Functions. The municipal functions of budgeting, personnel administration, financial administration (including purchasing and accounting), and planning, plus record-keeping and legal work, are classified as staff functions and are usually centrally organized because they serve the other agencies of the government rather than the public directly.

Line Functions. The municipal functions serving the people directly are line functions: police, fire protection, inspection, education, recreation, health, welfare corrections, public works, sanitation, transportation, housing, public utilities. These require elaborate field and headquarters organizations and demand a constant vigilance from the mayor or city manager if they are not to become semi-autonomous units, pursuing their own goals by methods convenient to themselves, and thus a threat to co-ordination, efficiency, and integrity.

Chapter 25

THE NATURE OF LAW AND ITS ENFORCEMENT

The state prescribes and enforces a body of rules governing human conduct. These generally agreed upon rules are the law. The sources of American law include the United States Constitution, United States statutes, federal rules and regulations; state constitutions, statutes, rules and regulations; local government ordinances, rules and regulations; and the common law.

CLASSIFICATION OF LAW

The classes into which law has been divided include many more than the traditional written-unwritten categorization.

Common Law and Equity. Common law refers to the body of rules evolved through custom and practice in the solution of controversies which gained acceptance throughout the king's realm. This common law of England is an American heritage. Equity also developed in England. This branch of law is resorted to primarily in those cases where ordinary law fails to provide a remedy. For example, law permits a government agent to destroy property, and later damages for the action may be recovered in court; equity on the other hand, by resort to its writ of injunction, may prevent the destruction.

International and Municipal. The law which governs a state in its relations with other countries is known as international law. Municipal law is the body of laws governing the internal affairs of a state: constitutions, statutes, charters.

Substantive and Procedural. Rights and duties are created and defined by substantive law. Procedural law relates to the means for the enforcement of rights and duties.

Public Law and Private Law. Public law treats the relationship between the government and the citizen. It is divided into four major fields: administrative law, international law, constitutional law, and criminal law. Private law regulates to the relations of citizen to citizen. The four classes of private law are: persons, property, contract, and torts.

Martial Law and Military Law. In times of disorder the limits of the executive's control over citizens in domestic territory are defined by martial law. Military law is applied to troops in war and peace.

Civil Law and Criminal Law. Civil law is concerned with such matters as property rights, contracts, torts, and domestic relations. In most instances the government is not a party to civil cases. Criminal law defines crimes and penalizes their commission. Crimes are usually classified as misdemeanors (minor crimes) and felonies (more serious crimes). All criminal actions are instituted in the name of the state or the people, against the perpetrator of the alleged infraction.

LAW ENFORCEMENT

In the field of civil law, the government provides rules to govern individuals in their relations with each other, and judicial tribunals in which controversies may be adjudicated.

Law enforcement is primarily concerned with the field of criminal law. In criminal law, the government assumes the extra responsibility of preventing violations of the law and punishing violators. American criminal law is to a large extent state law. Its enforcement is essentially a state function, a function which the various units of local government usually perform.

FEDERAL LAW ENFORCEMENT

At the present time there is a growing body of federal criminal law enforced by federal officers through federal courts. A partial list of federal offenses include: kidnaping, counterfeiting and forgery, espionage, Internal Revenue violations, narcotic violations, selective service violations, white slave traffic violations, and Food and Drug Act violations.

Federal Police. There is no unified United States police force operating throughout the nation. The detection of many of the violations previously mentioned is left to the administrative agencies. Some of the investigatory units of these agencies include the Secret Service Division, the Intelligence unit of the Bureau of Internal Revenue, the Bureau of Customs, the legal investigating division of many of the agencies exercising quasi-judicial functions and the Antitrust Division and Federal Bureau of Investigation of the Justice Department. The FBI investigates all violations of federal laws except those definitely assigned to other agencies. Although the many services and facilities of the FBI are available to state and local enforcement officials, this federal bureau seldom initiates the action or participates in local cases, unless federal laws, agents, or properties are implicated.

Department of Justice. The Department of Justice has general supervision over all federal prosecutions. The major share of the responsibility of proving guilt in the federal courts falls upon the United States District Attorneys and their assistants. U. S. District Attorneys are appointed by the President with the Senate's approval for terms of four years. There is an attorney in each judicial district.

The President also appoints, with Senate approval, United States marshals. In actuality, these marshals are federal sheriffs. They arrest violators, take care of prisoners, and carry out court orders. Violators of federal laws are kept in federal penal institutions or in approved state, county, and city jails.

STATE LAW ENFORCEMENT

The function of law enforcement in the state and local governments is handled by the various officers and agencies charged with preserving the peace, arresting violators of the law, and prosecuting these violators in the courts.

State Enforcement Agencies. The governor, the attorney general, the National Guard, and the state police are the agencies provided for criminal law enforcement at the state level. Unlike the President—who appoints the U. S. Attorney General, federal district attorneys, and U. S. marshals and can remove them—the state governor attempts to execute the laws with an elected attorney general, elected district attorneys, and very often elected sheriffs.

The majority of the states have state police systems with general jurisdiction to enforce all state laws. All of the states have some form of state police agency. For the most part, the state police force enforces the law outside the cities. In most states, as a matter of practice, local request precedes action by state authorities. A common restriction on the powers of state police is the denial of their use in connection with labor disputes.

Local Law Enforcement Agencies

To a considerable degree, basic responsibility for law enforcement is delegated by the state to the local units of government. The local officers concerned are many and varied. They include the sheriff, the prosecuting attorney, the local police, the constable, the coroner, and the grand jury.

Chapter 26

NATIONAL DEFENSE

During the years following the Second World War, federal expenditures for national defense have accounted for one-half or more of the national budget. American attempts to prepare and maintain an adequate military establishment have resulted in an increasing portion of the tax dollar being committed to defense efforts.

Congress and Defense. The federal Constitution vests Congress with considerable authority in the field of defense. Congress has the power to raise and support armies; to provide and maintain a navy; to declare war; to levy taxes and appropriate money for the common defense; to prescribe rules for the governmental regulation of our land and forces; to provide for calling up the state militia; and to make the laws necessary to effectuate these powers.

Declaration of War. Congress alone has the constitutional power to declare war. In practice, the President is in the most crucial position in the events which may lead to war. Congress has declared war only when called upon to do so by the chief executive. Some wars are determined by enemy attack, as for instance our entrance into the Second World War. President Harry S. Truman authorized the use of the United States troops in the United Nations Korean "police action" of 1950 without prior Congressional approval.

President and Defense. The power of the President in the field of national defense is derived from three sources of authority. He is commander-in-chief of the armed forces; he is the chief executive; and he is the recipient of a considerable delegation of legislative authority. As commander-in-chief the President appoints, with senatorial consent, all officers of the armed forces. During wartime and "cold war" periods, decisions on over-all strategy require presidential action.

Defense and Delegation of Powers. The First and Second World Wars required a full scale mobilization of American energy and materials. In both cases, Congress delegated considerable power to the President to bring about the shift from a peace to a war footing. In World War II, Congress limited the delegation either to the duration of the war or for a specified period. In the process of delegating wide discretionary powers to the chief executive Congress either creates the administrative machinery for exercising them or delegates the authority and lets the President determine the administrative mechanism to be used. Under either system the President administers the program put into effect.

NATIONAL DEFENSE ESTABLISHMENT

The lessons of World War I and World War II made it obvious that national defense depends upon the co-ordination of the military, the industrial, and the manpower efforts of the country. It is further apparent that such co-ordination is essential in peace time as well as during a war. In 1947 and 1949, Congress passed two national security acts for the purpose of providing a comprehensive program for the future security of the United States. The acts provided for the following administrative structure.

National Security Council. The function of the National Security Council is to "advise the President with respect to the integration of domestic, foreign, and military policies relating to the national security so as to enable the military services and the other departments and agencies of the government to co-operate more effectively in matters involving the national security." The National Security Council is located in the Executive Office of the President. The council is composed of the President, Vice-President, Secretary of Defense, Secretary of State, the director of International Cooperation Administration, and the director of the Office of Emergency Planning.

Central Intelligence Agency. The Central Intelligence Agency was established under the National Security Council for the purpose of co-ordinating the intelligence activities of the many government units in the interest of national security. It "correlates and evaluates intelligence relating to the national security, and provides for the appropriate dissemination of such intelligence within the government using, where appropriate, existing agencies and facilities."

Department of Defense. The National Security Act provided for the establishment of the Department of Defense as an executive department. It includes the Department of the Army, the Department of the Navy, the Department of the Air Force, the Armed Forces Policy Council, and the Joint Chiefs of Staff. While the Secretary of Defense has cabinet status, the Army, Navy, and Air Force Departments have "military" status. The Secretary of Defense establishes general policies and programs for the Department of Defense, directs the departments and agencies, eliminates duplication in fields of procurement, research, health, and transportation, and formulates and supervises the budget programs of the departments. Those powers not explicitly given to the Secretary of Defense are kept by the respective military departments.

In 1961, the Department of Defense took over many of the civil defense responsibilities formerly administered by the Office of Civil and Defense Mobilization, the successor to the Office of Defense Mobilization and the Federal Civil Defense Administration. Under the new plan, the Pentagon will be responsible for the fall-out shelter program, the present OCDM warning and communications system, and other civil defense plans and programs on a state and local level.

Department of Army. The responsibilities of the Department of the Army include providing support for the national and the international policy and security of the United States by planning, directing, and reviewing the military and civil operations of the army establishment. "The organization, training, and equipping of land forces of the United States for the conduct of prompt and sustained combat operations on land in accordance with plans for national security," are included in the operations of the army establishment. It supervises, and in time of war absorbs, the national guard.

Department of the Navy. As is true of the army and air force departments, the Secretary of the Navy is a civilian. The basic policy of this department is to maintain the navy and marine corps, as part of the Department of Defense, in sufficient strength and readiness to fulfill its responsibilities under the security laws. During wartime the Coast Guard is usually transferred from Treasury Department to Navy Department.

Department of Air Force. The air force "has primary responsibility for defending the United States against air attack; for gaining and maintaining general air supremacy; for defeating enemy air forces; for formulating joint doctrines and procedures, in co-ordination with the other services, for the defense of the United States against air attack; for providing the necessary units, equipment, and facilities for strategic air warfare; for providing air force units for joint amphibious and airborne operations; and for furnishing close combat and logistic air support for the army."

Armed Forces Policy Council. Serving as a "staff arm" to advise the Secretary of Defense on questions of policy in relation to the armed forces, is the Armed Forces Policy Council (within the Department of Defense). Membership on the Armed Forces Policy Council includes the Secretary of Defense, the Deputy Secretary of Defense, the secretaries of the three military departments—Army, Navy, and Air Force—plus the chiefs of staff of these three military departments, and the Chairman of the Joint Chiefs.

Joint Chiefs of Staff. The members of the Joint Chiefs of Staff are the top military advisers to the President and the Secretary of Defense. The Chief of Staff of the U. S. Army, the Chief of Staff of the U. S. Air Force, the Chief of Naval Operations, and the Chairman of the Joint Chiefs of Staff comprise the membership. All four are appointed by the President with the advice and consent of the Senate.

Chapter 27

GOVERNMENT AND BUSINESS

The twentieth century, particularly in contrast to the eighteenth and nineteenth centuries, has seen the rapid extension of government control over the economic order. The complex plan of the industrial world has led to governmental action both to regulate and to promote business and other economic activities. National, state, and local levels of government are involved in the regulation and promotion of business.

NATIONAL GOVERNMENT

The control exercised by the national government over business is derived, to a large extent, from its authority to regulate commerce. More than any other constitutional phrase, the phrase "commerce with foreign nations and among the several states" has needed to keep pace with changing aspects of our national life. All forms of traffic and intercourse crossing state and national boundaries may now be said to be under the jurisdiction of Congress. Commerce includes transportation of commodities, navigation, toll bridges, ferries across interstate rivers, traffic of all kinds, including the transmission of telephone, telegraph, and radio messages, the writing of insurance policies, and many others.

Foreign Commerce. In the regulation of commerce with foreign nations, Congress has adopted protective tariffs, levied tonnage duties, declared embargoes, enacted navigation and inspection laws, attempted to establish a merchant marine by financial and administrative aid, and regulated the flow of immigrants into the United States.

The Protective Tariff.   One of the major historic policies of the national government in the promotion of business has been the protective tariff. Inaugurated under the leadership of Alexander Hamilton, the protective tariff was, until the Civil War, successfully opposed by the nation's great surplus crop, cotton, but with the triumph of northern industrialism the protective tariff wall had become a fixed policy of the national government. Not even the postwar position of the United States as a creditor nation has served to reduce in any marked degree the tariff barriers. It is true that under the New Deal the Democratic party, as the historic opponent of high tariffs, has inaugurated a program of reciprocity agreements, but these agreements have served merely to adjust certain sections of the tariff to a lower level while the protective policy prevails. Thus, tariff barriers still exist in the contemporary interdependent world.

Promotion of Foreign Trade.   The national government has also been consistent in its policy of promotion of foreign trade opportunities for domestic surpluses. It maintains a world-wide chain of consular offices whose functions are to promote and aid the conduct of foreign trade. Congressional action in passing the Webb-Pomerene Export Act of 1918, creating the Export-Import Bank in 1934, and support for the Marshall Plan program has been an important factor in American foreign trade. The administration of the federal subsidy programs to encourage the development and maintenance of an American merchant marine has been transferred from the United States Maritime Commission to a federal Maritime Board of three members in the Department of Commerce.

Interstate Commerce.   Under its power to regulate commerce "among the several states," Congress has not only enacted a great body of river and harbor legislation providing for extensive internal improvements, but it has also extended its power to the regulation of railroads and other agencies of transportation as well as to the control of many of the corporations which are actively engaged in interstate business.

Stimulation and Regulation of Domestic Competition. At home, the national government has also had a long and extensive interest in the promotion and control of business activity. From the very beginning of the national government, patents, trademarks, and coyprights have been protected by federal law, and with the beginning of the industrial era, the promotion of controlled business activities became one of the primary concerns of the national government. The Sherman Anti-Trust Act of 1890 marked the determination of the national government to preserve domestic competition.

The establishment of the Department of Commerce in 1903 indicated the growth of an even wider interest, followed by the establishment of the Federal Trade Commission to control unfair business practices. Still more recently the program of the National Industrial Recovery Act and the Security and Exchange Act illustrate the entrance of the government into the regulation of detailed traditional business practices.

Transportation and Communication. In this field the national and state governments have engaged in the most extensive promotion and regulation, with promotion receiving the greater emphasis and regulation developing largely as a by-product. The building of national roads, of an extensive canal system, and the great program of promotion for a continental railway system are examples of the participation by the government in the development of a transportation network. The public domain and extensive public funds were used in building up a privately managed railway system. In the automobile era, all levels of government have gone extensively into the building of improved highways, until the expenditure for this purpose is second only to the expenditure for public education. The aviation industry is an even more recent beneficiary.

Increasing regulatory activity has accompanied the expansive promotion of transportation and communication. State regulation of railways, for example, has been followed by extensive federal regulation through the Interstate Commerce Commission. This federal regulation is now extended to the users of public highways and commercial airspace.

The merchant marine and the more recent development of aviation have also been objects of promotional and regulatory activities on the part of the government. Although government subsidies have not been prominent in this field, the federal government has increasingly exercised control over the business activities of the telegraph, telephone, radio, and more recently, television.

Interstate Commerce Commission. By the Act of 1887 Congress set up the Interstate Commerce Commission, the powers of which it has since steadily increased. It now has jurisdiction over interstate railroads, express and sleeping car companies, pipe lines (except for gas and water), motor carriers, water carriers, freight forwarders, and cable, telegraph, telephone, and wireless systems. Its powers include the fixing of rates for interstate carriers, the evaluation of the railroads, the enforcement of regulations, the formulation of a plan for railroad consolidation, and the consideration and review of consolidations, mergers, and acquisition of control of these carriers.

Federal Trade Commission. By a series of acts beginning with the Sherman Anti-Trust Act of 1890, the Congress has attempted to regulate or prevent combinations in restraint of trade. In 1915, the Federal Trade Commission was set up to prevent unfair methods of competition, to investigate corporations engaged in interstate activities, to report violations of antitrust laws, and to advise corporations in the ways of adjusting their practices to the law.

Securities and Exchange Commission. By the Securities Exchange Act of 1934, the Congress created the Securities and Exchange Commission and conferred upon it the power to supervise transactions in securities having interstate aspects or interstate complications. The commission is authorized to deny, suspend, or withdraw the registration of securities or exchanges which conflict with the rules and requirements, which it has seen necessary to set up.

Federal Communications Commission. By an act of 1934, the Congress also established a Federal Communications Commission with power to regulate foreign and interstate communication by wire or radio. Telephone, telegraph, and radio communications were thus brought into the field of regulation such as was applied to transportation for many years preceding.

Federal Power Commission. The Federal Power Commission was created by the Federal Water Power Act of 1920 and empowered by the Public Utility Act of 1935 to supervise water power projects on navigable streams, or affecting the interests of interstate commerce, or upon public lands, and to supervise the interstate movement of electric energy. When these powers are coupled with the controls of the Securities and Exchange Commission over the financial activities of electric utilities, the federal government is able to exercise thoroughgoing supervision over the production and sale of electrical power.

National Labor Relations Board. Created by the Wagner Act of 1935 and continued under the Taft-Hartley Act of 1947 and the Labor-Management Act of 1959, the National Labor Relations Board is empowered to ascertain who are employees' representatives for collective bargaining and to review complaints of violations of employees' rights under the law. Employees' rights include the right to organize and to bargain collectively. Employers are prohibited from engaging in "unfair labor practices" which are defined as interfering with or coercing employees in collective bargaining, maintaining company unions, discriminating against labor organizations in employment, discharging an employee for filing a complaint under the act, and refusing to bargain collectively with the representatives of employees. A labor union or its agent is prohibited from coercing an employer in the choice of his bargaining representative, refusing to bargain collectively with an employer, and using the strike to force any employer to recognize or bargain with a labor organization when another has been certified by the board as the representative of his employees.

Federal Aviation Agency. The Federal Aviation Act of 1958 created the Federal Aviation Agency as a successor to the Civil Aeronautics Administration and the Airways Modernization Board, and transferred to it the safety regulation authority of the Civil Aeronautics Board. The FAA is thus the central unit of the national government for air safety; it establishes and operates air navigation facilities and manages both civilian and military air traffic use of air space in the United States. It also gives assistance to the development of civil aviation in other countries.

FEDERAL ENTERPRISES

The United States government owns or is financially interested in about one hundred major business enterprises, representing a federal investment of over $20 billion. Some of these activities are among the following.

Postal Service. "Congress shall have power. . . . to establish post offices and post roads." This is the legal basis for the earliest and now the largest government business enterprise. This government monopoly operates through 39,000 post offices, employs several hundred thousand regular and temporary employees, and takes in well over two billion dollars a year in receipts.

Panama Canal. The federal government owns all the land in the Panama Canal Zone. The business enterprises there are the property of the Panama Canal and the Panama Canal Company. The supervision of the Panama Canal organization is located in the Secretary of the Army. Along with operating the canal, the Panama Canal unit runs a number of business enterprises including the water supply system, the electric system, the hospital, and the rental of land. The Panama Canal Company is an independent corporation. As an agency and instrumentality of the United States, and as an adjunct of the Panama Canal, the company conducts business operations incident to the care, maintenance, sanitation, operation, improvement, government, and protection of the Panama Canal and the Canal Zone.

Tennessee Valley Authority. The TVA is set up as a government corporation outside the executive departments. The major purpose of TVA is to foster "the orderly and proper physical, economic, and social development" of the area. It produces nitrate and phosphate products for use as fertilizers in peacetime and munitions in time of war, operates electric plants, and fosters soil conservation, diversification of industry. The corporation is financed by Congressional appropriation.

STATES

Business enterprises are subject, under the police power, to such regulation as may be reasonably necessary to protect public health, morals, welfare, and safety.

Corporations. Every state has a law outlining the conditions under which a corporation may be organized. A corporation is "domestic" in the state where it is incorporated, "foreign" in all other states. A corporation must obtain a license to do business in any state other than the one in which it is chartered. Many corporations organize in states offering attractive conditions of incorporation even though they expect to do all their business in other states.

Occupational Licensing. State occupational licensing is based on the theory that the public interest will suffer unless the qualifications and actions of people engaged in the occupations concerned are controlled. The tendency is toward the licensing and regulation of many more occupational groups. Generally speaking, states laws on the subject call for a license applicant to possess certain qualifications and pass an examination. The license, once granted, is usually subject to revocation for various specified reasons or offenses.

Antitrust Laws. Many states have legislation on the statute books aimed at preventing monopolistic practices in intrastate business. Not having jurisdiction over business

TENNESSEE VALLEY AUTHORITY

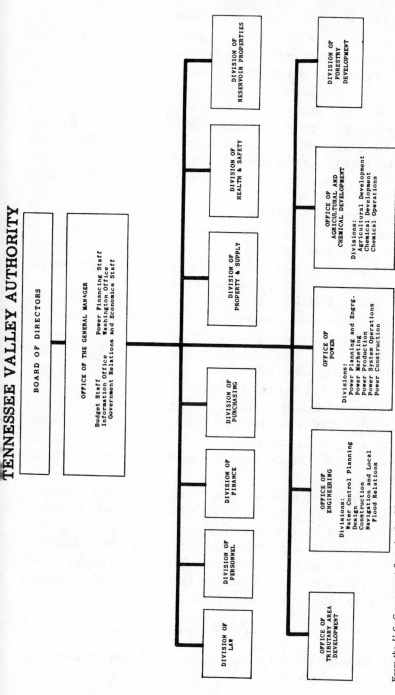

From the *U.S. Government Organization Manual, 1963–64.*

transactions of an interstate character, state officers find the enforcement of the antitrust laws a difficult task.

Price Control Acts.   Nearly forty states have enacted resale price maintenance laws. Such legislation allows manufacturers of trademarked or branded goods to fix the price at which their goods shall be sold by wholesalers and retailers. The purpose of these laws is to protect the producer against exploitation of the goodwill embodied in their trade name and to protect small independent stores from price cutting by chain stores.

Securities Regulation.   The provisions of state blue-sky laws usually require the licensing of securities dealers, the registration of securities offered for sale, and the authorization of a regulatory body to obtain court injunctions against the issuance or sale of fraudulent securities.

Public Utilities.   An enterprise which supplies an essential and widely used service to the public and enjoys grants of special privilege from the government is considered a public utility. Enterprises regarded as public utilities are usually those that provide electric light, gas, water, telephone, and railroad and bus service. The government seeks to insure the public satisfactory service at reasonable rates. Therefore, the public utilities enterprises are subjected to very stringent regulations. In this respect, the regulatory powers of state utilities commissions extend to nearly every phase of utility operations.

Liquor Regulation.   The objectives of state regulatory legislation covering the liquor trade include the divorce of the liquor business from organized crime, the prevention of the return of the saloon, and the collection of considerable revenue from the liquor trade. State liquor control systems are classified as: (a) prohibition system, (b) public monopoly system, (c) the licensing system.

STATE ENTERPRISES

Government ownership by the states is less extensive than federal ownership.

North Dakota.   The state which has the greatest variety of business enterprises is North Dakota. This state runs a flour mill, feed mill, grain elevator, and terminal elevator, all located in Grand Forks, with branch warehouses in many other cities. It is also an interesting fact that the Bank of North Dakota is a state-owned banking system.

Docks and Terminals.   Many seaboard states own and operate public dock facilities, grain elevators, and terminal facilities. The Port of New York Authority, a bi-state corporate agency, operates an extensive system of docks, terminals, and airports.

Other State Enterprises.   Several states have established systems of state dispensaries for the sale of liquor. Some states own airports, others operate systems of workmen's compensation, and some own and operate printing plants to supply the printing needs of their various governments.

City Governments

The city has the right to impose regulations or restrictions upon our use of our property or our exercise of our personal civil rights when such use interferes with the fundamental rights or privileges of our neighbors. In practice, this doctrine means that the city has in many respects regulated or restricted individuals and corporations in the enjoyment of the rights of both person and property. The following are examples of such restrictions.

Zoning.   For the purpose of conserving the health, safety, morals, and general welfare of a community, most communities have adopted a zoning plan. In general, zoning is the division of the community into districts or zones, with the regulation of such districts as to the use of the land, and the use, the height, and the area of buildings.

Building Codes.   One of the police power regulations designed for the protection of the public safety is the building code. This code requires a permit from the municipal authorities for the construction of all new buildings and for substantial additions to existing buildings. The specifications of construction, materials, installations, and inspection are usually included in the building code.

Licenses to Engage in Business. Many cities make the securing of licenses a prerequisite to engaging in certain types of business enterprise. In this way, both revenue and regulatory purposes are served. The kind of business establishments usually licensed by municipalities include taxicabs, barber shops, junk shops, pawnbrokers, pool halls, taverns, amusement places, and laundries.

MUNICIPAL ENTERPRISES

Government ownership is more common among cities than at the state and local level. It is especially widespread with respect to utility enterprises. More than two-thirds of all city water systems are owned by the public. In contrast, municipal ownership of electric plants or gas plants has not made much of a headway in the United States. New York and Chicago have established extensive city-owned subway systems, and other cities, such as Boston, have found it necessary to purchase privately-owned transportation systems and to assume their operation. The larger seacoast cities have interested themselves in public wharves and dock facilities. Ferries, markets, and airports are also examples of the municipal ownership of public utilities.

Chapter 28

GOVERNMENT FINANCE

The Constitution states that Congress has the power "to lay and collect taxes, duties, imposts, and excises, to pay the debts and provide for the common defense and general welfare of the United States." The limitations on Congressional taxing power include the constitutional requirements that all indirect taxes be uniform; that all direct taxes be apportioned according to population; that revenue laws shall not favor parts of one state over those of another; that export duties are prohibited; that interstate duties are prohibited; and that a tax must not violate due process.

The power to levy taxes for state purposes rests with the various state legislatures. Limitations imposed are those of the federal and state constitutions. The local taxing power is confined to those taxes which they are empowered by the state to levy.

Sources of Revenue

The acquisition of revenue for the support of public services is a major problem of government at each of the three levels—federal, state, and local.

Federal. In the fiscal year 1961, the personal income tax accounted for 52 per cent of the national government's revenues, the corporation income taxes produced 28 per cent, excise taxes amounted to 11 per cent, and all other receipts made up the remaining 9 per cent.

State.   The chief source of revenue for the state is the general sales tax. This tax produced about 23 per cent of the aggregate revenues of the states in 1959. Other significant state revenues are derived from motor fuel taxes, individual and corporate income taxes, property taxes, death and gift taxes, and license and privilege taxation. Nontax state revenue includes money from federal grants-in-aid and state enterprises.

Local.   The general property tax is still the chief source of local revenue, yielding more than half of all revenue collected by the local units of government. Sales taxes have been of increasing value as a source of revenue, particularly since the depression. Licenses, permits, and special assessments also provide substantial financial returns. Local nontax revenues include state grants-in-aid and income from municipal utility undertakings.

Duplication of Taxes.   The power to tax is a concurrent power. Both the state and federal governments may levy taxes on the same sources of revenue. Both units of government, for example, derive income from the income tax, taxes on gasoline, and taxes on tobacco. Proposed solutions for this duplication of taxes include the following suggestions: (a) the various levels of government should agree on a division of sources of revenue, (b) the tax offset device should be applied to many of the current duplicate taxes, (c) the federal government should collect all taxes and share the receipts with the lower levels.

Objects of Expenditure.   In the national government the estimated expenditures for fiscal year 1961 were about $80 billion. Of this total 54 per cent went for major national security programs, 11 per cent for interest on debt, 7 per cent for agriculture, 7 per cent for veterans, 5 per cent for debt retirement, and the remaining 16 per cent for all other national government functions, including conservation, health, housing, education, transportation, communication, general government and labor, commerce, finance, and industry.

The purposes of state and local expenditures cover a much

wider range than those of the national government. State expenditures are highest for welfare, schools, highways, and debt service. Local expenditures are greatest in the fields of education, debt service, welfare, and highways. In the cities, police and fire protection constitute large items in the budget.

Public Debts. Nearly every governmental unit has some power to borrow. State and local governments tend to be more restricted within certain limits than is the federal government. Congress has the power "to borrow money on the credit of the United States." Federal expenditures often exceed revenues. The estimated public debt of the federal government for 1960 was $285 billion. Generally speaking, the government borrows through the issuance of bonds.

The power of the states to incur indebtedness in large amounts is restricted in that most states require such borrowing to be approved by the voters in a referendum election or to be authorized by constitutional amendment. Other constitutional limitations on the contracting of indebtedness by states relate to the amount of indebtedness, the term of the bonds to be issued, and the taxes for payment of interest and principal. Local governments are restricted by constitutional provisions, statutory limitations, and the need to acquire the approval of the voters in a referendum election. Most of the bonds which are issued by the state and local units of government are done so in serial form of one kind or another.

Trends in Public Indebtedness. Just before the Second World War total state and local indebtedness amounted to about $20 billion, of which more than three-fourths was local. The federal debt at the time was just under $45 billion. During the war the federal debt was multiplied by six and the state and local indebtedness was reduced by 20 per cent. After the war and until the Korean incident, the national debt did not increase, but that of the states and local governments did. The gross governmental debt is now about $343 billion, of which $285 billion is federal, $58 billion state and local.

Public Budget

Prior to the First World War, public finance in the United States was the topic of very little deliberate planning. At the present time, careful fiscal planning through formal budget procedure is considered essential to the efficient administration of government at any level. A public budget is a comprehensive financial plan covering a definite period, based upon thoughtful estimates both of expenditures and revenue. Interest in budgeting on the part of American cities and states antedates, by many years, the start of the national budget system in 1921. The federal government, every state and many cities, counties, and other local units, now have some sort of budgeting system. While the budgetary procedures of the federal, state, and local governments vary greatly in detail, the underlying principles are everywhere the same.

Budget-Making Authority. The national government, the majority of the states, and most cities have an executive type budget. This type places the major responsibility for formulating the government's financial plan upon the chief executive. Usually he is provided with a staff unit to carry out the actual budgetary work. On the national level the responsibility for budget formulation is placed upon the President, who is assisted by the Bureau of the Budget.

Budget Preparation.   The first step in the budget process involves the request by the budget-making authority for "estimates." These estimates of needed expenditures for the coming fiscal period are provided by the agencies involved. Upon receipt of the requested data the budget authority reviews and revises the estimates. The second step usually involves conferences and hearings by means of which department heads are given an opportunity to justify their requests. Revised estimates become the program of proposed expenditures. The third step requires estimates of expected revenue. These estimates are drawn up by the budget authority or submitted by the government's chief financial officer. With the correlation of the expenditure estimate and revenue estimate

GENERAL ACCOUNTING OFFICE

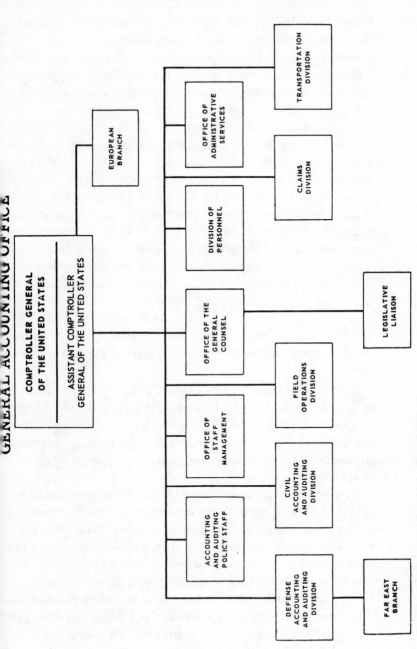

From the *U.S. Government Organization Manual, 1963–64.*

sides of the budget, the data is presented to the legislative body in the form of the budget document.

Budget and the Legislature.   The budget presented to the legislative body is only a plan for legislative guidance in financial matters. In the national government and in most states the legislative body is quite free to ignore the budget recommendations entirely and enact an appropriation measure of its own. In most legislative processes, the budget is acted upon in appropriate committees of both houses of the legislature. If appropriation and revenue bills are not submitted as part of the budget document, then they are usually drafted by the legislative committees dealing with appropriations and revenue. Public hearings on budget proposals are usually held by the committees, except at the federal level. The proposed legislation may provide for an itemized or a lump sum appropriation for a given department. Following action by both houses of the legislature, the bill goes to the chief executive for his signature. If dissatisfied he may veto the bill. Many governors may use the item veto, permitting them to strike out or to reduce any part of an appropriation bill.

Budget Execution.   The U..S. Treasury Department has custody of federal funds. Operating departments are advised by the treasury of the amount of money they may spend during the fiscal year. The Director of the Budget may apportion the financial appropriations for each agency month by month, or quarter by quarter.

In states and cities a somewhat similar procedure is followed, the operating agencies usually being closely supervised in their spending of appropriated funds. When the comptroller examines and approves claims against appropriation accounts before payment, it is known as the "preaudit." The postaudit is the analysis of expenditures, after disbursement, by an agency outside and independent of the administration. The important distinction between the administrative preaudit and the independent postaudit is widely ignored in the federal, the state, and the local governments.

Chapter 29

GOVERNMENT AND MONEY
AND BANKING

The currency powers of the national government are set forth in the national Constitution. From the earliest days the national and local governments have been interested in the regulation of the money system by control over the currency, the incorporation of banks (now subject to additional controls by the Federal Deposit Insurance Corporation), and the processes of bankruptcy.

The most important recent trend has been the emergence of the government as a major creditor in our economic system. The federal government has engaged on a very great scale in the provision of credit to farmers through the Farm Credit Administration, to business through the Reconstruction Finance Corporation, and indirectly to builders and home owners through mortgage insurance by the Federal Housing Administration. The states have been increasingly engaged in similar creditor activities. Through the Securities and Exchange Commission the federal government now regulates the operation of the stock and bond market systems and many of the fiscal activities of private business. There is a particularly extensive control over the activities of corporations engaged in the writing of insurance policies.

NATIONAL GOVERNMENT

Congress has power to coin money and regulate its value. Under this power it has not only provided for the coining of money in the constitutional sense, but it has also issued paper

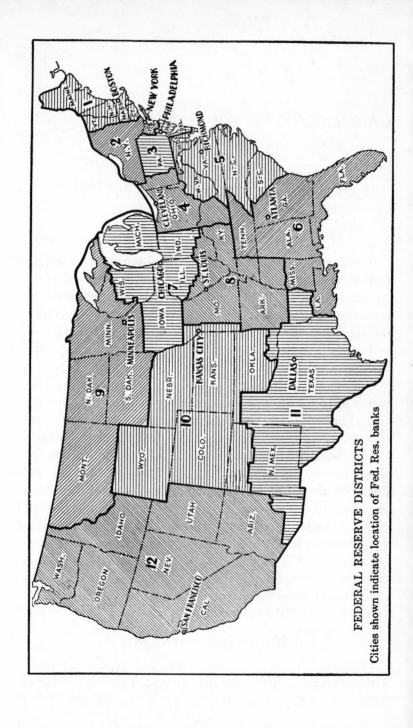

FEDERAL RESERVE DISTRICTS

Cities shown indicate location of Fed. Res. banks

money reinforced by legal tender acts. Under its implied powers, the Congress has extended its financial powers to include regulation of a major portion of the banking system.

Currency.   Congress established the first mint and adopted the bimetallic monetary standard in 1792. By law fifteen ounces of coined silver was exchangeable for one ounce of coined gold. This ratio between the two metals was later fixed at 16 to 1. In 1873, Congress enacted legislation that resulted in the abandonment of silver as a basic monetary metal. In the national presidential election of 1896, the restoration of bimetallism was a major issue. McKinley's defeat of Bryan in that election was a victory for the gold standard. In 1900, Congress passed the Gold Standard Act, making the gold dollar the unit of value and all other forms of money redeemable at face value in gold. A permanent fund of gold coin was to be created and maintained for redemption purposes.

In 1933, the gold standard was abandoned. Legal tender money was no longer freely exchangeable for gold. The President was empowered to "devalue" the dollar by not more than 60 per cent nor less than 40 per cent. Early the next year the weight of the gold dollar was reduced to 59.06 per cent of the former weight. In order to accumulate a stock of gold to serve as a metallic base for a paper currency, the gold purchased by the government was stored at Fort Knox, Kentucky.

In 1934, Congress enacted the Silver Purchase Act which set forth the policy of the United States to increase the ratio of silver to gold in the nation's monetary stock. Today the United States has a managed, inconvertible gold standard.

Present Forms of Currency.   The various kinds of American currency now in general circulation include: United States Treasury notes, silver certificates, federal reserve notes, silver dollars, and fractional currency.

Federal Reserve System.   Under the Federal Reserve Act of 1913 the country was divided into twelve banking districts with a federal reserve bank in each. All "national banks" are members of the system, and state banks may join. They are then entitled to the privileges of the system. One of these is the issuance of notes based upon securities and accepted by the federal reserve bank of their district. The board of governors of the Federal Reserve System, composed of seven members appointed for fourteen years by the President by and with the advice and consent of the Senate, is vested with broad supervisory powers.

The board determines generally monetary, credit, and operating policies for the system as a whole and formulates the rules and regulations necessary to carry out the purposes of the Federal Reserve Act. The board's principal duties consist of exerting an influence over credit conditions and supervising the Federal Reserve Banks and member banks. Each member of the Board of Governors is also a member of the Federal Open-Market Committee, whose membership in addition includes five representatives of the reserve banks. This committee is empowered to control the open market buying and selling of obligations of the United States, with regard to their bearing upon the general credit situation of the country.

Deposit Insurance. The Federal Deposit Insurance Corporation was set up in 1933. Members of the Federal Reserve System are automatically members; nonmember banks may apply for insurance. Deposits by individuals in insured banks are protected in full against loss up to $10,000. The insurance program is financed by annual assessments on the deposits of insured banks.

STATES

The Constitution of the United States denies the states the power to "coin money, emit bills of credit, or make anything but gold or silver legal tender in the payment of debts." The states may, however, charter banks and these banks may issue paper money, but such paper money may not be used as legal tender. The commercial banking systems controlled by the states are not to be confused with the commercial banking system controlled by the federal government.

State Banking Regulation.   State banks are created under state laws and are regulated, under state legislation, by state administrative offices. State banking regulations deal with such things as the organization of banking institutions, the minimum amount of capital stock for banks, the requirements concerning the amount and form of reserves, and provisions for examinations and reports. State chartered savings banks and building and loan associations are also regulated to insure greater security for depositors. State banks which become members of the Federal Reserve System, and others which have their deposits insured by the Federal Deposit Insurance Corporation, are subject to federal as well as state surveillance. The number of state banks is nearly twice that of national banks.

Small-Loan Business.   Most states have enacted laws to protect those people who borrow, on personal security, small sums of money to be repaid, in installments, within a few weeks or months. These statutes provide for a system of licensed and regulated small-loan or "personal finance" institutions.

Insurance.   Most states have regulatory laws in the field of insurance. The purpose of such regulation is to see that claims for insured losses are paid, unreasonable rates are not charged, and, in the case of life insurance, savings are secure. Insurance regulations include the licensing of both an insurance company and its agents; the denial of a license in the public interest; the revocation of license for cause; the restriction on the investment of assets; the requiring of reports; and the depositing of securities with the insurance department to guarantee payment of loss claims incurred within the state.

Prior to 1944, public regulation of insurance had been considered as being exclusively within the power of the states. Insurance was not considered commerce and hence was not subject, even in its interstate aspects, to congressional regulation. In 1944, the Supreme Court held that insurance is commerce and that insurance companies doing business across state lines should be prosecuted for violations of federal antitrust laws. The degree to which Congress may decide to enter the insurance field with regulatory legislation is as yet undetermined.

Chapter 30

GOVERNMENT AND NATURAL RESOURCES

Second only to the activities of the government in the promotion and regulation of the business system has been the interest in the promotion and control of agriculture.

Public Domain. Historically, the national government's first major interest in agriculture was seen in the increasingly liberal disposition of the public domain to individual farmers, culminating in the liberal homestead policy of the Lincoln administration. While a great portion of the public lands was granted to railroads or sold to land speculators, a widespread practice was to transfer a "homestead" (usually 160 acres) at a nominal fee to the individual homesteader.

AGRICULTURAL POLICIES

In the field of agriculture, the government's main policies are included in the following activities.

Scientific Research. Working mainly through the bureaus of the Agricultural Research Service of the Department of Agriculture, the federal government does extensive research for the assistance of farmers in soil chemistry, plant diseases and pests, agricultural engineering, plant industry, animal husbandry, dairy industry, weather, and many other fields. Few research agencies in the world are superior to those maintained for agriculture in the United States.

Agricultural Education. Beginning with the Morrill Act of 1862, the federal government has sponsored a system of land-grant colleges in the states. Around these agricultural

colleges a great network of college-level educational facilitie
has been built. These schools reach into every state and con
sist of specialized faculties, agricultural experiment stations
and a farm extension service serving every agricultural count
by way of a nation-wide staff of county agricultural agents

Agricultural Credit.   Modern farming requires capital
The government realized this and provided the Farm Loar
Act of 1916 which began the development of federal credi
aid to farmers, a program which now has many aspects
federal land banks, banks for co-operatives, commodit
credit, and extensive lending aids.

Agricultural Marketing.   Modern farming requires mod
ern marketing facilities. These are also provided to th
farmer through the Department of Agriculture, which com
piles and distributes crop and market news, establishes farm
produce standards, regulates buyers and warehousers as wel
as traders in agriculture "futures."

Farm Price Supports.   During the last three decades th
federal government has provided stability in farm prices b
combining acreage control with price guarantees and loan
up to 90 per cent of "parity." Parity is determined by th
price of the crops during a base period plus the rise in cos
of living.

Aid to Small Farmers.   The federal government also ex
tended special aid to farmers on marginal lands, tenant farm
ers, and migratory farm labor. This aid has included specia
loans, resettlement projects, and migratory labor camps.

Rural Electrification.   The federal government has als
embarked upon a program to bring electric power to th
farms, and has more than trebled the number of farms served

State Agricultural Activities

Every state has an executive department concerned wit
the welfare of the farmer. These departments carry out man
programs in co-operation with the federal agencies, an
many of them perform significant additional function
adapted to the special problems of the state's agricultura
industry.

NATURAL RESOURCES

During the first one hundred years of our history the natural resources of the country were actually ravaged. Since the last decade of the nineteenth century, when the conservation movement began, the scope of the conservation effort has been considerably broadened. Today, resources of the privately owned, as well as the publicly owned, areas of the country are subject to governmental control.

CONSERVATION POLICIES

The government's conservation activities have affected land use and water, forest, recreational, and mineral resources.

Land and Its Use. More than 20 per cent of the total national land area is "public land." The protection of this public domain and the prevention of the depletion of the soil of privately owned arable land threatened by erosion are major concerns of the national government. Through the Soil Conservation Service of the Department of Agriculture, the federal government seeks to increase the use of practices which control soil erosion by carrying out demonstrations and by co-operating with states, localities, and farmers in crop rotation, contouring, and many similar projects.

Water and Water Power. Congress exercises control over all navigable waters. Such control involves the damming of rivers, the development of water power, and the withdrawal of waters from navigable rivers and lakes. The Bureau of Reclamation in the Department of Interior has jurisdiction over irrigation projects on federal lands. It also operates and maintains reservoirs, canals, and other project facilities for privately owned lands. The Department of the Army and the Department of Interior do considerable work in flood control. The development of dams and waterpower on navigable waters and on public lands is controlled by the Federal Power Commission.

Forests and Wildlife. Under President Theodore Roosevelt the United States began a program to preserve and extend the forests of the country. The Forest Service of the Department of Agriculture conducts forestry research and demonstration projects along with the administration of more than a hundred and fifty national forests. It also conducts a research program on the various aspects of forest management and utilization.

The Fish and Wildlife Service in the Department of Interior, in co-operation with state fish and game agencies, is concerned with: the propagation of fish, the restrictions on the quantity of fishermen's catches, the restoration of wildlife, the protection of migratory birds, the licensing of hunters, and the provision and maintenance of many wildlife refuges. The promotion of the maximum current use and enjoyment of the wildlife resources, compatible with their perpetuity, is a prime objective of this service.

Minerals and Petroleum. The Geological Survey of the Department of Interior has the job of identifying, locating, and investigating mineral deposits. It also supervises oil, gas, and mining operations on the public domain. The Bureau of Mines in the Department of Interior conducts research on the reduction of waste through improved mining methods, more economical use of finished products, and the increased use of scrap materials. The bureau is also concerned with safety programs aimed at reducing mining accidents. In 1935, Congress approved an interstate compact for the conservation of oil and gas. By 1948, nineteen states, producing together more than 90 per cent of the country's gas and 80 per cent of the crude oil were participants in the compact program.

Another federal law enacted in 1935, the Connally Hot Oil Act, prohibits the interstate transportation of oil produced in excess of state restrictive regulations.

State Conservation Activities. The activities of the various state departments of conservation and special agencies for different types of conservation work include the protection of forests, the control of water resources, the protection of fish and game, and the completion of geological surveys. Most of these activities are conducted on a co-operative basis with the federal government.

Chapter 31

GOVERNMENT AND LABOR

The entrance of government into the promotion of labor interests and the regulation of labor activities has been a more recent growth than governmental interest in business and agriculture. The government entered this field at about the beginning of the nineteenth century and has continued and increased its labor activities since then.

Restriction of Immigration.   Early in the nineteenth century labor sought relaxation of the common-law doctrine of conspiracy by states in connection with recognition of labor unions and their right to strike. Later in the century labor demanded that the government restrict immigration to prevent the lowering of labor wage and hours standards in the United States. Starting with minor restrictions around 1900, labor gradually won stricter control over the entrance of competing immigrant laborers. In 1924, the Congress, by the imposition of a strict quota system, reduced immigration to a negligible factor in our economic system.

Labor Bureaus and Departments.   Late in the nineteenth century, in various states (Massachusetts 1869, New York 1886) labor caused the creation of labor bureaus whose function was to analyze working conditions and report them to the legislatures. A federal bureau of labor with similar functions was created in the Department of Interior in 1884.

Federal Department of Labor.   Labor won further service from the national government in 1903 with the establishment of the Department of Commerce and Labor, which ten years later was divided into two departments, the Department of Commerce and the Department of Labor. The latter has provided an extensive series of services to the labor movement in the United States.

Government Employment Agencies.   The government has also provided, both in the states and in the United States Department of Labor, public employment agencies which attempt to secure employment for qualified and employable workers.

In 1933, the United States Employment Service was established by the Wagner-Peyser Act. The Employment Service now maintains a nation-wide system of employment offices.

Workmen's Compensation Acts.   Another step in governmental services to labor has been the gradual establishment, by the states, of workmen's compensation systems which provide insurance payments to workmen injured or disabled through industrial accidents or occupational disease.

EARLY LABOR RELATIONS

In the second decade of the twentieth century, labor gradually won from the federal government a series of legislative measures which guarantee certain rights and privileges to the labor movement and provide additional services to labor. Most of the states enacted legislation: limiting the hours of labor of children, of women, and of men in dangerous occupations, regulating conditions of work and providing for methods of paying wages, collective bargaining, settlement of disputes, promoting conciliation, arbitration.

Child Labor Movement.   Unsuccessful in attempts to secure legislation or a constitutional amendment to prohibit child labor in the United States, the labor movement succeeded in securing the establishment of a Children's Bureau in the Department of Labor (now in the Department of Health, Education and Welfare) and the gradual prohibition of child labor. The Fair Labor Standards Act of 1938, effectively provided for the prohibition of child labor in most kinds of employment, the exceptions being those which may be classified in the now limited intrastate category.

Clayton Act. In 1915, labor won another substantial victory in national legislation in the Clayton Act, which was then described as "labor's Magna Charta." The Clayton Act exempted labor unions from the provisions of the antitrust act and attempted to give them a more favorable status in the courts.

Norris-LaGuardia Anti-Injunction Act. In 1932, through the Norris-LaGuardia Act, Congress took a further step in protecting the legal status of labor unions by declaring it "to be the public policy of the United States" that workers shall have the right to organize and join unions, and that the federal court shall not interfere by injunction in the exercise of this right. Specific acts—joining a union, paying dues, assembling peaceably, refusing to work, peaceably advising others to participate in these acts—are listed by statute as being not subject to injunction. Jury trial in contempt-of-court cases for violating labor injunctions was also provided.

New Deal Labor Relations

The New Deal brought a marked extension of governmental interest in labor activities, particularly in the guarantees extended to labor unions in their attempts at the establishment of collective bargaining systems and their relations with employers, and regarding workers' wages and hours.

Clause 7–A, National Industrial Recovery Act. The right to collective bargaining, which had been to some extent guaranteed by the Norris-LaGuardia Act of 1932, was guaranteed on a wider scale in the collective bargaining clause of the National Industrial Recovery Act, and became in greater or less degree a central feature of the industrial codes set up under that act.

National Labor Relations Act. This act, approved by Congress in 1935, continued the guarantees of Clause 7–A of the National Industrial Recovery Act, and created a National Labor Relations Board with power to prohibit unfair labor practices on the part of employers and to determine who the valid representatives of employees were by holding, if necessary, elections among workers within appropriate units.

Wages and Hours Board.   By an act of 1937, the Congress established national minimum standards for wages and maximum hours of labor per week, with standards to be gradually raised during 1939 and succeeding years. This act and the National Labor Relations Act represent by far the most important protection secured by the labor movement from the national government, and they are now paralleled in several instances by state laws providing the same guarantees with respect to interstate labor.

Recent Labor Relations

Taft-Hartley Act of 1947.   Passed over the veto of President Truman, this act was among the most controversial legislation of the decade. From the point of view of management, it redresses the pro-labor bias which management ascribed to the Wagner Act of 1935. From the point of view of labor, it deprives labor unions of hard-won gains and has a pro-management bias. Among its most debated provisions are those which prohibit the closed shop, require union leaders, but not management, to sign non-Communist affidavits, restore the use of the injunction in labor disputes, and outlaw jurisdictional strikes and secondary boycots. The act also authorizes the President to seek an eighty-day injunction when a strike threatens the national health or safety.

The Labor Reform Act of 1959.   This act is mainly concerned with the internal affairs of labor unions. It requires unions to report their constitutions, bylaws, and fiscal transactions to the Secretary of Labor; it also requires secret ballot union elections, protects union members in their rights under union rules, bans certain types of persons from union office, and tightens restrictions on secondary boycotts.

Chapter 32

SOCIAL SECURITY AND
PUBLIC HEALTH

The entrance of the government into the field of social security was long retarded by the powerful tradition of the Elizabethan poor laws.

Local Responsibility.   Within the framework of the Elizabethan poor law tradition, the United States had, until after the First World War, the theory of local responsibility for assistance to the aged and the needy. Such assistance was provided in institutions supported by the town or county and were familiar to several generations as "poor houses."

Growth of State Responsibility.   In the latter part of the nineteenth century, there was some movement toward a wider area of responsibility and state boards of charities or welfare were provided. Assistance was still, however, largely restricted to the Elizabethan pattern, though early in the twentieth century child welfare was to some extent made noninstitutional.

RISE OF NATIONAL RESPONSIBILITY

The crises of unemployment and insecurity brought by the depression in 1929 revolutionized the relationship of government to social security activities. The Elizabethan tradition was almost completely abandoned, and the thesis of local responsibility was radically modified.

National and State Responsibility.   The New Deal, particularly, emphasized the responsibilities of the national government as well as the state governments for assistance to the aged and the needy. As a result, emergency agencies were first set up under the New Deal to cope with the staggering problems of unemployment. These were paralleled in most states by state and local agencies engaged in supplementing the relief and assistance activities of the national government.

Reorganized State Departments. The era of the New Deal also brought the modernization of state departments of charities into state departments of welfare. These operated, in the most advanced states, under new statutes free from the Elizabethan tradition of institutional poor relief.

Recent National Policies

The emergency assistance program of the New Deal was crystallized in 1935 in the Social Security Act, which provides a permanent basis for the national government's activities in the field of social security. The act was designed to provide economic security through several forms of social insurance. The following are provisions of the act.

Public Assistance. The Social Security Act authorized federal grants to the states, under the supervision of the social security board, for three forms of public assistance: to provide income for the needy aged, the needy dependent children, and the needy blind. The federal government and the state governments share in paying for public assistance and in seeing that it is properly administered.

Unemployment Insurance. The act also authorized the board to extend grants to the states in support of approved unemployment compensation systems. There is a national guarantee of costs of administration and a national payroll tax, 90 per cent of which is deductible by the employer on his federal return if his state levies a payroll tax. Many variations in provisions and administration exist among the states.

Federal Old-Age Benefits. This act also set up a nationally administered and financed system of old-age benefits to persons who have spent their active years in commerce and industry. Under a 1946 amendment to the Social Security Act, survivors of qualified veterans of the Second World War may receive benefits under the old age and survivors insurance program.

Grants for Public Health, Maternal and Child Welfare, Vocational Rehabilitation. The activities of the Public Health Service, the Maternal and Child Welfare services of the Children's Bureau, and the vocational rehabilitation program of the Office of Education were also extended.

Social Security Act of 1950. The Socal Security Act underwent a major overhauling. Coverage was extended in terms of both numbers and classes of beneficiaries. The kinds and amounts of protection afforded were also changed by the 1950 and subsequent legislation. The programs affected, in varying degrees, were old age and survivors insurance, public assistance, and unemployment insurance.

Department of Health, Education, and Welfare. Reorganization Plan 1 of 1953 established the Department of Health, Education, and Welfare and, in doing so, abolished the Federal Security Agency. (The Federal Security Agency had been created by President F. D. Roosevelt in 1939 to integrate the administration of the federal security activities.) Differing slightly in purpose and emphasis, the Department of Health, Education, and Welfare is responsible for improving the administration of the Public Health Service, Office of Education, Social Security Administration, Office of Vocational Rehabilitation, Food and Drug Administration, and Saint Elizabeths Hospital. The Department of Health, Education, and Welfare is thus the administrative keystone of the American social security program. The national government and the state and local governments co-operate on a wide scale in the provision of extensive forms of social insurance, the like of which was undreamed of under the Elizabethan tradition.

State and Local Agencies. States maintain homes for deaf, dumb, and blind, for children, and for incurables. Counties or townships still maintain alms houses, poor farms, and similar institutions. Many classes, especially the aged, need institutional care. Improvements have occurred through the segregation of different classes of inmates and the regional location of institutions in a few states.

GOVERNMENT AND PUBLIC HEALTH

The entrance of the government into the field of public health has been retarded by a tradition similar to the Elizabethan tradition in public assistance.

Local Responsibility. As in the field of public assistance, there is a long theory of local responsibility for public health. Not until 1869 did health problems reach the state level, when Massachusetts in that year established a department of health.

State Health Departments. Beginning with the Massachusetts department in 1869, the theory of state responsibility has been extended gradually to all the states of the Union; each state now has a state health code, which is supplemented in the majority of the states by administrative divisions for enforcement. Industrial states, such as New York, Pennsylvania, and Illinois, have extensive state health departments; New York, for instance, spends more than $4,000,000 a year for the enforcement of state health standards. Several states have set up separate departments of mental hygiene to administer their mental health programs and institutions; New York, for example, spends more than $100,000,000 a year to cover the current operating expenses of its mental institutions. Although the state governments perform many health services, supervise and control local health activities, and give financial grants to local units of government, the major responsibility for the initiation and administration of most public health programs still remains with the local units of government.

United States Public Health Service. Supplementing the extensive health administrative agencies in the large cities, the nation-wide county health units, and the extensive state departments of health, is the United States Public Health Service, a division of the Department of Health, Education and Welfare. This bureau makes surveys and investigations into the administration of public health standards, does extensive research work, and pays particular attention to national attempts to eradicate specific diseases and other health hazards.

Grants-in-Aid to States. Federal services in the field of public health also receive impetus in the provisions of the Social Security Act for aid to states in child and maternal welfare, in public health education, and in the training of public health personnel. More recently the federal grants-in-aid to state and local governments for health purposes have been extended to cover the control of venereal diseases, tuberculosis, cancer, mental health, and the assistance of state and local units in maintaining full time general health services and in constructing of local hospitals.

Chapter 33

EDUCATION AND HOUSING

Public education is one of the most firmly established American traditions. Even in the colonies there were the beginnings of public education. At the close of the Revolution the gradual emergence of a concern for education was an aid to the development of representative government.

The Growth of Local School Administration. Education is still primarily administered by local districts with state and some federal assistance. These local district organizations have been organized with professional teaching and administrative personnel. In most districts the governing authority is an elective board, which is usually divorced from other administrative units. Public education is the largest single enterprise engaged in by the state and local governments.

The Growth of State Responsibility. By the middle of the nineteenth century, state governments had assumed general responsibility for the maintenance of a uniform educational system and subsequent progress has been extensive. Almost every state now has a system of state control over educational standards, including the curriculum and the selection of teaching personnel, and an extensive program of state fiscal assistance to local schools. In Delaware, New Hampshire, and North Carolina the administration and financing of local schools is highly centralized.

Public Higher Education. The growth of publicly supported higher education in the latter part of the nineteenth century and the beginning of the twentieth century was correspondingly extensive. Every state now has some form of publicly supported higher education and the American state universities have become a significant factor in the expansion of higher education in the United States.

United States Office of Education. The federal government has extended its assistance to public education through the establishment and extension of the Office of Education, now a part of the Department of Health, Education, and Welfare. Its activities are primarily in the field of information, statistics, research, and other professional assistance to local and state educational enterprises. Additional federal activities in the field of public education include the provision of funds for vocational education, state college agricultural programs, and, until 1955, the G.I. Bill of Rights.

Beginning in the late 1950's, major financial assistance by the national government to the states and educational institutions became a new national policy.

GOVERNMENT AND HOUSING

The twentieth century has seen the growth of the housing problem from a local urban headache to a national crisis. Two great wars and a long economic depression have limited housing construction to less than normal volume, while rapid urbanization and steady population growth has increased demand at higher than normal rates. Moreover, obsolescence has proceeded almost unchecked.

Until the middle 1930's housing was regarded as a problem for solution by the private housing industry and by local governments.

Federal Housing Act of 1934. This act represented the federal government's first direct entrance into the construction and management of low-rental housing, and into financial assistance to limited-dividend private corporations which construct low-rental housing.

Wagner-Steagall Act of 1937. Under this act the federal government entered the housing field more vigorously. The U. S. Housing Authority was established with an initial borrowing power of $500,000,000. Its function was to loan to state and local housing authorities up to 90 per cent of building costs or to make other financial assistance available in the form of capital grants or annual contributions. Under the stimulus of this act, many state and local agencies came into being and public housing became a significant governmental activity.

Defense and War Housing. The expansion of employment and the building up of new urban centers due to war production brought new housing problems, and, as a result, the federal government entered heavily into new housing activities. The National Housing Agency was established in 1942, and all federal housing activities were consolidated under its direction.

Postwar Housing Programs. In 1947, the war-time housing agency was made permanent under the new title of the Housing and Home Finance Agency. The Housing Act of 1949 gave this agency responsibility for a long-range federally-sponsored housing program in which construction of public housing and financial assistance for the private construction of low-cost housing are both emphasized. The Housing Act of 1950 provides for loans to colleges and universities to assist in providing student and faculty housing. The Housing Act of 1954 expanded the responsibilities of the Agency to approve and certify certain urban renewal programs.

In 1961, Congress approved the housing program proposed by President Kennedy, greatly expanding the preceding housing activities of the national government.

State and Local Programs. Almost every state and many cities now have their own housing programs, in addition to their participation in the federal program.

Chapter 34

INTERNATIONAL ORGANIZATIONS

One of the most significant developments in the course of American foreign policy in recent decades has been our increased participation in international agencies. The form and nature of the existing international organizations to maintain peace and security through collective action are the latest variants of many ideas, many institutions, and many practices of the past.

UNITED NATIONS SYSTEM

The purposes of the United Nations are to maintain international peace and security; to develop friendly relations among nations; to co-operate internationally in solving international economic, social, cultural, and humanitarian problems; and to be a center for harmonizing the actions of nations in attaining common ends.

Membership. All peace-loving nations which accept the obligations of the United Nations Charter and, in the judgment of the organization, are able and willing to carry out the obligations are eligible for membership. The original members of the UN are those countries which signed the Declaration by the United Nations in 1942, or took part in the San Francisco Conference, and later signed and ratified the Charter.

PRINCIPAL ORGANS

The management of the affairs of the United Nations Organization is vested in the following organs.

General Assembly.   All the member states are represented in the General Assembly where each member has one vote. The Assembly makes recommendations on the principles of international co-operation, discusses any questions or matters within the scope of the Charter and, except for not being able to make recommendations on matters which the Security Council is dealing with, it "may make recommendations to the members of the United Nations or to the Security Council or to both on any such questions or matters." The Assembly initiates studies and makes recommendations to promote international political co-operation; receives and considers reports from the Security Council and other organs of the United Nations; supervises, through the Trusteeship Council, the execution of the Trusteeship Agreements; and considers and approves the budget of the United Nations.

Security Council.   The Security Council is composed of five permanent members: China, Great Britain, France, Russia, and the United States, and six nonpermanent members elected by the General Assembly for terms of two years. Voting on all matters other than questions of procedure is by an affirmative vote of seven members, including the concurring votes of the five major powers. The Security Council's functions include the investigation of disputes or situations which might lead to conflict, the determination of the existence of a threat to the peace and the recommendation of action, the motivation of members to apply economic sanctions and other measures short of war to prevent or stop aggression, the instigation of military action against an aggressor, and the recommendation of new members for admission to the United Nations. The Council functions continuously. Its major functional subordinate units are the Military Staff Committee, the Atomic Energy Commission, and the Commission for Conventional Armaments.

Economic and Social Council.   The Economic and Social Council is composed of eighteen members elected by the General Assembly for a three-year term. This council is responsible for the economic and social activities of the United

Nations. It initiates studies, calls international conferences, and makes recommendations relative to international, social, economic, and cultural affairs. The council works through commissions and committees, such as the Fiscal Commission, the Social Commission, and the Population Commission. It also co-ordinates the activities of the specialized agencies affiliated with the United Nations.

Trusteeship Council. A fourth major organ of the United Nations is the Trusteeship Council. This council is composed of countries administering trust territories, the big five powers, and enough nonadministering trust members, elected by the General Assembly, to create a balance between the administering and nonadministering groups. The Trusteeship Council supervises the administration of the trust territories. In this respect, it considers reports and accepts and examines petitions, and provides for visits of delegations to trust territories.

International Court of Justice. The fifth organ, the principal judicial body of the United Nations, is the International Court at the Hague. It consists of fifteen judges, elected by the General Assembly and the Security Council. All members of the United Nations are permitted to refer cases to the court for advisory opinions on legal questions. Countries who are not members of the UN can also become a party to the statute of the court. Individuals cannot refer cases to the court.

Secretariat. The last of the six principal organs of the United Nations organization is the Secretariat. It is composed of the Secretary General appointed by the General Assembly upon the recommendation of the Security Council and "such staff as the organization may require." The Secretary General is the chief administrative officer of the United Nations. He may bring to the attention of the Security Council any matter which in his opinion may threaten the maintenance of international peace and security. The Secretary General is assisted by an international staff.

Specialized Agencies

Organizations established by inter-governmental agreements and having wide responsibilities in economic, social, cultural, educational, health, and related fields are brought into relationship with the United Nations. The activities of the following agencies are co-ordinated by the Economic and Social Council.

International Labor Organization.   Concerned with promoting social justice the International Labor Organization seeks to improve, through international action, labor conditions and living standards and to promote economic and social stability. The governing body of the ILO is composed of representatives of governments, management, and labor.

Food and Agricultural Organization of the United Nations.   The FAO considers methods for raising the levels of nutrition and standards of living through improvements in the production and distribution of food and agricultural products.

United Nations, Educational, Scientific, and Cultural Organization.   UNESCO collaborates in the advancement of the mutual knowledge and understanding of peoples through various means of communication. It also aims to maintain, increase, and diffuse knowledge.

International Civil Aviation Organization.   ICAO has as its primary purpose the study of problems of international civil aviation and the establishment of international standards and regulations for civil aviation.

International Bank for Reconstruction and Development. The International Bank was established in 1945 for the purpose of assisting in the long-term reconstruction of countries damaged by war and in the development of underprivileged territories. These functions are performed by making loans, participating in loans, and guaranteeing loans.

International Monetary Fund.   The fund was, with the bank, part of the Bretton Woods agreement of 1945. It is concerned with promoting international monetary co-operation and exchange stability, and avoiding competitive exchange depreciations.

World Health Organization. The prime purpose of WHO is the attainment of the highest possible level of health for all peoples. Other specialized agencies working with the United Nations include the International Trade Organization, the International Refugee Organization, and the Universal Postal Union.

INDEX GUIDE TO THE CONSTITUTION

PREAMBLE

ARTICLE I

Legislative Department: organization, powers, and restraints.

ARTICLE II

Executive Department: powers, restraints, duties, and election of the President.

ARTICLE III

Judicial Department: powers, restraints. Definition of treason.

ARTICLE IV

Powers of the states. Relation of states and territories to the federal government.

ARTICLE V

Method of amending Constitution. Guarantee of equal representation of states in the United States Senate.

ARTICLE VI

Provision for national debts. Supremacy of the United States Constitution, Federal laws and treaties. Pledge of national and state officials to uphold Constitution. No religious test required as qualification to public office.

ARTICLE VII

Method for ratification of the Constitution.

AMENDMENTS

The first ten Amendments are frequently referred to as the *Bill of Rights*.

I   Freedom of religion, of speech, and of the press.
        Right to petition.

II   Right to keep and bear arms.

III   Soldiers in time of peace.

IV   Right of search.

V   Protection of accused in capital crimes.

VI   Right to speedy trial for accused.

VII   Trial by jury in lawsuits.

VIII   Excessive bail or unusual punishment forbidden.

IX   Peoples' rights retained.

X   Undelegated powers revert to the states.

XI   Exemption of states from suit.

XII   New method of electing President (Supersedes **part of** Article II, Sec. 1).

XIII   Slavery prohibited.

XIV   Protection of citizens' rights.
        Apportionment of representatives in Congress
           (Supersedes part of Article I, Sec. 2).
        Status of officials engaged in insurrection.
        Validity of war debt.

XV   Right of citizens to vote.

XVI   Income tax.

XVII   Election of senators.
        Senatorial vacancies.

XVIII   Prohibition of intoxicating liquors.

XIX   Woman suffrage.

XX   Abolition of "lame duck" session of Congress.
        Change in the date of assembly.

XXI   Repeal of Eighteenth Amendment.

XXII   Limitation of an individual President's service to two elected terms.

XXIII   Right of residents of the District of Columbia to vote.

CONSTITUTION OF THE UNITED STATES

Adopted September 17, 1787
Effective March 4, 1789

WE the people of the United States, in order to form a more perfect union, establish justice, insure domestic tranquillity, provide for the common defense, promote the general welfare, and secure the blessings of liberty to ourselves and our posterity, do ordain and establish this Constitution for the United States of America.

ARTICLE I

SECTION 1. All legislative powers herein granted shall be vested in a Congress of the United States, which shall consist of a Senate and House of Representatives.

SECTION 2. 1. The House of Representatives shall be composed of members chosen every second year by the people of the several States, and the electors in each State shall have the qualifications requisite for electors of the most numerous branch of the State legislature.

2. No person shall be a representative who shall not have attained to the age of twenty-five years, and been seven years a citizen of the United States, and who shall not, when elected, be an inhabitant of that State in which he shall be chosen.

3. Representatives and direct taxes [1] shall be apportioned among the several States which may be included within this Union, according to their respective numbers, which shall be determined by adding to the whole number of free persons, including those bound to service for a term of years, and excluding Indians not taxed, *three fifths of all other persons*.[2] The actual enumeration shall be made within three years after the first meeting of the Congress of the United States, and within every subsequent term of ten years, in such manner as they shall by law direct. The number of representatives shall not exceed one for every thirty thousand, but each State shall have at least one rep-

[1] See the 16th Amendment.
[2] See the 14th Amendment.

resentative; and until such enumeration shall be made, the State of New Hampshire shall be entitled to choose three, Massachusetts eight, Rhode Island and Providence Plantations one, Connecticut five, New York six, New Jersey four, Pennsylvania eight, Delaware one, Maryland six, Virginia ten, North Carolina five, South Carolina five, and Georgia three.

4. When vacancies happen in the representation from any State, the executive authority thereof shall issue writs of election to fill such vacancies.

5. The House of Representatives shall choose their speaker and other officers; and shall have the sole power of impeachment.

SECTION 3. 1. The Senate of the United States shall be composed of two senators from each State, *chosen by the legislature thereof,*[1] for six years; and each senator shall have one vote.

2. Immediately after they shall be assembled in consequence of the first election, they shall be divided as equally as may be into three classes. The seats of the senators of the first class shall be vacated at the expiration of the second year, of the second class at the expiration of the fourth year, and of the third class at the expiration of the sixth year, so that one third may be chosen every second year; and if vacancies happen by resignation, or otherwise, during the recess of the legislature of any State, the executive thereof may make temporary appointments until the next meeting of the legislature, which shall then fill such vacancies.[1]

3. No person shall be a senator who shall not have attained to the age of thirty years, and been nine years a citizen of the United States, and who shall not, when elected, be an inhabitant of that State for which he shall be chosen.

4. The Vice President of the United States shall be President of the Senate, but shall have no vote, unless they be equally divided.

5. The Senate shall choose their other officers, and also a President *pro tempore,* in the absence of the Vice President, or when he shall exercise the office of the President of the United States.

[1] See the 17th Amendment.

6. The Senate shall have the sole power to try all impeachments. When sitting for that purpose, they shall be on oath or affirmation. When the President of the United States is tried, the chief justice shall preside: and no person shall be convicted without the concurrence of two thirds of the members present.

7. Judgment in cases of impeachment shall not extend further than to removal from office, and disqualifications to hold and enjoy any office of honor, trust or profit under the United States: but the party convicted shall nevertheless be liable and subject to indictment, trial, judgment and punishment, according to law.

SECTION 4. 1. The times, places, and manner of holding elections for senators and representatives, shall be prescribed in each State by the legislature thereof; but the Congress may at any time by law make or alter such regulations, except as to the places of choosing senators.

2. The Congress shall assemble at least once in every year, and such meeting shall be on the first Monday in December, unless they shall by law appoint a different day.

SECTION 5. 1. Each House shall be the judge of the elections, returns and qualifications of its own members, and a majority of each shall constitute a quorum to do business; but a smaller number may adjourn from day to day, and may be authorized to compel the attendance of absent members, in such manner, and under such penalties as each House may provide.

2. Each House may determine the rules of its proceedings, punish its members for disorderly behavior, and, with the concurrence of two thirds, expel a member.

3. Each House shall keep a journal of its proceedings, and from time to time publish the same, excepting such parts as may in their judgment require secrecy; and the yeas and nays of the members of either House on any question shall, at the desire of one fifth of those present, be entered on the journal.

4. Neither House, during the session of Congress, shall, without the consent of the other, adjourn for more than three days, nor to any other place than that in which the two Houses shall be sitting.

SECTION 6. 1. The senators and representatives shall receive a compensation for their services, to be ascertained by law, and paid out of the Treasury of the United States. They shall in all cases, except treason, felony, and breach of the peace, be privileged from arrest during their attendance at the session of their respective Houses, and in going to and returning from the same; and for any speech or debate in either House, they shall not be questioned in any other place.

2. No senator or representative shall, during the time for which he was elected, be appointed to any civil office under the authority of the United States, which shall have been created, or the emoluments whereof shall have been increased during such time; and no person holding any office under the United States shall be a member of either House during his continuance in office.

SECTION 7. 1. All bills for raising revenue shall originate in the House of Representatives; but the Senate may propose or concur with amendments as on other bills.

2. Every bill which shall have passed the House of Representatives and the Senate, shall, before it becomes a law, be presented to the President of the United States; if he approves he shall sign it, but if not he shall return it, with his objections to that House in which it shall have originated, who shall enter the objections at large on their journal, and proceed to reconsider it. If after such reconsideration two thirds of that House shall agree to pass the bill, it shall be sent, together with the objections, to the other House, by which it shall likewise be reconsidered, and if approved by two thirds of that House, it shall become a law. But in all such cases the votes of both Houses shall be determined by yeas and nays, and the names of the persons voting for and against the bill shall be entered on the journal of each House respectively. If any bill shall not be returned by the President within ten days (Sundays excepted) after it shall have been presented to him, the same shall be a law, in like manner as if he had signed it, unless the Congress by their adjournment prevent its return, in which case it shall not be a law.

3. Every order, resolution, or vote to which the concurrence of the Senate and the House of Representatives may be necessary

(except on a question of adjournment) shall be presented to the President of the United States; and before the same shall take effect, shall be approved by him, or being disapproved by him, shall be repassed by two thirds of the Senate and House of Representatives, according to the rules and limitations prescribed in the case of a bill.

SECTION 8. The Congress shall have the power

1. To lay and collect taxes, duties, imposts, and excises, to pay the debts and provide for the common defense and general welfare of the United States; but all duties, imposts, and excises shall be uniform throughout the United States;

2. To borrow money on the credit of the United States;

3. To regulate commerce with foreign nations, and among the several States, and with the Indian tribes;

4. To establish a uniform rule of naturalization, and uniform laws on the subject of bankruptcies throughout the United States;

5. To coin money, regulate the value thereof, and of foreign coin, and fix the standard of weights and measures;

6. To provide for the punishment of counterfeiting the securities and current coin of the United States;

7. To establish post offices and post roads;

8. To promote the progress of science and useful arts, by securing for limited times to authors and inventors the exclusive right to their respective writings and discoveries;

9. To constitute tribunals inferior to the Supreme Court;

10. To define and punish piracies and felonies committed on the high seas, and offenses against the law of nations;

11. To declare war, grant letters of marque and reprisal, and make rules concerning captures on land and water;

12. To raise and support armies, but no appropriation of money to that use shall be for a longer term than two years;

13. To provide and maintain a navy;

14. To make rules for the government and regulation of the land and naval forces;

15. To provide for calling forth the militia to execute the laws of the Union, suppress insurrections and repel invasions;

16. To provide for organizing, arming, and disciplining the militia, and for governing such part of them as may be employed in the service of the United States, reserving to the States respectively the appointment of the officers, and the authority of training the militia according to the discipline prescribed by Congress;

17. To exercise exclusive legislation in all cases whatsoever, over such district (not exceeding ten miles square) as may, by cession of particular States, and the acceptance of Congress, become the seat of the government of the United States, and to exercise like authority over all places purchased by the consent of the legislature of the State in which the same shall be, for the erection of forts, magazines, arsenals, dockyards, and other needful buildings: and

18. To make all laws which shall be necessary and proper for carrying into execution the foregoing powers, and all other powers vested by this Constitution in the government of the United States, or in any department or officer thereof.

SECTION 9. 1. The migration or importation of such persons as any of the States now existing shall think proper to admit, shall not be prohibited by the Congress prior to the year one thousand eight hundred and eight, but a tax or duty may be imposed on such importation, not exceeding ten dollars for each person.

2. The privilege of the writ of *habeas corpus* shall not be suspended, unless when in cases of rebellion or invasion the public safety may require it.

3. No bill of attainder or *ex post facto* law shall be passed.

4. No capitation, or other direct, tax shall be laid, unless in proportion to the census or enumeration hereinbefore directed to be taken.[1]

5. No tax or duty shall be laid on articles exported from any State.

[1] See the 16th Amendment.

6. No preference shall be given by any regulation of commerce or revenue to the ports of one State over those of another: nor shall vessels bound to, or from, one State be obliged to enter, clear, or pay duties in another.

7. No money shall be drawn from the Treasury, but in consequence of appropriations made by law; and a regular statement and account of the receipts and expenditures of all public money shall be published from time to time.

8. No title of nobility shall be granted by the United States: and no person holding any office of profit or trust under them, shall, without the consent of the Congress, accept of any present, emolument, office, or title, of any kind whatever, from any king, prince, or foreign State.

SECTION 10. 1. No State shall enter into any treaty; alliance, or confederation; grant letters of marque and reprisal; coin money; emit bills of credit; make anything but gold and silver coin a tender in payment of debts; pass any bill of attainder, *ex post facto* law, or law impairing the obligation of contracts, or grant any title of nobility.

2. No State shall, without the consent of the Congress, lay any imposts or duties on imports or exports, except what may be absolutely necessary for executing its inspection laws: and the net produce of all duties and imposts laid by any State on imports or exports, shall be for the use of the Treasury of the United States; and all such laws shall be subject to the revision and control of the Congress.

3. No State shall, without the consent of the Congress, lay any duty of tonnage, keep troops, or ships of war in time of peace, enter into any agreement or compact with another State, or with a foreign power, or engage in war, unless actually invaded, or in such imminent danger as will not admit of delay.

ARTICLE II

SECTION 1. 1. The executive power shall be vested in a President of the United States of America. He shall hold his office during the term of four years, and, together with the Vice President, chosen for the same term, be elected as follows:

2. Each State shall appoint, in such manner as the legislature thereof may direct, a number of electors, equal to the whole number of senators and representatives to which the State may be entitled in the Congress: but no senator or representative, or person holding an office of trust or profit under the United States, shall be appointed an elector.

The electors shall meet in their respective States, and vote by ballot for two persons, of whom one at least shall not be an inhabitant of the same State with themselves. And they shall make a list of all the persons voted for, and of the number of votes for each; which list they shall sign and certify, and transmit sealed to the seat of the government of the United States, directed to the president of the Senate. The president of the Senate shall, in the presence of the Senate and House of Representatives, open all the certificates, and the votes shall then be counted. The person having the greatest number of votes shall be the President, if such number be a majority of the whole number of electors appointed; and if there be more than one who have such majority, and have an equal number of votes, then the House of Representatives shall immediately choose by ballot one of them for President; and if no person have a majority, then from the five highest on the list the said House shall in like manner choose the President. But in choosing the President, the votes shall be taken by States, the representation from each State having one vote; a quorum for this purpose shall consist of a member or members from two thirds of the States, and a majority of all the States shall be necessary to a choice. In every case, after the choice of the President, the person having the greatest number of votes of the electors shall be the Vice President. But if there should remain two or more who have equal votes, the Senate shall choose from them by ballot the Vice President.[1]

3. The Congress may determine the time of choosing the electors, and the day on which they shall give their votes; which day shall be the same throughout the United States.

4. No person except a natural born citizen, or a citizen of the United States, at the time of the adoption of this Constitution,

[1] Superseded by the 12th Amendment.

shall be eligible to the office of President; neither shall any person be eligible to that office who shall not have attained to the age of thirty-five years, and been fourteen years a resident within the United States.

5. In case of the removal of the President from office, or of his death, resignation, or inability to discharge the powers and duties of the said office, the same shall devolve on the Vice President, and the Congress may by law provide for the case of removal, death, resignation, or inability, both of the President and Vice President, declaring what officer shall then act as President, and such officer shall act accordingly, until the disability be removed, or a President shall be elected.

6. The President shall, at stated times, receive for his services a compensation, which shall neither be increased nor diminished during the period for which he shall have been elected, and he shall not receive within that period any other emolument from the United States, or any of them.

7. Before he enter on the execution of his office, he shall take the following oath or affirmation:—"I do solemnly swear (or affirm) that I will faithfully execute the office of President of the United States, and will to the best of my ability, preserve, protect and defend the Constitution of the United States."

SECTION 2. 1. The President shall be commander in chief of the army and navy of the United States, and of the militia of the several States, when called into the actual service of the United States; he may require the opinion, in writing, of the principal officer in each of the executive departments, upon any subject relating to the duties of their respective offices, and he shall have power to grant reprieves and pardons for offenses against the United States, except in cases of impeachment.

2. He shall have power, by and with the advice and consent of the Senate, to make treaties, provided two thirds of the senators present concur; and he shall nominate, and by and with the advice and consent of the Senate, shall appoint ambassadors, other public ministers and consuls, judges of the Supreme Court, and all other officers of the United States, whose appointments are not herein otherwise provided for, and which shall be established by law: but the Congress may by law vest the appointment of

such inferior officers, as they think proper, in the President alone, in the courts of law, or in the heads of departments.

3. The President shall have power to fill up all vacancies that may happen during the recess of the Senate, by granting commissions which shall expire at the end of their next session.

SECTION 3. He shall from time to time give to the Congress information of the state of the Union, and recommend to their consideration such measures as he shall judge necessary and expedient; he may, on extraordinary occasions, convene both Houses, or either of them, and in case of disagreement between them with respect to the time of adjournment, he may adjourn them to such time as he shall think proper; he shall receive ambassadors and other public ministers; he shall take care that the laws be faithfully executed, and shall commission all the officers of the United States.

SECTION 4. The President, Vice President, and all civil officers of the United States, shall be removed from office on impeachment for, and conviction of, treason, bribery, or other high crimes and misdemeanors.

ARTICLE III

SECTION 1. The judicial power of the United States shall be vested in one Supreme Court, and in such inferior courts as the Congress may from time to time ordain and establish. The judges, both of the Supreme and inferior courts, shall hold their offices during good behavior, and shall, at stated times, receive for their services, a compensation, which shall not be diminished during their continuance in office.

SECTION 2. 1. The judicial power shall extend to all cases, in law and equity, arising under this Constitution, the laws of the United States, and treaties made, or which shall be made, under their authority;—to all cases affecting ambassadors, other public ministers and consuls;—to all cases of admiralty and maritime jurisdiction;—to controversies to which the United States shall be a party;—to controversies between two or more States;—between a State and citizens of another State; [1]—between citizens of different States;—between citizens of the same State claiming

[1] See the 11th Amendment.

lands under grants of different States, and between a State, or the citizens thereof, and foreign States, citizens or subjects.

2. In all cases affecting ambassadors, other public ministers and consuls, and those in which a State shall be party, the Supreme Court shall have original jurisdiction. In all the other cases before mentioned, the Supreme Court shall have appellate jurisdiction, both as to law and to fact, with such exceptions, and under such regulations as the Congress shall make.

3. The trial of all crimes, except in cases of impeachment, shall be by jury; and such trial shall be held in the State where the said crimes shall have been committed; but when not committed within any State, the trial shall be at such place or places as the Congress may by law have directed.

SECTION 3. 1. Treason against the United States shall consist only in levying war against them, or in adhering to their enemies, giving them aid and comfort. No person shall be convicted of treason unless on the testimony of two witnesses to the same overt act, or on confession in open court.

2. The Congress shall have power to declare the punishment of treason, but no attainder of treason shall work corruption of blood, or forfeiture except during the life of the person attained.

ARTICLE IV

SECTION 1. Full faith and credit shall be given in each State to the public acts, records, and judicial proceedings of every other State. And the Congress may by general laws prescribe the manner in which such acts, records and proceedings shall be proved, and the effect thereof.

SECTION 2. 1. The citizens of each State shall be entitled to all privileges and immunities of citizens in the several States.[1]

2. A person charged in any State with treason, felony, or other crime, who shall flee from justice, and be found in another State, shall on demand of the executive authority of the State from which he fled, be delivered up to be removed to the State having jurisdiction of the crime.

[1] See the 14th Amendment, Sec. 1.

3. No person held to service or labor in one State under the laws thereof, escaping into another, shall, in consequence of any law or regulation therein, be discharged from such service or labor, but shall be delivered up on claim of the party to whom such service or labor may be due.[2]

SECTION 3. 1. New States may be admitted by the Congress into this Union; but no new State shall be formed or erected within the jurisdiction of any other State; nor any State be formed by the junction of two or more States, or parts of States, without the consent of the legislatures of the States concerned as well as of the Congress.

2. The Congress shall have power to dispose of and make all needful rules and regulations respecting the territory or other property belonging to the United States; and nothing in this Constitution shall be so construed as to prejudice any claims of the United States, or of any particular State.

SECTION 4. The United States shall guarantee to every State in this Union a republican form of government, and shall protect each of them against invasion; and on application of the legislature, or of the executive (when the legislature cannot be convened) against domestic violence.

ARTICLE V

The Congress, whenever two thirds of both Houses shall deem it necessary, shall propose amendments to this Constitution, or, on the application of the legislatures of two thirds of the several States, shall call a convention for proposing amendments, which in either case, shall be valid to all intents and purposes, as part of this Constitution when ratified by the legislatures of three fourths of the several States, or by conventions in three fourths thereof, as the one or the other mode of ratification may be proposed by the Congress; Provided that no amendment which may be made prior to the year one thousand eight hundred and eight shall in any manner affect the first and fourth clauses in the ninth section of the first article; and that no State, without its consent, shall be deprived of its equal suffrage in the Senate.

[2] See the 13th Amendment.

ARTICLE VI

1. All debts contracted and engagements entered into, before the adoption of this Constitution, shall be as valid against the United States under this Constitution, as under the Confederation.[1]

2. This Constitution, and the laws of the United States which shall be made in pursuance thereof; and all treaties made, or which shall be made, under the authority of the United States, shall be the supreme law of the land; and the Judges in every State shall be bound thereby, anything in the Constitution or laws of any State to the contrary notwithstanding.

3. The senators and representatives before mentioned, and the members of the several State legislatures, and all executive and judicial officers, both of the United States and of the several States, shall be bound by oath or affirmation to support this Constitution; but no religious test shall ever be required as a qualification to any office or public trust under the United States.

ARTICLE VII

The ratification of the conventions of nine States shall be sufficient for the establishment of this Constitution between the States so ratifying the same.

Done in Convention by the unanimous consent of the States present the seventeenth day of September in the year of our Lord one thousand seven hundred and eighty-seven, and of the independence of the United States of America the twelfth. In witness whereof we have hereunto subscribed our names.

[Names omitted]

———————

Articles in addition to, and amendment of, the Constitution of the United States of America, proposed by Congress, and ratified by the legislatures of the several States pursuant to the fifth article of the original Constitution.

[1] See the 14th Amendment, Sec. 4.

AMENDMENTS

First Ten Amendments passed by Congress Sept. 25, 1789.
Ratified by three-fourths of the States December 15, 1791.

ARTICLE I

Congress shall make no law respecting an establishment of religion, or prohibiting the free exercise thereof; or abridging the freedom of speech, or of the press; or the right of the people peaceably to assemble, and to petition the government for a redress of grievances.

ARTICLE II

A well regulated militia, being necessary to the security of a free State, the right of the people to keep and bear arms, shall not be infringed.

ARTICLE III

No soldier shall, in time of peace be quartered in any house, without the consent of the owner, nor in time of war, but in a manner to be prescribed by law.

ARTICLE IV

The right of the people to be secure in their persons, houses, papers, and effects, against unreasonable searches and seizures, shall not be violated, and no warrants shall issue, but upon probable cause, supported by oath or affirmation, and particularly describing the place to be searched, and the persons or things to be seized.

ARTICLE V

No person shall be held to answer for a capital, or otherwise infamous crime, unless on a presentment or indictment of a grand jury, except in cases arising in the land or naval forces, or in the militia, when in actual service in time of war or public danger; nor shall any person be subject for the same offense to be twice put in jeopardy of life or limb; nor shall be compelled in any criminal case to be a witness against himself, nor be deprived of life, liberty, or property, without due process of law; nor shall private property be taken for public use without just compensation.

ARTICLE VI

In all criminal prosecutions, the accused shall enjoy the right to a speedy and public trial, by an impartial jury of the State and district wherein the crime shall have been committed, which district shall have been previously ascertained by law, and to be informed of the nature and cause of the accusation; to be confronted with the witnesses against him; to have compulsory process for obtaining witnesses in his favor, and to have the assistance of counsel for his defense.

ARTICLE VII

In suits at common law, where the value in controversy shall exceed twenty dollars, the right of trial by jury shall be preserved, and no fact tried by a jury shall be otherwise reëxamined in any court of the United States, than according to the rules of the common law.

ARTICLE VIII

Excessive bail shall not be required, nor excessive fines imposed, nor cruel and unusual punishments inflicted.

ARTICLE IX

The enumeration in the Constitution of certain rights shall not be construed to deny or disparage others retained by the people.

ARTICLE X

The powers not delegated to the United States by the Constitution, nor prohibited by it to the States, are reserved to the States respectively, or to the people.

ARTICLE XI

Passed by Congress March 5, 1794. Ratified January 8, 1798.

The judicial power of the United States shall not be construed to extend to any suit in law or equity, commenced or prosecuted against one of the United States by citizens of another State, or by citizens or subjects of any foreign State.

ARTICLE XII

Passed by Congress December 12, 1803. Ratified September 25, 1804.

The electors shall meet in their respective States, and vote by ballot for President and Vice President, one of whom, at least, shall not be an inhabitant of the same State with themselves; they shall name in their ballots the person voted for as President, and in distinct ballots, the person voted for as Vice President, and they shall make distinct lists of all persons voted for as President and of all persons voted for as Vice President, and of the number of votes for each, which lists they shall sign and certify, and transmit sealed to the seat of the government of the United States, directed to the President of the Senate;—The President of the Senate shall, in the presence of the Senate and House of Representatives, open all the certificates and the votes shall then be counted;—The person having the greatest number of votes for President, shall be the President, if such number be a majority of the whole number of electors appointed; and if no person have such majority, then from the persons having the highest numbers not exceeding three on the list of those voted for as President, the House of Representatives shall choose immediately, by ballot, the President. But in choosing the President, the votes shall be taken by States, the representation from each State having one vote; a quorum for this purpose shall consist of a member or members from two thirds of the States, and a majority of all the States shall be necessary to a choice. And if the House of Representatives shall not choose a President whenever the right of choice shall devolve upon them, before the fourth day of March next following, then the Vice President shall act as President, as in the case of the death or other constitutional disability of the President. The person having the greatest number of votes as Vice President shall be the Vice President, if such number be a majority of the whole number of electors appointed, and if no person have a majority, then from the two highest numbers on the list, the Senate shall choose the Vice President; a quorum for the purpose shall consist of two thirds of the whole number of Senators, and a majority of the whole number shall be necessary to a choice. But no person constitutionally ineligible to the office of President shall be eligible to that of Vice President of the United States.

ARTICLE XIII

Passed by Congress February 1, 1865. Ratified December 18, 1865.

SECTION 1. Neither slavery nor involuntary servitude, except as punishment for crime whereof the party shall have been duly convicted, shall exist within the United States, or any place subject to their jurisdiction.

SECTION 2. Congress shall have power to enforce this article by appropriate legislation.

ARTICLE XIV

Passed by Congress June 16, 1866. Ratified July 23, 1868.

SECTION 1. All persons born or naturalized in the United States, and subject to the jurisdiction thereof, are citizens of the United States and of the State wherein they reside. No State shall make or enforce any law which shall abridge the privileges or immunities of citizens of the United States; nor shall any State deprive any person of life, liberty, or property, without due process of law; nor deny to any person within its jurisdiction the equal protection of the laws.

SECTION 2. Representatives shall be opportioned among the several States according to their respective numbers, counting the whole number of persons in each State, excluding Indians not taxed. But when the right to vote at any election for the choice of electors for President and Vice President of the United States, representatives in Congress, the executive and judicial officers of a State, or the members of the legislature thereof, is denied to any of the male inhabitants of such State, being twenty-one years of age, and citizens of the United States, or in any way abridged, except for participation in rebellion, or other crime, the basis of representation therein shall be reduced in the proportion which the number of such male citizens shall bear to the whole number of male citizens twenty-one years of age in such State.

SECTION 3. No person shall be a senator or representative in Congress, or elector of President and Vice President, or hold any office, civil or military, under the United States, or under any State, who having previously taken an oath, as a member of Congress, or as an officer of the United States, or as a member of any

State legislature, or as an executive or judicial officer of any State, to support the Constitution of the United States, shall have engaged in insurrection or rebellion against the same, or given aid or comfort to the enemies thereof. But Congress may by a vote of two thirds of each House, remove such disability.

SECTION 4.   The validity of the public debt of the United States, authorized by law, including debts incurred for payment of pensions and bounties for services in suppressing insurrection or rebellion, shall not be questioned. But neither the United States nor any State shall assume or pay any debt or obligation incurred in aid of insurrection or rebellion against the United States, or any claim for the loss or emancipation of any slave; but all such debts, obligations, and claims shall be held illegal and void.

SECTION 5.   The Congress shall have power to enforce, by appropriate legislation, the provisions of this article.

ARTICLE XV

Passed by Congress February 27, 1869. Ratified March 30, 1870.

SECTION 1.   The right of citizens of the United States to vote shall not be denied or abridged by the United States or by any State on account of race, color, or previous condition of servitude.

SECTION 2.   The Congress shall have power to enforce this article by appropriate legislation.

ARTICLE XVI

Passed by Congress July 12, 1909. Ratified February 25, 1913.

The Congress shall have power to lay and collect taxes on incomes, from whatever source derived, without apportionment among the several States, and without regard to any census or enumeration.

ARTICLE XVII

Passed by Congress May 16, 1912. Ratified May 31, 1913.

The Senate of the United States shall be composed of two senators from each state, elected by the people thereof, for six years; and each senator shall have one vote. The electors in each State shall have the qualifications requisite for electors of the most numerous branch of the State legislature.

When vacancies happen in the representation of any State in the Senate, the executive authority of such State shall issue writs of election to fill such vacancies: *Provided,* That the legislature of any State may empower the executive thereof to make temporary appointments until the people fill the vacancies by election as the legislature may direct.

This amendment shall not be so construed as to affect the election or term of any senator chosen before it becomes valid as part of the Constitution.

ARTICLE XVIII

Passed by Congress December 17, 1917. Ratified January 29, 1919.

After one year from the ratification of this article, the manufacture, sale, or transportation of intoxicating liquors within, the importation thereof into, or the exportation thereof from the United States and all territory subject to the jurisdiction thereof for beverage purposes is hereby prohibited.

The Congress and the several States shall have concurrent power to enforce this article by appropriate legislation.

This article shall be inoperative unless it shall have been ratified as an amendment to the Constitution by the legislatures of the several States, as provided in the Constitution, within seven years from the date of the submission hereof to the states by Congress.

ARTICLE XIX

Passed by Congress June 5, 1919. Ratified August 26, 1920.

The right of citizens of the United States to vote shall not be denied or abridged by the United States or by any State on account of sex.

The Congress shall have power by appropriate legislation to enforce the provisions of this article.

ARTICLE XX

Passed by Congress March 3, 1932. Ratified January 23, 1933.

SECTION 1. The terms of the President and Vice President shall end at noon on the 20th day of January, and the terms of

Senators and Representatives at noon on the 3d day of January, of the years in which such terms would have ended if this article had not been ratified; and the terms of their successors shall then begin.

SECTION 2.   The Congress shall assemble at least once in every year, and such meeting shall begin at noon on the 3d day of January, unless they shall by law appoint a different day.

SECTION 3.   If, at the time fixed for the beginning of the term of the President, the President-elect shall have died, the Vice President-elect shall become President. If a President shall not have been chosen before the time fixed for the beginning of his term, or if the President-elect shall have failed to qualify, then the Vice President-elect shall act as President until a President shall have qualified; and the Congress may by law provide for the case wherein neither a President-elect nor a Vice President-elect shall have qualified, declaring who shall then act as President, or the manner in which one who is to act shall be selected, and such person shall act accordingly until a President or Vice President shall have qualified.

SECTION 4.   The Congress may by law provide for the case of the death of any of the persons from whom the House of Representatives may choose a President whenever the right of choice shall have devolved upon them, and for the case of the death of any of the persons from whom the Senate may choose a Vice President whenever the right of choice shall have devolved upon them.

SECTION 5.   Sections 1 and 2 shall take effect on the 15th day of October following the ratification of this article.

SECTION 6.   This article shall be inoperative unless it shall have been ratified as an amendment to the Constitution by the legislatures of three-fourths of the several States within seven years from the date of its submission.

ARTICLE XXI

Passed by Congress February 20, 1933. Ratified December 5, 1933.

SECTION 1.   The Eighteenth Article of amendment to the Constitution of the United States is hereby repealed.

SECTION 2. The transportation or importation into any State, Territory, or possession of the United States for delivery or use therein of intoxicating liquors in violation of the laws thereof, is hereby prohibited.

SECTION 3. This article shall be inoperative unless it shall have been ratified as an amendment to the Constitution by conventions in the several States, as provided in the Constitution, within seven years from the date of the submission thereof to the States by the Congress.

ARTICLE XXII

Passed by Congress March 24, 1947. Ratified February 26, 1951.

SECTION 1. No person shall be elected to the office of the President more than twice, and no person who has held the office of President, or acted as President, for more than two years of a term to which some other person was elected President shall be elected to the office of President more than once. But this article shall not apply to any person holding the office of President when this article was proposed by the Congress, and shall not prevent any person who may be holding the office of President, or acting as President, during the term within which this article becomes operative from holding the office of President or acting as President during the remainder of such term.

SECTION 2. This article shall be inoperative unless it shall have been ratified as an amendment to the Constitution by the legislatures of three-fourths of the several States within seven years from the date of its submission of the States by the Congress.

ARTICLE XXIII

Passed by Congress June 16, 1960. Ratified March 29, 1961.

SECTION 1. The District constituting the seat of Government of the United States shall appoint in such manner as the Congress may direct:

A number of electors of President and Vice President equal to the whole number of Senators and Representatives in Congress to which the District would be entitled if it were a State, but in no event more than the least populous state; they shall be in addition to those appointed by the states, but they shall be considered, for the purposes of the election of President and Vice President, to be electors appointed by a state; and they shall meet in the District and perform such duties as provided by the twelfth article of amendment.

SECTION 2. The Congress shall have the power to enforce this article by appropriate legislation.

ARTICLE XXIV

Passed by Congress Sept. 14, 1962. Ratified Jan. 23, 1964.

SECTION 1. The right of citizens of the United States to vote in any primary or other election for President or Vice President, for electors for President or Vice President, or for Senator or Representative in Congress, shall not be denied or abridged by the United States or any State by reason of failure to pay any poll tax or other tax.

SECTION 2. The Congress shall have the power to enforce this article by appropriate legislation.

SELECTED REFERENCES

Chapter 1

Hyneman, C. S. *The Study of Politics: The Present State of American Political Science,* 1959, Univ. of Illinois Press.

Young, R., ed. *Approaches to the Study of Politics,* 1958, Northwestern Univ. Press.

Chapter 2

Dimock & Dimock. *American Government in Action,* 1951, Rinehart.

Hall, Sikes, Stoner, & Wormuth. *American National Government,* 1949, Harper.

MacIver, R. M. *The Web of Government,* 1947, Macmillan.

Riemer, N. *Problems of American Government,* 1952, McGraw-Hill.

Smith & Zurcher, *Dictionary of American Politics,* 1955, Barnes & Noble.

Wilson, F. G. *The American Political Mind,* 1949, McGraw-Hill.

Chapter 3

Boorstin, D. J. *The Americans: The Colonial Experience,* 1958, Random House.

MacDonald, Webb, Lewis, & Strauss. *Outside Readings in American Government,* 1952, Crowell.

Munro, W. B. *The Government of the United States,* 1946, Macmillan.

Swarthout & Bartley. *Principles and Problems of American National Government,* 1955, Oxford Univ. Press.

Chapter 4

Adams, R. G. *Political Ideas of the American Revolution,* 1958, Barnes & Noble.

Burnett, E. C. *The Continental Congress,* 1941, Macmillan.

Chitwood, O. P. *A History of Colonial America,* 1948, Harper.

Greene, E. B. *The Revolutionary Generation, 1763–1790,* 1943, Macmillan.

Hamilton, Madison, & Jay. *The Federalist* (ed. by M. Beloff), 1948, Macmillan.

Jensen, M. *The Articles of Confederation,* 1948, Univ. of Wisconsin Press.

———. *New Nation,* 1950, Knopf.

MacDonald, Webb, Lewis, & Strauss. *Outside Readings in American Government,* 1952, Crowell.

McLaughlin, A. C. *A Constitutional History of the United States,* 1935, Appleton-Century.

Munro, W. B. *The Government of the United States,* 1946, Macmillan.

Smelser, M. *An Outline of American Colonial and Revolutionary History,* 1950, Barnes & Noble.

Smith, J. H. *Appeals to the Privy Council from the American Plantations,* 1950, Columbia Univ. Press.

Chapter 5

Corwin, E. S. *The Constitution and What It Means Today,* 1954, Princeton Univ. Press.

Dimock & Dimock. *American Government in Action,* 1951, Rinehart.

Fenn, P. T. *The Development of the Constitution,* 1948, Appleton-Century.

Finer, H. *The Theory and Practice of Modern Government,* 1949, Holt.

Kelly & Harbison. *The American Constitution: Its Origins and Development,* 1955, Norton.

Munro, W. B. *The Government of the United States,* 1946, Macmillan.

MacDonald, Webb, Lewis, & Strauss. *Outside Readings in American Government,* 1952, Crowell.

Smelser, M. *An Outline of American Colonial and Revolutionary History,* 1950, Barnes & Noble.

Swarthout & Bartley. *Principles and Problems of American National Government,* 1955, Oxford Univ. Press.

Swisher, C. B. *The Growth of Constitutional Power in the United States,* 1946, Univ. of Chicago Press.

Van Doren, C. *The Great Rehearsal,* 1948, Viking.
White, L. D. *The Federalists,* 1948, Macmillan.

Chapter 6

Brownlow, L. *The President and the Presidency,* 1953, Chicago Univ. Press.
Corwin, E. S. *The President: Office and Powers,* 1948, New York Univ. Press.
Finer, H. *The Presidency: Crisis and Regeneration,* 1960, Univ. of Chicago Press.
Hall, Sikes, Stoner, & Wormuth. *American National Government: Law and Practice,* 1949, Harper.
Herring, P. *Presidential Leadership,* 1940, Rinehart.
Laski, H. *The American Presidency,* 1958, Grosset.
MacDonald, Webb, Lewis, & Strauss. *Outside Readings in American Government,* 1952, Crowell.
Munro, W. B. *Government of the United States,* 1946, Macmillan.
Neustadt, R. *Presidential Power: The Politics of Leadership,* 1960, Wiley.
Patterson, C. P. *Presidential Government of the United States,* 1947, Univ. of North Carolina Press.
Riemer, N. *Problems of American Government,* 1952, McGraw-Hill.
Rossiter, C. *The American Presidency,* 1960, New American Library.
Swarthout & Bartley. *Principles and Problems of American National Government,* 1955, Oxford Univ. Press.
Tugwell, R. G. *Enlargement of the Presidency,* 1960, Doubleday.

Chapter 7

Appleby, P. H. *Policy and Administration,* 1949, Univ. of Alabama Press.
Fenno, R. *The President's Cabinet,* 1959, Harvard Univ. Press.
Graves, W. B. *Public Administration,* 1950, Heath.
Hobbs, E. H. *Behind the President,* 1954, Public Affairs Press.
The Hoover Commission Report, 1949, McGraw-Hill.
MacDonald, Webb, Lewis, & Strauss. *Outside Readings in American Government,* 1952, Crowell.

Munro, W. B. *The Government of the United States,* 1946, Macmillan.

Riemer, N. *Problems of American Government,* 1952, McGraw-Hill.

Swarthout & Bartley. *Principles and Problems of American National Government,* 1955, Oxford Univ. Press.

United States Government Organization Manual, published annually, U.S. Gov't Printing Office.

White, L. D. *Introduction to the Study of Public Administration,* 1955, Macmillan.

Chapter 8

Bernstein, M. H. *Regulating Business by Independent Commissions,* 1955, Princeton Univ. Press.

Cushman, R. E. *The Independent Regulatory Commissions,* 1941, Oxford Univ. Press.

MacDonald, Webb, Lewis, & Strauss. *Outside Readings in American Government,* 1952, Crowell.

Munro, W. B. *The Government of the United States,* 1946, Macmillan.

Riemer, N. *Problems of American Government,* 1952, McGraw-Hill.

Schwartz, B. *The Professor and the Commissions,* 1959, Knopf.

Swarthout & Bartley. *Principles and Problems of American National Government,* 1955, Oxford Univ. Press.

Chapter 9

Emmerich, H. *Essays on Federal Reorganization,* 1950, Univ. of Alabama Press.

The Hoover Commission Report, 1949, McGraw-Hill.

Hyneman, C. S. *Bureaucracy in a Democracy,* 1950, Harper.

MacDonald, Webb, Lewis, & Strauss. *Outside Readings in American Government,* 1952, Crowell.

Millett, J. D. *Government and Public Administration,* 1959, McGraw-Hill.

Riemer, N. *Problems of American Government,* 1952, McGraw-Hill.

United States Government Organization Manual, published annually, U.S. Gov't Printing Office.

Swarthout & Bartley. *Principles and Problems of American National Government,* 1955, Oxford Univ. Press.

Waldo, D. *The Administrative State,* 1948, Ronald.

Chapter 10

Bernstein, M. H. *The Job of the Federal Executive,* 1958, Brookings.

Carpenter, W. S. *The Unfinished Business of Civil Service Reform,* 1952, Princeton Univ. Press.

Hall, Sikes, Stoner, & Wormuth. *American National Government,* 1949, Harper.

The Hoover Commission Report, 1949, McGraw-Hill.

MacDonald, Webb, Lewis, & Strauss. *Outside Readings in American Government,* 1952, Crowell.

Sayre, Wallace S., ed. *The Federal Government Service,* 1955, American Assembly.

Stahl, O. G. *Public Personnel Administration,* 1956, Harper.

Swarthout & Bartley. *Principles and Problems of American National Government,* 1955, Oxford Univ. Press.

United States Government Organization Manual, published annually, U.S. Gov't Printing Office.

Van Riper, P. *History of the United States Civil Service,* 1958, Row.

Chapter 11

Acheson, D. *A Citizen Looks at Congress,* 1957, Harper.

Bailey, S. K. *Congress Makes a Law,* 1950, Columbia Univ. Press.

Burns, J. M. *Congress on Trial,* 1949, Harper.

Galloway, G. B. *The Legislative Process in Congress,* 1953, Crowell.

Gross, B. M. *The Legislative Struggle,* 1953, McGraw-Hill.

Kefauver & Levin. *A Twentieth-Century Congress,* 1947, Essential Books.

MacDonald, Webb, Lewis, & Strauss. *Outside Readings in American Government,* 1952, Crowell.

Riddick, F. M. *The United States Congress: Organization and Procedure,* 1949, National Capital Pubs.

Riemer, N. *Problems of American Government,* 1952, McGraw-Hill.

Swarthout & Bartley. *Principles and Problems of American National Government,* 1955, Oxford Univ. Press.

Truman, D. B. *The Congressional Party,* 1959, Wiley.

Voorhis, H. J. *Confessions of a Congressman,* 1947, Doubleday.

Walker, H. *The Legislative Process: Lawmaking in the United States,* 1948, Donald.

White, W. S. *Citadel: The Story of the U.S. Senate,* 1957, Harper.

Wilson, Woodrow. *Congressional Government,* 1958, Smith, Peter.

Chapter 12

Dahl, R. A. *Congress and Foreign Policy,* 1950, Harcourt.

Drury, A. *Advise and Consent,* 1959, Doubleday.

Harris, J. P. *The Advise and Consent of the Senate,* 1953, Univ. of California Press.

Posey & Huegli. *Government for Americans,* 1953, Row.

Swarthout & Bartley. *Principles and Problems of American National Government,* 1955, Oxford Univ. Press.

Taylor, T. *The Grand Inquest,* 1955, Simon and Schuster.

Chapter 13

Cheever, D. S. *American Foreign Policy and the Separation of Powers,* 1952, Harvard Univ. Press.

Cushman, R. E. *Leading Constitutional Decisions,* 1955, Appleton-Century.

Frank, J. *Courts on Trial,* 1949, Princeton Univ. Press.

———. *Law and the Modern Mind,* 1949, Coward-McCann.

Freund, P. A. *On Understanding the Supreme Court,* 1949, Little, Brown.

Haines, C. G. *The Role of the Supreme Court in American Government,* 1944, Univ. of California Press.

Hall, Sikes, Stoner, & Wormuth. *American National Government: Law and Practice,* 1949, Harper.

McCloskey, R. *The American Supreme Court,* 1961, Univ. of Chicago Press.

MacDonald, Webb, Lewis, & Strauss. *Outside Readings in American Government,* 1952, Crowell.

Mason, A. T. *Brandeis: A Free Man's Life,* 1946, Viking.

———. *The Supreme Court from Taft to Warren,* 1958, Louisiana State Univ. Press.

Munro, W. B. *The Government of the United States,* 1946, Macmillan.

Pritchett, C. H. *The Roosevelt Court: A Study in Judicial Politics and Values, 1937–1947,* 1948, Macmillan.

Riemer, N. *Problems of American Government,* 1952, McGraw-Hill.

Sunderland, E. R. *Judicial Administration,* 1948, Callaghan.

Swarthout & Bartley. *Principles and Problems of American National Government,* 1955, Oxford Univ. Press.

Swisher, C. B. *The Supreme Court in Its Modern Role,* 1958, N.Y. Univ. Press.

Wendell, M. *The Relations Between Federal and State Courts,* 1949, Columbia Univ. Press.

Westin, A. F. *The Anatomy of a Constitutional Law Case,* 1958, Macmillan.

Chapter 14

Acheson, D. G., *Power and Diplomacy,* 1958, Harvard Univ. Press.

Bailey, T. A. *A Diplomatic History of the American People,* 1955, Appleton-Century.

Chamberlain & Snyder, eds. *American Foreign Policy,* 1948, Rinehart.

Harris, S. E. *The European Recovery Program,* 1948, Harvard Univ. Press.

Hoskins, H. L. *The Atlantic Pact,* 1949, Public Affairs Press.

Kennan, G. F. *American Diplomacy: 1900–1950,* 1950, Univ. of Chicago Press.

Lippmann, W. *The Cold War: A Study in United States Foreign Policy,* 1947, Harper.

London, K. *How Foreign Policy Is Made,* 1950, Van Nostrand.

MacDonald, Webb, Lewis, & Strauss. *Outside Readings in American Government,* 1952, Crowell.

Munro, W. B. *The Government of the United States,* 1946, Macmillan.

Riemer, N. *Problems of American Government,* 1952, McGraw-Hill.

Stuart, G. H. *The Department of State,* 1950, Macmillan.

Swarthout & Bartley. *Principles and Problems of American National Government,* 1955, Oxford Univ. Press.

Wright, Q. X., ed. *A Foreign Policy for the United States,* 1947, Univ. of Chicago Press.

Chapter 15

Anderson, W. *American Government,* 1953, Holt.

Barber, J. *Hawaii: Restless Rampart,* 1941, Bobbs-Merrill.

Department of State. *The United States and Non-self Governing Territories,* 1947, U. S. Gov't Printing Office.

Hilscher, H. H. *Alaska Now,* 1948, Little, Brown.

Konvitz, M. R. *The Alien and the Asiatic in American Law,* 1946, Cornell Univ. Press.

Munro, W. B. *The Government of the United States,* 1946, Macmillan.

Swarthout & Bartley. *Principles and Problems of American National Government,* 1955, Oxford Univ. Press.

United States National Resources Committee. *The Problem of a Changing Population,* 1938, U. S. Gov't Printing Office.

Vincent, J. C. *America's Future in the Pacific,* 1947, Rutgers Univ. Press.

Chapter 16

Anderson, W. *Federalism and Intergovernmental Relations,* 1953, Public Administration.

———. *The Nation and the States, Rivals or Partners,* 1955, Univ. of Minnesota Press.

Council of State Governments. *The Book of States,* published annually, The Council.

———. *Federal Grants-in-Aid,* 1949, The Council.

Finer, H. *The Theory and Practice of Modern Government,* 1949, Holt.

Graves, W. B. *American State Government,* 1953, Heath.

Leach & Suggs. *The Administration of Interstate Compacts,* 1959, Louisiana State Univ. Press.

MacDonald, A. F. *American State Government and Administration,* 1955, Crowell.

MacMahon, A. W., ed. *Federalism: Mature and Emergent,* 1955, Doubleday.

Munro, W. B. *The Government of the United States,* 1946, Macmillan.

Quattlebaum, C. A. *Federal Educational Activities and Educational Issues before Congress: A Report Prepared in the Legislative Reference Service of the Library of Congress,* 1951.

White, L. D. *The States and the Nation,* 1953, Louisiana State Univ. Press.

Chapter 17

Corwin, E. S. *Liberty Against Government,* 1948, Louisiana State Univ. Press.

Cushman, R. E. *Civil Liberties in the United States,* 1956, Cornell Univ. Press.

Emerson & Haber, eds. *Political and Civil Rights in the U.S.,* 1953, Dennis.

Gellhorn, W. *Individual Freedom and Governmental Restraints,* 1956, Louisiana State Univ. Press.

Gosnell, H. F. *Democracy, the Threshold of Freedom,* 1948, Ronald.

Hand, L. *The Bill of Rights,* 1958, Harvard Univ. Press.

Hartmann, E. G. *The Movement to Americanize the Immigrant,* 1948, Columbia Univ. Press.

Hocking, W. E. *Freedom of the Press: A Framework of Principle,* 1947, Univ. of Chicago Press.

Konvitz, M. R. *The Alien and the Asiatic in American Law,* 1946, Cornell Univ. Press.

Munro, W. B. *The Government of the United States,* 1946, Macmillan.

President's Committee on Civil Rights. *To Secure These Rights,* 1947, U.S. Gov't Printing Office.

Vose, C. E. *Caucasians Only,* 1959, Univ. of California Press.

Weintraub, R. G. *How to Secure These Rights,* 1949, Doubleday.

Woodward, C. Vann, *The Strange Career of Jim Crow,* 1958, Oxford Univ. Press.

Chapter 18

Allen, R. S., ed. *Our Sovereign State,* 1949, Vanguard.

Binkley, W. E. *American Political Parties,* 1945, Knopf.

Bone, H. A. *American Politics and the Party System,* 1955, McGraw-Hill.

Campbell, A., et al. *The American Voter,* 1960, Wiley.

Ehrmann, H. W., ed. *Interest Groups on Four Continents,* 1958, Univ. of Pittsburgh Press.

Heard, A. *The Costs of Democracy,* 1960, Univ. of North Carolina Press.

Hesseltine, W. B. *The Rise and Fall of the Third Parties,* 1948, Public Affairs Press.

Kent, F. R. *The Democratic Party,* 1928, Century.

Key, V. O. *Politics, Parties, and Pressure Groups,* 1952, Crowell.

MacDonald, Webb, Lewis, & Strauss. *Outside Readings in American Government,* 1952, Crowell.

McKean, D. D. *Party and Pressure Politics,* 1949, Houghton Mifflin.

Merriam & Gosnell. *The American Party System,* 1949, Macmillan.

Munro, W. B. *The Government of the United States,* 1953, Macmillan.

Myers, W. S. *The Republican Party,* 1931, Century.

Odegard & Helms. *American Politics,* 1947, Harper.

Ranney & Kendall. *Democracy and the American Party System,* 1956, Harcourt.

Riemer, N. *Problems of American Government,* 1952, McGraw-Hill.

Shannon, J. B. *Money and Politics,* 1959, Random House.

Chapter 19

Adrian, C. *State and Local Governments,* 1960, McGraw-Hill.

Bates, F. G., et al. *State Governments,* 1954, Harper.

Graves, W. B., et al. *American State Government and Administration,* 1949, Council of State Governments.

———. *American State Governments,* 1953, Heath.

———., ed. *Major Problems in State Constitutional Revision,* 1960, Public Administration Service.

Hall, Sikes, Stoner, & Wormuth. *American National Government: Law and Practice,* 1949, Harper.

MacDonald, A. F. *American State Government and Administration,* 1955, Crowell.

MacDonald, Webb, Lewis, & Strauss. *Outside Readings in American Government,* 1952, Crowell.

National Municipal League. *Model State Constitution,* 1948, The League.

O'Rourke & Campbell. *Constitution-Making in a Democracy,* 1943, Johns Hopkins.

Snider, C. F. *American State and Local Government,* 1950, Appleton-Century.

Chapter 20

Bates, F. G., et al. *State Governments,* 1954, Harper.

Council of State Governments. *Our State Legislature,* 1949, The Council.

Fordham, J., *The State Legislative Institution,* 1959, Univ. of Pennsylvania Press.

Graves, W. B. *American State Government,* 1953, Heath.

MacDonald, A. F. *American State Government and Administration,* 1955, Crowell.

MacDonald, Webb, Lewis, & Strauss. *Outside Readings in American Government,* 1952, Crowell.

Peel, R. V. *State Government Today,* 1948, Univ. of New Mexico Press.

Snider, C. F. *American State and Local Government,* 1950, Appleton-Century.

Weeks, O. D. *Research in the American Legislative Process,* 1947, Ohio State Univ. Press.

Zeller, B., ed. *American State Legislatures,* 1954, Crowell.

Chapter 21

Bates, F. G., et al. *State Governments,* 1954, Harper.

Bollens, J. C. *Administrative Reorganization in the States Since 1939,* 1947, Univ. of California Press.

Council of State Governments. *The Book of States,* published annually, The Council.

———. *Reorganizing State Governments,* 1950, The Council.

Graves, W. B. *American State Government,* 1953, Heath.

Lipton, L. *The American Governor: From Figurehead to Leader,* 1939, Univ. of Chicago Press.

MacDonald, A. F. *American State Government and Administration,* 1955, Crowell.

MacDonald, Webb, Lewis, & Strauss. *Outside Readings in American Government,* 1952, Crowell.

Ransone, C. B. *The Office of Governor in the United States,* 1956, Univ. of Alabama Press.

Schlesinger, J. A. *How They Became Governor,* 1957, Bur. of Bus. & Econ. Res., Michigan State Univ.

Snider, C. F. *American State and Local Government,* 1950, Appleton-Century.

Chapter 22

Bates, F. G., et al. *State Governments,* 1954, Harper.

Callison, I. P. *Courts of Injustice,* 1956, Twayne.

Council of State Governments. *The Book of States,* published annually, The Council.

——. *The Courts of Last Resort,* 1950, The Council.

——. *Trial Courts,* 1951, The Council.

Crouch & McHenry. *California Government,* 1950, Univ. of California Press.

Frank, J. *Courts on Trial,* 1949, Princeton Univ. Press.

Graves, W. B. *American State Governments,* 1953, Heath.

MacDonald, Webb, Lewis, & Strauss. *Outside Readings in American Government,* 1952, Crowell.

Munro, W. B. *The Government of the United States,* 1946, Macmillan.

Peltason, J. W. *Missouri Plan for Selection of Judges,* 1945, Univ. of Missouri Press.

Sunderland, E. R. *Judicial Administration,* 1948, Callaghan.

Vanderbilt, A. T., ed. *Minimum Standards of Judicial Administration,* 1949, Oceana.

Wendell, M. *The Relations Between Federal and State Courts,* 1949, Columbia Univ. Press.

Chapter 23

Anderson W. *Units of Government in the United States,* 1949, Holt.

Bollens, J. C. *Special District Governments in the United States,* 1957, Univ. of California Press.

Lancaster, L. W. *Government in Rural America,* 1952, Van Nostrand.

MacDonald, Webb, Lewis, & Strauss. *Outside Readings in American Government,* 1952, Crowell.

Munro, W. B. *Government of the United States,* 1946, Macmillan.

National Municipal League. *Model County Charter,* 1956, The League.

Snider, C. F. *American State and Local Government,* 1950, Appleton-Century.

————. *Local Government in Rural America,* 1957, Appleton-Century.

Vidick & Bensman. *Small Town in Mass Society,* 1958, Smith, Peter.

Wager, P. W., ed. *County Government Across the Nation,* 1950, Univ. of North Carolina Press.

Weidner, E. W. *The American County—Patchwork of Boards,* 1946, National Municipal League.

Chapter 24

Adrian, C. *Governing Urban America,* 1955, McGraw-Hill.

Bogue, D. J. *The Structure of the Municipal Community,* 1949, Univ. of Michigan Press.

Bromage, A. W. *Introduction to Municipal Government and Administration,* 1950, Appleton-Century.

Fisher, R. M., ed. *The Metropolis in Modern Life,* 1955, Doubleday.

Jones, V. *Metropolitan Government,* 1942, Univ. of Chicago Press.

Kneier, C. M. *City Government in the United States,* 1947, Harper.

MacCorkle, S. A. *American Municipal Government and Administration,* 1948, Heath.

MacDonald, A. F. *American City Government and Administration,* 1951, Crowell.

MacDonald, Webb, Lewis, & Strauss. *Outside Readings in American Government,* 1952, Crowell.

National Municipal League. *Model City Charter,* 1948, The League.

Reed, T. H. *Municipal Management,* 1941, Macmillan.

Sayre & Kaufman. *Governing New York City: Politics in the Metropolis,* 1960, Russell Sage.

Schultz, E. B. *American City Government,* 1949, Stackpole & Heck.

Stewart, F. M. *A Half Century of Municipal Reform,* 1950, Univ. of California Press.

Wood, R. C. *Suburbia: Its People and Their Politics,* 1959, Houghton Mifflin.

Chapter 25

Appleby, P. H. *Morality and Administration in Democratic Government,* 1952, Louisiana State Univ. Press.

Graham, G. A. *Morality in American Politics,* 1952, Random House.

Hall, Sikes, Stoner, & Wormuth. *American National Government: Law and Practice,* 1949, Harper.

MacDonald, Webb, Lewis, & Strauss. *Outside Readings in American Government,* 1952, Crowell.

Millspaugh, A. C. *Local Democracy and Crime Control,* 1936, Brookings.

———. *Crime Control by the National Government,* 1937, Brookings.

Smith, B. *Police Systems in the United States,* 1949, Harper.

United States Senate. *Kefauver Committee Report on Organized Crime,* 1951, Didier Pubs.

Chapter 26

Corwin, E. S. *Total War and the Constitution,* 1947, Knopf.

Furnies, E. S. *American Military Policy,* 1957, Rinehart.

Huntington, S. P. *The Soldier and the State,* 1958, Harvard Univ. Press.

Huzar, E. *The Purse and the Sword,* 1950, Cornell Univ. Press.

Janowitz, M. *The Professional Soldier,* 1960, Free Press.

Kintner, W. R., et al. *Forging A New Sword,* 1958, Harper.

Millis, W. *Arms and Men,* 1956, New American Library.

———., et al. *Arms and the State,* 1958, Twentieth Century.

Posey & Huegli. *Government for Americans,* 1953, Row.

Swarthout & Bartley. *Principles and Problems of American National Government,* 1955, Oxford Univ. Press.

Chapter 27

Dearing & Owen. *National Transportation Policy,* 1949, Brookings.

Dimock, M. E. *Business and Government,* 1961, Holt.

Edwards, C. D. *Maintaining Competition,* 1949, McGraw-Hill.

Mannings & Potter. *Government and the American Economy,* 1950, Holt.

Federal Trade Commission. *The Concentration of Productive Facilities,* 1949, U.S. Gov't Printing Office.

Kaplan, A. D. H. *Big Enterprise in a Competitive System,* 1954, Brookings.

————. *Small Business,* 1948, McGraw-Hill.

MacDonald, Webb, Lewis, & Strauss. *Outside Readings in American Government,* 1952, Crowell.

McCormick, E. T. *Understanding the Securities Act and the S.E.C.,* 1949, American Book.

Mund, V. A. *Government and Business,* 1955, Harper.

Munro, W. B. *The Government of the United States,* 1946, Macmillan.

Pegrum, D. F. *Regulation of Industry,* 1949, Irwin.

Redford, E. S. *Administration of National Economic Control,* 1952, Macmillan.

Rohlfing, C. C., et al. *Business and Government,* 1949, Foundation Press.

Thompson & Smith. *Public Utility Economics,* 1941, McGraw-Hill.

Chapter 28

Blough, R. *The Federal Taxing Process,* 1952, Prentice-Hall.

Bureau of the Budget. *The Federal Budget in Brief,* published annually, U.S. Gov't Printing Office.

Burkhead, J. *Government Budgeting,* 1956, Wiley.

Hall, Sikes, Stoner, & Wormuth. *American National Government: Law and Practice,* 1949, Harper.

MacDonald, Webb, Lewis, & Strauss. *Outside Readings in American Government,* 1952, Crowell.

Munro, W. B. *The Government of the United States,* 1946, Macmillan.

Strayer, P. J. *Fiscal Policy and Politics,* 1958, Harper.

Chapter 29

Bach, G. L. *Federal Reserve Policy-Making,* 1950, Knopf.

Hall, Sikes, Stoner, & Wormuth. *American National Government: Law and Practice,* 1949, Harper.

Kemmerer & Kemmerer. *The ABC of the Federal Reserve System,* 1950, Harper.

MacDonald, Webb, Lewis, & Strauss. *Outside Readings in American Government,* 1952, Crowell.

Senate Committee on Banking and Currency. *Federal Reserve Policy and Economic Stability, 1951–57* (Senate Report 2500, 85th Congress, 2nd Session), 1958, U.S. Gov't Printing Office.

Chapter 30

Clark, W. H. *Farms and Farmers: The Story of American Agriculture,* 1945, Page.

Clawson & Held. *The Federal Lands: Their Use and Management,* 1957, Johns Hopkins.

Jarrett, H., ed. *Perspectives on Conservation,* 1958, Johns Hopkins.

Hall, Sikes, Stoner, & Wormuth. *American National Government: Law and Practice,* 1949, Harper.

Harding, T. S. *Two Blades of Grass: A History of Scientific Development in the United States Department of Agriculture,* 1947, Univ. of Oklahoma Press.

MacDonald, Webb, Lewis, & Strauss. *Outside Readings in American Government,* 1952, Crowell.

Manning & Potter. *Government and the American Economy,* 1950, Holt.

Pinchot, G. *Breaking New Ground,* 1947, Harcourt.

Renne, R. R. *Land Economics,* 1947, Harper.

Riemer, N. *Problems of American Government,* 1952, McGraw-Hill.

Swarthout & Bartley. *Principles and Problems of American National Government,* 1955, Oxford Univ. Press.

Wengert, N. *Natural Resources and the Political Struggle,* 1955, Random House.

Chapter 31

Dimock, M. E. *Business and Government,* 1953, Holt.

Hartley, F. A. *Our New National Labor Policy,* 1948, Funk & Wagnalls.

Kaltenbòrn, H. S. *Government Adjustment of Labor Disputes,* 1943, Didier Pubs.

MacDonald, Webb, Lewis, & Strauss. *Outside Readings in American Government,* 1952, Crowell.

Miller, G. W. *American Labor and the Government,* 1948, Prentice-Hall.

Millis & Brown. *From the Wagner Act to Taft-Hartley,* 1950, Univ. of Chicago Press.

Morris, R. B. *Government and Labor in Early America,* 1946, Columbia Univ. Press.

Petro, S. *Power Unlimited: The Corruption of Union Leadership,* 1959, Ronald.

Riemer, N. *Problems of American Government,* 1952, McGraw-Hill.

Staniford, E. F. *Recent State Labor Legislation,* 1949, Univ. of California Press.

Sultan, P. *Labor Economics,* 1957, Holt.

Wollett, D. H. *Labor Relations and Federal Law,* 1949, Univ. of Washington Press.

Chapter 32

Burns, E. M. *The American Social Security System,* 1949, Houghton Mifflin.

———. *Social Security and Public Policy,* 1956, McGraw-Hill.

Gagliardo, D. *American Social Insurance,* 1955, Harper.

Ginzberg, E. *A Pattern for Hospital Care,* 1949, N.Y. State Hospital Study.

Hall, Sikes, Stoner, & Wormuth. *American National Government: Law and Practice,* 1949, Harper.

Larson, A. *Know Your Social Security,* 1959, Harper.

Livingston, H. E. *National Health Insurance,* 1950, Public Affairs Bulletin 85, Legislative Reference Service.

MacDonald, A. F. *American State Government and Administration,* 1955, Crowell.

MacDonald, Webb, Lewis, & Strauss. *Outside Readings in American Government,* 1952, Crowell.

Manning & Potter. *Government and the American Economy,* 1950, Holt.

Meriam, L. *Relief and Social Security,* 1946, Brookings.

Mustard, H. S. *Government in Public Health,* 1945, Harvard Univ. Press.

Riemer, N. *Problems of American Government,* 1952, McGraw-Hill.

Rosen, G. *A History of Public Health,* 1958, Doubleday.

Simmons, J. E., ed. *Public Health in the World Today,* 1949, Harvard Univ. Press.

Somers & Somers. *Doctors, Patients, and Health Insurance,* 1961, Brookings.

Stern, B. J. *Medical Services by Government: Local, State, and Federal,* 1946, Oxford Univ. Press.

Chapter 33

Allen, H. P. *The Federal Government and Education,* 1950, McGraw-Hill.

Fisher, R. M. *Twenty Years of Public Housing,* 1959, Harper.

Hall, Sikes, Stoner, & Wormuth. *American National Government: Law and Practice,* 1949, Harper.

Harris, S. E. *How Shall We Pay for Education?* 1948, Harvard Univ. Press.

House and Home Finance Agency. *The Housing Situation,* 1949, U.S. Gov't Printing Office.

Joint Committee on Housing. *Final Majority Report, Housing Study and Investigation* (House Report 1564, 80th Congress, 2nd Session), 1948, U.S. Gov't Printing Office.

MacDonald, Webb, Lewis, & Strauss. *Outside Readings in American Government,* 1952, Crowell.

President's Commission on Higher Education. *Higher Education for American Democracy,* 1947, U.S. Gov't Printing Office.

Quattlebaum, C. A. *Federal Aid to Elementary and Secondary Education,* 1948, Public Adm.

———. *Federal Educational Activities and Educational Issues before Congress: A Report Prepared in the Legislative Reference Service of the Library of Congress,* 1951.

Rockefeller Brothers Fund. *The Pursuit of Excellence: Manpower and Education,* 1958, Doubleday.

Straus, N. *The Seven Myths of Housing,* 1945, Knopf.

Chapter 34

Chase, E. P. *The United Nations in Action,* 1950, McGraw-Hill.

Eichelberger, C. M. *UN: The First Fifteen Years,* 1960, Harper.

Fenwick, C. G. *The Inter-American Regional System,* 1949, McMullan.

Goodrich, L. M. *The United Nations,* 1959, Crowell.

Hall, Sikes, Stoner, & Wormuth. *American National Government: Law and Practice,* 1949, Harper.

Levi, W. *Fundamentals of World Organization,* 1950, Univ. of Minnesota Press.

MacDonald, Webb, Lewis, & Strauss. *Outside Readings in American Government,* 1952, Crowell.

MacLaurin, J. *The United Nations and Power Politics,* 1951, Allen.

Riemer, N. *Problems of American Government,* 1952, McGraw-Hill.

Swarthout & Bartley. *Principles and Problems of American National Government,* 1955, Oxford Univ. Press.

United Nations. *Everyman's United Nations,* 1953, Int. Doc. Service-Columbia Univ. Press.

INDEX

SELF-SCORING EXAMINATION WITH ANSWERS

By Samuel Smith, Ph.D.

A Quick-Reference Aid to the Study of the U.S. Constitution and American Government

---

This self-scoring examination consists of three parts:

1. **VISUAL QUIZ** (on pages A, B, C, and D) with 28 questions. The answers (a, b, c, or d) must be written on the blank lines in the left and right margins of the page. After answering questions 1–28, the reader turns page B so that the correct printed answers appear next to his written answers. He can at once find his errors, analyze them, and study the explanations.

2. **COMPARISON TEST** (on pages E, F, G, and H) with 40 questions. The answers (T for True, or F for False) must be written on the blank lines in the left and right margins of the page. After answering questions 1–40, the reader turns page F so that the correct printed answers appear next to his written answers. He can at once find his errors, analyze them, and study the explanations.

3. **VISUAL SYNOPSIS** (on pages I, J, K, L, M, N, and O). Page I shows an over-all view of the federal governmental structure. This part includes 15 essay-type questions (on pages I, L, and M). The reader writes out answers in his own words and then compares his answers with the printed information on pages I–M. Additional important facts to review are given on pages N and O.

A

PART I. VISUAL QUIZ

For all questions 1–28, write your answers (a, b, c, or d) on the numbered lines in the margins. When you have answered all 28 questions, turn page B so that the printed answers on pages C and D will appear next to your answers. Study answer to questions you missed.

1.____

2.____

3.____

4.____

5.____

6.____

7.____

8.____

9.____

10.____

11.____

12.____

13.____

14.____

1. The Declaration of Independence expresses the
(a) divine rights theory of government
(b) government contract theory
(c) theory that the state arises from force
(d) evolutionary theory of origin of government

2. Voluntary associations replace the state under
(a) a totalitarian form of government
(b) individualism
(c) collectivism
(d) anarchism

3. By 1775 colonial assemblies had exclusive control over
(a) local government
(b) waging Indian wars
(c) taxes and appropriations
(d) colonial administration

4. In the colony of Virginia, the governor was
(a) appointed by the king
(b) elected annually
(c) selected by the Council
(d) chosen by the proprietor

5. Under Articles of Confederation
(a) each state had 1 vote
(b) the national courts were the supreme authority
(c) Congress imposed heavy taxes
(d) Congress elected the President

6. Authors of *The Federalist* were
(a) Samuel Adams and Patrick Henry
(b) Hamilton, Madison, and Jay
(c) Washington and Franklin
(d) Jefferson, Madison, and Jay

7. The Bill of Rights prohibited
(a) racial discrimination
(b) slavery
(c) excessive bail and cruel punishments
(d) suits against the states

8. The power of judicial review is
(a) enumerated
(b) reserved
(c) delegated
(d) implied

9. Eighteen specific powers of Congress are
(a) enumerated in the U.S. Constitution
(b) delegated to the states
(c) inherent
(d) implied

10. Constitutional amendments must be ratified by
(a) national referendum
(b) two-thirds of Congress
(c) legislatures or conventions in three-fourths of states
(d) two-thirds of state conventions called for this purpose

11. Recognition of foreign governments is a power of the
(a) Senate
(b) President
(c) State Department
(d) American ambassador

12. A bill of attainder refers to
(a) a retroactive law
(b) punishment of an individual without trial by legislative act
(c) an ex post facto law
(d) a *true bill*

13. Separation of powers is mainly a
(a) means for preventing dictatorship
(b) limitation on Congress
(c) restriction on the executive
(d) device to promote efficiency

14. In the vast majority of highly centralized governments,
(a) the national executive tends to be weak
(b) powers of local government tend to decline
(c) efficiency is impossible
(d) local initiative increases

RT I. VISUAL QUIZ (CONT.)

estions 15–28

DTE: Write your answers to questions 15–28 on the numbered lines at the right.

B

15.Due process refers mainly to
(a)police powers against crime
(b)moral behavior of individuals
(c)search of home without warrant
(d)limits on arbitrary government

16.A minority of voters can elect
a President
(a)only if several candidates run
(b)only by means of proportional
representation
(c)because of election-at-large
(d)because unit rule is illegal

17.All members of the President's
Cabinet are
(a)approved by the House
(b)appointed (with Senate approval) by
and responsible to President
(c)subject to impeachment in Supreme Court under Constitution
(d)subject to orders of Congress

18.The President can lawfully suspend or remove
(a)a member of Congress
(b)a quasi-judicial officer
(c)any judge too old to serve
(d)no judicial officer

19.The President can lawfully
(a)appropriate funds for defense
(b)revive an expired statute
(c)declare war without Congress
(d)involve the nation in war by order-
ing armed intervention abroad

20.If a treaty voids a federal law,
(a)the treaty is always superior
(b)the law takes precedence
(c)the most recent law or treaty is
considered valid
(d)it cannot bind future Presidents

21.If a President waits 10 days, then
returns unsigned bill to Congress,
(a)the bill is automatically killed
(b)a 2/3 vote for its passage is
required
(c)the bill becomes law
(d)Congress must vote on the bill
again and resubmit it

22.The Commission form of city government
(a)combines legislative and executive functions in one body
(b)divides authority between city
manager and elected council
(c)is the Commission-Manager plan
(d)makes use of proportional representation

23.The House has great influence on
foreign policy mainly because
(a)it must approve treaties
(b)it must approve war declaration
(c)it originates all revenue bills
(d)it has power to impeach the
Secretary of State

24.The President can make rules
with the force of law
(a)if Congress so empowers him
(b)without Senate approval
(c)only after Congress adjourns
(d)whenever Atty. Gen. approves

25.Congress' power to take a census
and reapportion House seats is
(a)mandatory under Constitution
(b)usurped by Census Bureau
(c)concurrent with that of States
(d)subject to judicial control

26.Third parties are retarded by
(a)proportional representation
(b)the single-member representative
district system
(c)use of the Australian ballot
(d)direct election of Senators

27.The U.S. Supreme Court can
(a)veto any act of Congress
(b)invalidate a bill when it is
still in committee
(c)decide only specific cases
(d)render pre-trial decisions

28.In federal court civil cases,
(a)injunctions are not permissible
(b)felonies are often prosecuted
(c)the govt. may be a plaintiff
(d)the U.S. can usually be sued
without its consent

(b)

(d)

(c)

(a)

(a)

(b)

(c)

(d)

(a)

(c)

(b)

(b)

(a)

(b)

1. The Declaration of Independence expresses the contract theory binding the king to rule justly. The king's violations of the contract released the people from their obligation to obey it and justified them in creating free and independent states.

2. Voluntary associations replace the state under anarchism, which considers the state an unnecessary restriction on liberty. Both collectivism and totalitarianism require centralized control.

3. By 1775 colonial assemblies had exclusive control over initiating tax laws and making appropriations. Governor was commander-in-chief, directed colonial and local administrations.

4. In the colony of Virginia, the governor was appointed by king as in all royal colonies; in charter colonies, elected annually; in proprietary, chosen by proprietor.

5. Under Articles of Confederation each state had 1 vote (& 2 to 7 congressmen), reflecting state sovereignty. There were no national courts, no taxing power, and no central executive.

6. Authors of The Federalist were Madison and Jay, working with Hamilton, not Jefferson. Adams opposed Constitution without a Bill of Rights. Washington decisively favored Constitution.

7. The Bill of Rights prohibited excessive bail, cruel punishments, government expropriation, conviction without fair trial, denial of free speech, etc., unreasonable searches. Ignored slavery.

8. The power of judicial review is implied because of (1)supremacy of Constitution and (2)duty of federal courts to disregard statute conflicting with Constitution.

9. Eighteen specific powers of Congress are enumerated in Art.I of Constitution. Implied powers are those necessary to execute specific enumerated powers. Inherent powers are those essential to sovereignty.

10. Constitutional amendments must be ratified by three-fourths of state legislatures or conventions. State can change its negative vote but not its acceptance once voted. Congress may set time limit; otherwise, proposal remains before the states.

11. Recognition of foreign governments is a power of the President, who acts by receiving envoys from abroad, appointing a diplomat, negotiating a treaty, or issuing a proclamation.

12. A bill of attainder refers to legislative condemnation without trial or other legal protection. A true bill is grand jury endorsement approving an indictment. (a) and (c) are identical.

13. Separation of powers is mainly a means of preventing dictatorship. The Constitution also contains checks and balances by which one division may partly control another.

14. In the vast majority of highly centralized governments, powers of local government tend to decline and to be taken over by the central government, especially by the executive. As U.S. national problems grew more complex, federal powers greatly expanded.

15. Due process refers mainly to limits on arbitrary government. It protects individuals from unfair trials and unjust laws (5th and 14th Amendments).

16. A minority of voters can elect a President because election-at-large method permits choice of many electors by narrow margins and nullifies huge majorities for electors in some other states.

17. All members of the President's Cabinet are responsible to President, who appoints (with Senate approval usually granted) and can remove them or suspend cabinet meetings; all civil officers are subject to removal by impeachment.

18. The President can lawfully suspend or remove no judicial or quasi-judicial or quasi-legislative officers. Judges can be impeached by House and tried by Senate.

19. The President can lawfully direct troops to intervene abroad and thus involve the nation in war, but only Congress can appropriate necessary funds. Senate could obstruct his appointments.

20. If a treaty voids a federal law, the courts will usually enforce the more recent expression of public will in law or treaty. Executive agreements, which are not submitted to Senate, fall under different rule.

21. If a President waits 10 days, then returns unsigned bill to Congress, the bill becomes law unless Congress has adjourned during the 10-day period, in which case the bill is void, as if it had been vetoed. This is the "pocket veto" whch cannot be overridden by houses of Congress.

22. The Commission form of city government concentrates legislative and executive powers in one elected body. Since each Commissioner heads a department, there is danger of administrative inefficiency, arbitrary decisions, and political interference.

23. The House has great influence on foreign policy mainly because it originates all money bills. Only the Senate votes on treaties. But both Houses must concur for war declaration. Secretary is responsible to President.

24. The President can make rules with the force of law when Congress grants him power to do so and sets forth objectives consistent with the U.S. Constitution.

25. Congress' power to take a census and reapportion House seats is mandatory. Article I requires reapportionment among states on basis of population. Census Bureau acts as agent of Congress.

26. Third parties are retarded by single-member district system nullifying minority vote in district. Proportional representation gives voice to minority, tending to create splinter parties.

27. The U.S. Supreme Court can decide specific cases brought by persons affected by a law. Only courts can decide what the law is and whether it conflicts with Constitution.

28. In federal court civil cases, the federal government may be a defendant or a plaintiff, but never a prosecutor; it cannot be sued without its consent. Injunctions are often granted.

(d)	15._____
(c)	16._____
(b)	17._____
(d)	18._____
(d)	19._____
(c)	20._____
(c)	21._____
(a)	22._____
(c)	23._____
(a)	24._____
(a)	25._____
(b)	26._____
(c)	27._____
(c)	28._____

(Study questions you missed. Then go on to Part II.)

E

PART II. COMPARISON TEST

For all questions 1–40, write your answers (T for True, or F for False) on the numbered lines in the margins. Then turn page F so that the printed answers on pages G and H appear next to your answers. Study answers to questions you missed.

1.———
2.———
3.———
4.———
5.———
6.———
7.———
8.———
9.———
10.———
11.———
12.———
13.———
14.———
15.———
16.———
17.———
18.———
19.———
20.———

1. **The 11th Amendment**
   prohibits the U.S. Supreme Court from taking action against the states.
2. **Delegates to the Constitutional Convention**
   were originally instructed to amend the Articles of Confederation, not to write a new Constitution.
3. **The legislative powers of state governments are**
   delegated to them by the national government and may be withdrawn by Congress.
4. **In 1789 all but a few believed that the vote should be granted**
   to all citizens, including the poorest nontaxpayers.
5. **The U.S. Constitution provides for freedom of speech**
   in time of peace, but not during war emergencies when military leaders control public opinion.
6. **The Populist Party of the 1890's advocated**
   a tax policy now part and parcel of the governing process.
7. **The U.S. Constitution provides that in national elections**
   all citizens 21 years or older will have the opportunity to vote.
8. **When the President vetoes a bill,**
   he may ignore it or return it unsigned to either House of Congress that he chooses.
9. **Urban areas in many states**
   are underrepresented in their legislature in proportion to their population.
10. **The U.S. Constitution**
    allows states to make interstate compacts which become effective when approved by Congress.

11. **American citizenship may be given up voluntarily**
    at any time, including a period of war emergency.
12. **The Pendleton Act of 1883 provided for**
    establishment of a Civil Service Commission and a Bureau of the Budget.
13. **Secretaries of the Army, Navy, and Air Force are subordinate**
    to the Joint Chiefs of Staff.
14. **The basis of U.S. citizenship is application of two factors:**
    the jus soli and the jus sanguinis.
15. **The U.N. Charter gives a veto power to**
    all 5 largest Powers for use in the Assembly and the Council.
16. **American municipalities are rightly considered creatures**
    of the federal government under the Constitution.
17. **A home rule charter for the typical American city**
    allows it perfect freedom to make its own laws without restriction.
18. **The U.S. Supreme Court may**
    declare part of a law unconstitutional without invalidating the entire law.
19. **The Supreme Court held that**
    Congress can create quasi-legislative bodies and prescribe the sole grounds for dismissal.
20. **Members of Congress cannot be arrested**
    during attendance at or on the way to Congress even on charges of committing a felony.

F

21. Congress can, if it chooses to do so,
    reorganize the executive branch of the federal government.

22. The size of the House of Representatives
    varies automatically with increases in population every ten years.

23. The Federal Government's principal source of revenue is
    the income made possible by the 16th Amendment.

24. To become a law a bill in Congress must be
    reported favorably by a standing committee of majority party.

25. The main purpose of efforts to reorganize state governments is
    to give less authority to the legislature and to decentralize.

26. If a majority on the Supreme Court cannot agree on a decision,
    the case must be settled outside of the federal courts.

27. Nominations in direct primary elections
    are regulated only by state laws, not by Congress.

28. Ability to read and write English
    is an unconstitutional requirement to keep some minorities from voting.

29. The Hatch Act limited the political campaign expenditures in national elections to 3 million dollars.

30. The functions and powers of a county govt. are usually
    granted by the state in a charter which lists each of the functions and powers.

31. In most states the Atty. General
    is nominated by the governor and approved by the state's legislature.

32. The 15th Amendment to the U.S. Constitution
    extended the franchise to all citizens, including illiterates and the insane.

33. In the case of McCulloch v. Maryland,
    the U.S. Supreme Court prevented a state from interfering with federal govt. activities.

34. In the case of Brown v. Bd. of Educ. of Topeka
    the Supreme Court reversed its "separate but equal" doctrine.

35. In 1959 an act passed by Congress
    admitted the territory of Hawaii into the U.S. as the 50th state of the Union.

36. In all suits at common law in state and federal courts,
    the 6th Amendment to the Constitution requires a jury trial.

37. A person violating both a state and a federal law in one act
    cannot be prosecuted by both state and federal officers.

38. The 8th Amendment provides that
    all accused persons must be released on reasonable bail.

39. The Civil Rights Act of 1957
    empowered new Division in Justice Dept. to get court injunctions to protect voting rights.

40. The U.S. Supreme Court has
    authority to judge qualifications of candidates for the House and Senate.

G

Compare your answers with the printed answers. Study answers to any questions you missed.

(F) 1. The 11th Amendment merely exempts states from suits by citizens of other states or of
(T) foreign countries.

(F) 2. Delegates to the Constitutional Convention
(F) substituted a new constitution which became effective when
(F) ratified by nine states.

(F) 3. The legislative powers of state governments are
(T) reserved, not delegated, but must give way to Constitutional federal
(F) powers in case of conflict.

(F) 4. In 1789 all but a few believed that the vote should be granted
(F) only to the property owners and
(F) the taxpayers.

(F) 5. The U.S. Constitution provides for freedom of speech
(T) at all times. But it is limited
(F) by government's power of self-preservation.

(F) 6. The Populist Party of the 1890's advocated
(F) a graduated income tax made possible by the 16th Amendment.

(T) 7. The U.S. Constitution provides that in national elections
(F) states set voting qualifications except as to race, sex, or poll tax payments.

(F) 8. When the President vetoes a bill, he returns it unsigned to the house
(F) of origin with his objections within 10 days.

(T) 9. Urban areas in many states have increased their legislative
(T) representation due to Supreme Court decisions on apportionment.

(F) 10. The U.S. Constitution prohibits any state from making agreements with other states without the consent of Congress.

11. American citizenship may be given up voluntarily in wartime but only with the approval of the U.S. Atty. Gen.

12. The Pendleton Act of 1883 provided for a Civil Service Commission, but the Bureau of the Budget was set up in 1921.

13. Secretaries of the Army, Navy, and Air Force are subordinate to the Secy. of Defense, who is a civilian member of Cabinet.

14. The basis of U.S. citizenship is application of two factors: birthplace; nationality of one's parents.

15. The U.N. Charter gives a veto power to 5 major Powers for use only in the Security Council.

16. American municipalities are rightly considered creatures of state govt. which approves charters and grants specific powers.

17. A home rule charter for the typical American city grants much freedom, but subject to state and federal laws.

18. The U.S. Supreme Court may negate invalid parts of a law but let valid parts stand if separable from the other parts.

19. The Supreme Court held that Congress can restrict the President from dismissing commissioners of quasi-legislative or regulatory bodies.

20. Members of Congress cannot be arrested for anything said in their speeches, but they can be arrested at any time for treason or a felony.

PART II. COMPARISON TEST (CONT.)
Answers to Questions 21–40

Compare your answers with the printed answers. Study answers to any questions you missed.

21. Congress can, if it chooses to do so,
create executive depts. and withhold funds from them.

22. The size of the House of Representatives
is fixed by statute at 435 members (1941 amendment provides equal-proportions method of reapportionment).

23. The Federal Government's principal source of revenue is
income tax: individual tax yields 50%; corporation tax 30%.

24. To become a law a bill in Congress must be
passed by both Houses in identical form, submitted to President.

25. The main purpose of efforts to reorganize state governments is
to increase powers of the governor over executive departments.

26. If a majority on the Supreme Court cannot agree on a decision,
the decision of the next lower court will be enforced.

27. Nominations in direct primary elections
are subject to state regulation (e.g., Conn. does not use primaries).

28. Ability to read and write English
is not a constitutional requirement if Congress provides other language standards.

29. The Hatch Act limited the political campaign expenditures
amt. spent by natl. party but not amt. spent by state or local groups.

30. The functions and powers of a county govt. are usually
delegated to the county govt. by the state in its statute laws or its constitution or both.

31. In most states the Atty. General is elected by the voters and is often quite independent of the governor and the majority party.

32. The 15th Amendment to the U.S. Constitution
merely guaranteed voting rights irrespective of race, color, or previous condition of servitude.

33. In the case of McCulloch v. Maryland,
the Supreme Court prevented Md. from taxing and thus controlling a United States bank.

34. In the case of Brown v. Bd. of Educ. of Topeka
the Court invalidated race discrimination in public schools.

35. In 1959 an act passed by Congress
changed the status of Hawaii effective after a referendum of approval by the Hawaiian people.

36. In all suits at common law in state and federal courts,
the 7th Amendment grants jury trial if more than $20 is involved.

37. A person violating both a state and a federal law in one act
broke both laws, can be prosecuted by state and federal govts.

38. The 8th Amendment provides that bail must be reasonable; it may be refused in capital crimes.

39. The Civil Rights Act of 1957
permits contempt proceedings against persons violating court orders protecting voting rights.

40. The U.S. Supreme Court has
no power to judge qualifications for Congress; each House judges qualifications of its own members.

(T)	21._____
(F)	22._____
(T)	23._____
(F)	24._____
(F)	25._____
(F)	26._____
(T)	27._____
(F)	28._____
(T)	29._____
(F)	30._____
(F)	31._____
(F)	32._____
(T)	33._____
(T)	34._____
(T)	35._____
(F)	36._____
(T)	37._____
(T)	38._____
(T)	39._____
(F)	40._____

I

PART III. VISUAL SYNOPSIS

Write answers to questions I–V, below, and compare your answers with facts on pages J and K. Then go on to questions VI and VII on page L.

THE U.S.CONSTITUTION

I. What are the 6 processes whereby the Constitution has been greatly modified? Explain how each of these processes has changed provisions or applications of the Constitution. (See Page J)

II. What are 6 basic principles underlying the U.S. Constitution? (See Page J)

LEGISLATURE	EXECUTIVE	JUDICIARY
III. Name 6 types of non-legislative and 8 types of legislative powers of Congress.	IV. (See Page K) What 11 kinds of activities are within the scope of the President's authority?	V. (See Page K) State the main classes of legal cases decided by the federal courts.

11 DEPTS. (In Order of Possible Succession to Presidency)

1. State Dept.: conducts foreign affairs; controls overseas representatives; negotiates treaties; work in international agencies; information services; passports; acts as home office.

2. Treasury:collects customs, duties, and taxes; prints money; supervises federal expenditures; manages public debt; directs Secret Service, Narcotics Squad, national banks.

3. Defense:runs Army, Navy,Air Force, and advisory agencies.

4. Justice:Attorney General, legal adviser of Pres., conducts U.S. cases; FBI, federal prisons; immigration and naturalization; executes federal court orders.

5. Post Office:mail; postal savings; stamps.

6. Interior:fish and wildlife; mineral resources; public lands management; water and power development; Indian affairs; national parks; Geological Survey; reclamation; Bureau of Mines.

7. Agriculture:research on soils, forestry, etc.; training and advisory programs; marketing (data and regulation); aid to farmers (credit and insurance; rural electrification).

8. Commerce:foreign trade; Patent Office; Census Bureau; Civil Aeronautics Admin.; public roads; Bureau of Standards; Business Economics; Geodetic Survey.

9. Labor:statistics; employment services; administers labor laws.

10. Health, Education, and Welfare: research; social security programs; Food and Drug Admin.; aid for handicapped persons. (Not in line of succession to Presidency.)

11. Housing and Urban Development: plans, administers, and coordinates federal housing programs. (Not in line of succession to Presidency.)

INDEPENDENT AGENCIES, responsible to Congress and the President, combine legislative and judicial functions. Their technical experts facilitate execution of Congressional policies. Independent agencies are of several types:

(1) regulating agencies, which combine legislative and judicial functions and operate in accord with Administrative Procedure Act of Congress. Examples: Civil Service Comm.; Fed. Communications Comm.; Fed. Trade Comm.; Interstate Commerce Comm.; Natl. Labor Relations Board (NLRB); Securities Exchange Comm.; U.S. Tariff Comm.

(2) agencies outside departmental system: e.g., Agency for Internatl. Development; Central Intelligence Agency; Export-Import Bank; Fed. Reserve System; Natl. Aeronautics and Space Admin. (NASA); Natl. Mediation Bd.; Selective Service System; Veterans Administration.

(3) govt. corporations: e.g., Fed. Deposit Insurance Corp.; Tenn. Valley Authority (TVA).

THE U.S.CONSTITUTION
ratified by 9 states, June 1788 (excluding NY and Va.)

sets forth 6 fundamental principles: (1)Popular sovereignty with limited government. (2)Federalism, with power shared by states and central government. (3)Powers not enumerated must be reserved for the states or people. (4)Supremacy of national government protected from state taxation or interference—U.S. courts to decide conflicts. (5) Separation of powers among executive, legislative, and judicial branches. (6)Supremacy of the judiciary in deciding Constitutional issues.

The Constitution has changed through 6 processes:(1)amendment;(2)passage of laws by Congress;(3)judicial interpretation;(4)influence of political parties;(5)influence of President;(6)changing customs. (See discussion of the 6 processes, below.)

The Constitution has 7 Articles and 24 Amendments(1-10,Bill of Rights)
Articles:

I.Legislative dept.:organization, powers, restraints

II.Executive dept.:powers, restraints, duties, election of President

III.Judicial dept.:powers, restraints, treason defined

IV.Powers of states. Relation of states and territories to federal government

V.Method of amending Constitution

VI.National debts; supremacy of Constitution, federal laws and treaties; pledge of officials; no religious test for public office

VII.Method for ratification

Amendments:

1-10:Bill of Rights. 11:Exemption of states from suit. 12:New method of electing President. 13:Slavery prohibited. 14:Protection of citizen's rights(due process). 15:Right to vote. 16:Income tax. 17:Popular election of senators. 18:Prohibition. 19:Woman suffrage. 20:Abolition of lame duck session. 21: Repeal of 18th. 22:Limitation of President to 2 elective terms. 23: Wash., D.C., voting rights. 24: Poll tax prohibited in federal elections.

Passage of Laws by Congress:
Congress interprets broadly its duties stated or implied by the Constitution. E.g., it established the Civil Service System (1883) under Art.II Sec.2 which gives Congress authority to vest the appointment of "such inferior officers . . . in the President alone, in the courts of law, or in the heads of depts." Laws regulating mfg., farming, and public utilities are other examples of broad interpretation.

Judicial Interpretation:
The courts have changed the interpretations to meet changing conditions. Thus, minimum wage laws and federal taxes on state employees were once invalid. Marbury v. Madison(1803)set precedent for court supremacy in interpretation.

Influence of Political Parties:
Political parties have modified the Constitution through method of electing President and pressure on Congress and President. Even minor parties have influenced interpretation by popularizing social reforms later espoused by the two major parties.

Influence of President:
The President has often applied his own interpretations of the Constitution, as in claiming right to send troops abroad to protect American property.

Changing Customs:
Changing customs have modified the Constitution, as in development of the President's Cabinet or legislative committees, or "senatorial courtesy" (whereby senator blocks appointment of objectionable nominee from his home state).

K

NOTE: The information below answers questions III–V and also includes basic
additional facts about the three branches of the federal government.

LEGISLATURE	EXECUTIVE	JUDICIARY
Non-legislative powers: constituent; electoral; judicial; executive; administrative; and investigative. Its legislative powers are: enumerated; implied; resultant; emergency; mandatory; permissive; exclusive; and concurrent.	Powers cover: law enforcement; military; appointment and removal; foreign affairs; pardon and reprieve; messages to Congress; veto; special sessions of Congress; budget; executive ordinances; contacts with political leaders.	Decides cases involving: the Constitution; federal laws; treaties; admiralty and maritime affairs; foreign representatives or nations; U.S. as a party; different states or citizens of different states.
Two senators from each of 50 states; house membership for each based on population as determined by Census Bureau. State designation of Congressional districts permits gerrymandering. Representative must be 25 yrs. or older, resident of his state, and U.S. citizen 7 yrs. or more. Each house judges election results and qualifications of its members. House term, 2 yrs.; Senate, 6 yrs. Senator must be 30 yrs. or older, resident of his state, U.S. citizen 9 yrs. or more; 17th Amendment provided for direct election by people instead of by state legislatures. In House, Speaker is majority leader; in Senate, U.S. Vice-Pres. presides. A bill is referred to 1 of 20 standing committees in House, to 1 of 16 in Senate; these are decisive for legislation.	White House Office has several Special Assts. to the President and various administrative and personal secretaries. **Bureau of the Budget** prepares and supervises budget; advises on work of all govt. agencies and on proposed legislation. **Council of Economic Advisors** advises Pres. on economic problems and policies, helps him prepare economic reports. **National Security Council** assists Pres. to execute programs, domestic and foreign, to safeguard national security. **Office of Emergency Planning** aids in mobilization of national resources for defense. **Office of Science and Tech.** QUALIFICATIONS: Pres. and Vice-Pres.—35 yrs. or older, U.S. resident 14 yrs. or more, native-born citizen. REMOVAL: only by impeachment.	U.S. Supreme Court (Chief Justice, 8 Assoc. Justices) judges original cases (1) affecting ambassadors, etc. and (2) involving a state; it judges all other cases of law and constitutionality which come to it on appeal or writ from state courts or are referred to it from lower federal courts. The 90 district courts (about 300 judges) render decisions which can be appealed to Circuit Courts (11 in 11 circuits). Circuit Court decisions are usually final unless Supreme Court intervenes, to decide a major constitutional or legal point. Special courts: U.S. Court of Claims (suits vs. U.S.); U.S. Court of Customs and Patent Appeals; U.S. Customs Court; Territorial Courts; Court of Military Appeals; Tax Court. Federal judges are nominated by Pres., confirmed by Senate. They can be removed only by impeachment.

VISUAL SYNOPSIS   (CONT.)

NOTE: For essay-type questions VI–XV (pages L and M) write your answers out and compare them with the information on pages L, M, and N.

VI. Discuss ten important constitutional cases. (Compare your answers with the list below.)

VII. Discuss the basic constitutional rights of citizens and states. (Compare your answer with the list below.)

CONSTITUTIONAL CASES

1. **Marbury** v. **Madison** (1803) voided act of Congress giving court greater jurisdiction than that fixed in Art. III.
2. **Dartmouth Coll.** v. **Woodward** (1819): corporate charters cannot be nullified by a state.
3. **McCulloch** v. **Md.** (1819): state cannot tax (and thus possibly destroy) a U.S. instrumentality.
4. **Dred Scott** v. **Sanford** (1857): slave not a citizen with right to sue in U.S. courts.
5. **Wabash, St. Louis, and Pacific** v. **Ill.** (1886): state cannot regulate that portion of interstate journey in state.
6. **Lochner** v. **N.Y.** (1905): state fixing of maximum hrs. violates freedom of contract (14th Amend.). Reversed in Bunting v. Oregon, 1917).
7. **Adkins** v. **Children's Hospital** (1923): federal regulation of minimum wages unconstitutional (reversed in West Coast Hotel v. Parrish, 1937).
8. **N.L.R.B.** v. **Jones & Laughlin** (1937): industries organized on natl. scale are subject to interstate commerce power of Congress.
9. **U.S.** v. **Darby** (1941): upheld Fair Labor Standards Act setting maximum hrs. and minimum wages and also prohibiting interstate shipment of goods produced by child labor.
10. **Brown** v. **Bd. of Educ. of Topeka** (1954): race segregation in public schools unconstitutional (reversing "separate but equal" doctrine of Plessy v. Ferguson, 1896).

CONSTITUTIONAL RIGHTS

1. Writ of habeas corpus requires prompt justice for any prisoner. Art. I, Sec. 9.
2. Bills of attainder and ex post facto laws prohibited. Art I, Secs. 9, 10.
3. Jury trial in criminal cases, Art. III, Sec. 3; in civil cases, 7th Amendment.
4. Treason narrowly defined to protect innocent and heirs of guilty. Art. III.
5. Laws vs. freedoms of speech, religion, press, or assembly forbidden. 1st Amendment.
6. Peacetime right to refuse quartering of soldiers in one's home. 3rd Amendment.
7. Protection vs. unreasonable searches and seizures. 4th Amendment.
8. Double jeopardy forbidden; no criminal prosecution unless grand jury indicts; no one compelled to testify against self- due process of law to protect life, liberty, property. 5th Amendment.
9. Prompt, public trial of accused person in state and district of the crime; charges and witnesses to be presented; right to legal counsel. 6th Amendment.
10. Jury trial in civil cases involving $20 or more in value. 7th Amendment.
11. Excessive bail or fines and cruel punishments prohibited. 8th Amendment.
12. Freedom to vote irrespective of race, color, sex; qualifications must apply to all. 15th and 19th Amendments.
13. State laws must not impair obligations of a contract. Art. I, Sec. 10.
14. Each state must give citizens of other states the same privileges and immunities as those accorded to its own citizens. 14th Amendment.
15. Each state must give full faith and credit to acts of other states. Art. IV.

COLONIAL GOVERNMENTS

VIII. What documents and practices of the mother country formed the basis for American traditions of self-government?

IX. Who had final authority in the colonies in 1775?

COLONIAL GOVERNMENTS

Traditions of self-govt. were based on the British Magna Charta, Petition of Right, Bill of Rights (1689), common law, independent judiciary, bicameral legislature. In 1775 royal colonies were governed by officers of the King; laws in proprietary colonies (except Md.) were subject to Royal approval; not so in charter colonies.

ARTICLES OF CONFEDERATION

X. What were 5 principal features of the Articles of Confederation?

XI. State reasons for the failure of the Confederation.

ARTICLES OF CONFEDERATION, 1781

Features state sovereignty; unicameral govt. by delegates of state legislatures; no central executive or judiciary; authority— no power over taxes, commerce, tariff barriers, individuals; amendments required unanimity. Failure due to: financial troubles, currency depreciation, commercial warfare, lack of state cooperation.

CONSTITUTIONAL CONVENTION

XII. Who were the delegates to the Constitutional Convention?

XIII. Describe the Virginia Plan.

CONSTITUTIONAL CONVENTION, 1787

11 states sent delegates, mainly leading lawyers, businessmen, politicians. Each state had 1 vote; majority ruled.

Virginia Plan proposed lower house elected by people, upper house by lower house from list submitted by state legislatures. State's voting power in Congress to depend on taxes paid, population or both. Congress could veto state laws. Congress to choose national executive and national judges.

Pinckney Plan proposed Pres. with 7-yr. term chosen by Congress (bicameral as above); each legislator to have 1 vote.

New Jersey Plan: 1-house Congress to elect Pres. who elects judges. Each state to have equal representation in Congress.

Conn. Compromise: House based on population; Senate representation equal for all states.

Three-fifths Compromise: three-fifths of slaves counted for direct taxes and for representation in Congress.

EARLY STATE GOVERNMENTS

XIV. What were the democratic principles of the early state governments of 1775-1781?

XV. In what respect were they undemocratic?

EARLY STATE GOVERNMENTS, 1775-1781

The Revolutionary state govts. observed principles of popular sovereignty, limited govt., individual rights, separation of powers, and legislative supremacy. But all the states sharply limited suffrage. Governors had little power; most of them were elected (by the people or the legislatures) for 1-yr. terms.

Usually the lower house, elected by the voters for 1-yr. term, favored the rank and file. The upper house, elected by the voters or by the lower house for 1 to 5 yr. terms, often favored property owners. In most states, judges were appointed by governor or legislature (popularly elected in Ga.) and could be removed by legislature.

Conn. and R.I. retained their charters.

Mass. did not adopt her constitution until 1780.

TYPES OF GOVERNMENT

Anarchist: opposes all govt. controls. **Individualist:** favor govt. action to preserve order and protect personal rights. **Totalitarianism:** advocates govt. control over all important matters (Communists oppose private ownership; fascist totalitarians accept it). **Collectivist:** demands more govt. control in matters affecting public welfare, with less reliance on individual's self-direction.

Major Types: autocracy (1-man rule); oligarchy (rule by few); democracy (rule by people directly or, in a republic, by their representatives mainly); unitary (1 central authority provided); federal (power shared with states).

The U.S. is a federal, democratic republic (people in 50 states elect representatives) with a written constitution and Presidential govt. Great Britain is a unitary democracy with an unwritten constitution and a parliamentary govt. (the executive is responsible to the legislature). Soviet Russia is a totalitarian dictatorship which claims to be progressing toward a collective, Communist state; it differs from Socialism elsewhere, which advocates a more peaceful, gradual increase in collective authority without dictatorship. Laissez-faire is the theory directly opposed to increased govt. control of individuals.

MODERN STATE GOVERNMENTS

State Constitutions: contain bill of rights; provide for legislative, executive, and judicial depts.; define relations between state and local govts.; fix qualifications for suffrage; and often regulate important matters, such as taxation, finance, public utilities, etc. Constitutional conventions (except in R.I.) can propose revisions for popular referendum. Some state legislatures have appointed commissions to prepare the proposals.

State Legislatures: range in size from 49 members in 1-house system of Neb. to 417 in 2-chamber system of N.H. Terms are 2 or 4 yrs. (senators serve 2 yrs. in 15 states, 4 yrs. in 35 states; representatives serve 2 yrs. in 45 states). Constitutions in 36 states give legislatures control over apportionment of seats. Legislatures enact laws on education, elections, finance, highways, insurance, labor, libraries, mental health, taxes, water resources, status and work of women, etc.

State Judiciary: highest court; superior; county or district or circuit courts; and special courts (surrogate, municipal, justices of the peace, juvenile, magistrates', small claims, etc.). Often the judges are elected (in a few states appointed by legislature or governor).

Executive: in 36 states governor serves 4 yrs., in 14 he serves 2 yrs. Highest officers (Secy. of State, Treasurer, Auditor, Atty. Gen.) usually elected; in many states lesser officers appointed by governor.

THEORIES OF ORIGINS OF GOVERNMENT

Elements necessary for any govt. are: people; territory; unity; political institutions; sovereign power; and continuity.

Competing Theories:

Divine Rights, with the king as the inheritor of authority from a divine source—the historical basis of monarchy.

Govt. Contract theory (adopted in the Declaration of Independence) that govt. is based on an agreement between the people and their rulers.

Force Theory (of govt. through right of conquest) is always inadequate explanation.

Anthropological (or **Evolutionary**) theory states that govt. developed when customs became fixed and had to be enforced by some authority—the favored theory.

O

MODERN LOCAL GOVERNMENT

County Govts. (ranging from 3 in Del. to 254 in Texas): officers derive powers from state govts.; administer state laws; collect local taxes, prosecute criminals; supervise elections, educational institutions, health and welfare programs, highway construction and maintenance, etc. Bd. of Supervisors and other county officials, such as sheriff, clerk, superintendent of schools, coroner, assessor, treasurer, and recorder of deeds are usually elected.

Towns: in New England are the principal units of local government; elsewhere towns or townships are subordinate to counties.

Municipal Govts.: operate under charter system as corporations with proprietary and governmental powers. Charters may be: special—granted by legislature; general—identical for all cities in state; classified—based on population groupings; optional—with cities choosing their form through a referendum; home-rule—in about 200 cities in 24 states.

Types of City Govt.: Mayor-council (elected mayor and city council); commission plan (5 members replace mayor and council), combining legislative with executive powers; council-manager plan (manager selected by city council to direct city affairs); and proportional-representation-city manager plan (with commissioners elected by proportional representation).

PASSAGE OF LAW

Each committee of Congress reports on original or amended bill which (if cleared by majority leader in Senate or Rules Committee in House) is debated, amended, and approved before being sent to the other house where their committee reports. The bill is debated, etc., in 2nd house. Conferees meet to iron out differences; the bill is then sent to the President.

SUCCESSION TO PRESIDENCY

By law of 1947: Speaker of House follows Vice-Pres.; then Pres. pro tem of Senate, Secs. of State, Treasury, Defense, Atty. Gen., Postmaster Gen., Secs. of Interior, Agriculture, Commerce, and Labor.

U.S. SUPREME COURT

Concurring and dissenting opinions are usually written; if majority cannot agree, lower court decision stands.

Justices may retire at full pay at age 65, following 15 years of service, or at age 70, following 10 years of service.

FIELDS OF STUDY

Besides political theory, major fields of study include: constitutions and constitutional law (written or unwritten, with interpretations by courts, legislatures, or executives); international relations and organizations, including international law and diplomacy; comparative govt.; political processes, such as parties, elections, propaganda, law-making; and public administration (especially fiscal, personnel, and judicial problems involved in the management of public affairs).